CW01269748

Bridgend Library & Information Service MSS

Gwasanaeth Llyfrgell a Gwybodaeth Pen-y-bont ar Ogwr

Please return/renew this item by the last date below

Dychwelwch/Adnewyddwch erbyn y dyddiad olaf y nodir yma

MAESTEG LIBRARY
(01656) 754835

10/15

WEDI'I GYMRYD ODDI AR Y CYFLENWAD
WITHDRAWN FROM STOCK

14 DEC 2015

-5 MAR 2018

-9 APR 2020

www.bridgend.gov.uk/libraries

Gwalia Patagonia

© Hugo Pedel, courtesy of Wiki Commons licence

Gwalia Patagonia

Jon Gower

Gomer

Published in 2015 by
Gomer Press, Llandysul, Ceredigion, SA44 4JL

ISBN 9 781 84851 884 1

A CIP record for this title is available from the British Library.
© Copyright: Jon Gower 2015

Jon Gower asserts his moral right under the
Copyright, Designs and Patents Act 1988
to be identified as the author of this work.

All rights reserved. No part of this book may be reproduced,
stored in a retrieval system, or transmitted in any form
or by any means, electronic, electrostatic, magnetic tape, mechanical,
photocopying, recording or otherwise without permission
in writing from the above publishers.

This book is published with the financial support of the
Welsh Books Council.

Printed and bound in Wales at
Gomer Press, Llandysul, Ceredigion
www.gomer.co.uk

This book is dedicated to the late, great Nigel Jenkins, author of *Gwalia in Khasia*, a fine poet and fabulous writer, a tutelary spirit for many of his students and a deeply generous man. The light of his star shines undiminished.

© Jon Gower

Contents

Prologue	xi
1. New Found Land	1
2. From Gwalia to Patagonia	14
3. The Great Emptiness	67
4. Terra Gigantica	79
5. The Welsh and the Tehuelche	86
6. Puerto Madryn	105
7. Trelew (Lewis Jones-town)	109
8. Making tracks	118
9. Ariel and Martha	128
10. El Hospital	134
11. The Artisan	137
12. Gaiman	140
13. Eluned	152
14. Little Nell	159
15. To the Yellow House	162
16. Waldo Williams and Bod Iwan	170
17. The Welsh in Chatwinland	176
18. Naming the Land	185
19. *Frutas*	192
20. Elvin and Amanda	202
21. Esquel	210
22. Land of the Condor	218
Acknowledgements	233
Bibliography	237

© Jon Gower

GWALIA PATAGONIA: *A VISIT TO THE SITE, IN SOUTH AMERICA, OF THE MOST ENDURING OVERSEAS VENTURE EVER SUSTAINED BY THE WELSH.*

All the royalties from this book will be donated to Ysgol y Cwm in Esquel.

Residing amidst the water and surrounded by twilight, Kóoch desired to behold the strange world. To this end, he removed himself into distant space, and failing to see clearly, raised his hand to scratch at the shadows ...

(From a Tehuelche creation myth)

The government shall encourage European immigration and may not restrict, limit or burden with any tax whatsoever, the entrance into Argentine territory of foreigners who arrive for the purpose of tilling the soil ...

(Article 25 of the Constitution of Argentina, 1853)

This is the old flag which guided our forefathers to battle long ago. It was dormant for centuries in Wales, and now it spreads its wings in a remote country. The power of the whole of Patagonia, from the Atlantic to the Andes, meets here to create the Welsh Colony for ourselves and our people for ever. I can imagine the time when this flag will be honoured on sea and land. Being alone in a far-off country does not matter, and it is worth facing any danger to be beneath its shade for just an hour. It is sunset: now I must lower the flag carefully and set it as a pillow, so as to sleep on it and dream of splendid things to come.

(One of the first settlers, Edwin Cynrig Roberts, on raising the Welsh flag at Punta Cuevas)

Prologue

At the end of Richard Llewellyn's hugely popular coal-and-soap opera, *How Green Was My Valley*, the book's hero, Huw Morgan, leaves his valley in south Wales, perhaps forever. The wildly overwritten sequel, *Up Into the Singing Mountain*, written twenty-one years later, finds him transported a long, long way from the populous, teeming terraces and a skyline punctuated by the skeletal iron of the pithead wheels, to a strange world:

> It was joyous songs to the beauty to be endured about three weeks and all the Atlantic Ocean later when I saw Port Madryn. A few old sheds and huts, and some baulks and planks for a dock, and nothing but low hills of pampas bush, and rain in hanging clouds, and the shine of mud by the mile.

Huw Morgan has left an industrial, coal-hewing and very close community, full of people living cheek by jowl, to go to a place which is a byword for emptiness, a place, as Bruce Chatwin put it, 'of black fogs and whirlwinds at the end of the habited world'. It is a grand place to both lose oneself and find oneself. Chatwin wasn't the only writer to see Patagonia as somewhere set very far apart from ordinary life, a beyond-place, or a place beyond, where one should pause first before venturing. In his leviathan novel *Moby Dick*, the great American novelist Herman Melville employs 'Patagonian' as a byword for marvel and danger:

> Then the wild and distant seas where he rolled his island bulk; the undeliverable, nameless perils of the whale: these, with all the attendant marvels of a thousand Patagonian sights and sounds, helped sway me to my wish.

Huw Morgan's intention in braving the Melvillean whirlwinds and nameless perils is to disentangle or distance himself from his socially proscribed love for Bron, his brother's widow. He goes about as far away from her as he possibly can, travelling to the 'final capes of exile', yet without completely severing his links with Wales and Welshness. *Up Into the Singing Mountain* sees Huw join the struggling settlers who have come from Wales, finding that the tightly-knit pioneer community is consumed by the self-same violent passions and fierce prejudices that drove him from his homeland. When Huw reaches the aforementioned peaks, those singing mountains, though, there are epiphanies awaiting him – the mountains various and glorious in their colours:

> … the mountains all round us were like dreams, every one a different colour, and you could think yourself gone fast asleep or gone in the head to see a pure yellow mountain next to one blue, and purple the next, and apricot, and then a red, and green, and orange and scarlet and darker green and paler blue, but in a sunset of crimson clouds it was easy to believe that you were finished with the Earth and waiting below the Throne for your turn to hear the Voice.

But life isn't over and the Earth isn't finished with Huw, and there is even more celestial majesty to unfurl, in another Damascene-style revelation:

> One morning I woke to see the first light on the peaks, among all those tips of colour only a little breath of lilac, no more, and a tent of burning green above for a sky, with a gold coin for a moon, and a brilliance of stars, and families were singing prayers along the train, and I remember my mother and father living in a Light even more beautiful through the years, and as though told by Abraham, I knew then, that if a little part of Earth can have more peace and wonder, Beyond must have much more …

The novel which completes the trilogy, *Green, Green the Mountain Now*, finds Huw is now a successful Patagonian businessman, ready to return home to Wales, in a peregrinatory novel full of Llewellyn's usual hyper-oxygenating prose. But you don't come here, to Llewellyn's novels – any more than you go to Chatwin's travelogues – if you want the facts and the history of Patagonia. When Llewellyn, his face blackened by the sun, his demeanour mischievous, met R. Bryn Williams, the indefatigable historian of the Welsh colony, y Wladfa, he freely admitted that he wasn't interested in history other than as the stuff of the novel, the material for fiction. But it's a place where facts rival fiction, competing against them.

In both physical and mental cartographies, Patagonia is a long, long way from Wales: 7,000 miles away, with great stretches of the North Atlantic and South Atlantic in between. There is certainly little of the green, green grass of home. What grows here is often monotonously grey – tough and stunted – wiry desert shrubs on parched, vast scrubland. This region of South America, covering parts of southern Argentina and Chile, is mostly a dry, barren plateau, extending from the Colorado River in central Argentina to the Strait of Magellan, and ranging from the Andes to the Atlantic coast. This is a terrain of salt lakes and sparse vegetation, beaten by flensing winds, of sandy, rocky desert, bare, bleak hills and not enough grass to feed an Argentine shrew. You can cross this land for days and not see a soul. Only that wind keeps you company, and it only wants to keen for the dead; the other doomed and demented travellers who passed this way. Sorry, it's all too easy to romanticize the place, to rhapsodize about its strangeness and its harshness. It's a huge patch of planet, testing the boundlessness of any imagination. 'The hedge defines the mind's limits,' says an R. S. Thomas poem. But here, in this great, aching emptiness, there are no hedges and very few fence posts, and the sky truly is boundless.

On the map of the world, this is where the great continent of South America begins to narrow and fracture, its coastline jagged, crimped and crenellated, before land contracts and diminishes, to end as a gnarly, rocky finger, a finisterre in Tierra del Fuego, arthritically pointing the way to the South Pole. Yet y Wladfa, the Welsh-speaking colony in Argentina, the one Huw Morgan joined, feels somehow closer to Wales because of the bridge of language, the still-open doors of Bethel chapel in Gaiman, and the persistence of customs imported long ago from the homeland. Thus, it has a hold on the Welsh imagination because *it can feel like home*, though set in a landscape of defining emptiness which can also seem defeatingly enormous.

Little wonder, then, that y Wladfa has spawned books and films and TV documentaries by the dozen, much like that factory of books examining the Spanish Civil War where, ultimately, there will be more volumes written about its atrocities than there were people who died in it.

There's the famous, albeit probably apocryphal, story of not one but four camera crews who found themselves at the annual South American

Eisteddfod in Trelew, trying unsuccessfully to keep out of each others' shots, like mad actors trapped in some Gabriel García Márquez story. Yes, the settlement, now celebrating 150 years since its establishment in 1865, still exerts a powerful pull on the imagination.

And the books and the films keep on coming. There's been *Separado!* (2010), the debut film by former Super Furry Animals lead singer Gruff Rhys and director Dylan Goch – a zany and restlessly inventive account of his search for his musical relative, René Griffiths, who turns out to have been living in Cardiff all along. (I see René around sometimes; a desperately handsome man who once tried to establish a *vicuña* farm in Pembrokeshire.)

On the big screen, director Marc Evans's film, *Patagonia* (2010), chronicles two parallel road trips; one winding through the concertinaed hillscapes of Wales and the other extending along the long, mainly carless roads of Patagonia. Patagonia may consist of an awful lot of wind-scorched scrub, but it's a fertile source of material for creatives of all hues. As this book goes to print, the artist Marc Rees is preparing the first ever co-production between Theatr Genedlaethol Cymru and National Theatre Wales. To be performed in the Royal Opera House's enormous, and enormously unexpected set storage spaces in Abercwmboi (an area which was home to many of the earliest settlers who went to y Wladfa), it promises to be a rich and multi-layered experience, splicing together a play called *Yr Archentwr* from the 1960s and texts collected by Marc on his travels around Patagonia. It will also meld dance with film, and feature a driving, central dramatic narrative by the playwright Roger Williams. Intriguingly, one of the roles will be filled by a Patagonian actress, Elizabeth Fernandez, who came over to Wales to improve her Welsh. Elizabeth doesn't have Welsh roots, but she decided to learn the language at the age of 15. She took a job in the National History Museum in St. Fagans (which helps make this a bit of a Disney tale), and now plays the part of Gabriela Gonzalez in the soap opera *Pobol y Cwm*, set in the fictional village of Cwmderi. It's a bit of a magical realist tale in itself.

This veritable manufactory of histories, travel books, learnéd articles, films, radio broadcasts and television programmes creates something much more than a comprehensive record of a tough land and its denizens. As Chris Moss says in his immensely readable *Patagonia: A Cultural History*, it all amounts to the Welsh 'forging a national epic' from an enterprise which one reviewer of a Welsh-language account of the settlement was forced to describe as 'at once bold, bungling and rather magnificent'.

It *is* magnificent, this story of how 162 people fled cultural and linguistic persecution by crossing the South Atlantic on an old tea clipper. It's a story familiar to most Welsh speakers, part of the story bank raided for inspiration by school teachers, writers and broadcasters throughout the land. But is also a story of bungling so, well, bungling, that it almost led to complete and utter disaster for the entire cohort of settlers.

They were tempted to South America by enticements such as those listed in Hugh Hughes' *Llawlyfr y Wladychfa Gymreig*, a sort of settlers' handbook, which acted as an advert for the adventure, describing the shoulder-high, 'tall, strong grasses' in 'luscious pastures' with abundant wild cattle, not to mention an amenable climate not dissimilar to Wales. This latter was a meteorological sleight of hand easily achieved by comparing mean temperatures for Buenos Aires in the north and Port Famine in the south. It was enough to make a farmer of the bald Welsh hills, living a hardscrabble life, believe that he could make it here, away from prohibitive regimes of rates, and he could own, yes, *own* his own land. The pauper could be king of all he surveyed in this *tierra de nadie*, this no-man's land where, crucially, no men had previously staked their claims. There was the official promise of 300 acres of land for each settler, and this a land where horses could be reared for their hides and command a good price on the British market. And the handbook and its advocates cheerfully assessed a whole diverse economy that would be available to the new settlers, who could gather *guano* (the accumulated dropping of seabirds, rich in nitrates), process salt, hew coal, capture wild horses, make iron and make hay, and rear both sheep and cattle. It stressed that such resources were only there for those willing to work hard, and underlined the hardships involved, but, people who were already inured to hardship would have probably filtered out such warnings, or failed to heed them properly. After all: why spoil a comforting dream?

His biographer, E. G. Bowen, suggested that Hugh Hughes had read 'everything that was available to him about the country at the time … but … had merely selected from what he had read that which he considered favourable to his argument, and discarded all evidence to the contrary'. One feels that the Advertising Standards Authority, had it existed at the time, would have had a field day. But then again, this was happening all over the world, with countries keen as can be to attract new migrants like birds to a lighthouse beam. Labour was capital, or, rather, could become capital, and there were new frontiers everywhere, from the American West to the Australian outback, where land lay to be claimed, gained and pioneered.

Reaching the promised land

When the first boatload of settlers from Wales made landfall in South America, they did not find the land described in the handbooks and the various adverts which encouraged them to give up everything and venture to a completely foreign land. There was no milk, or honey: neither were there wild cattle – big as prehistoric aurochs – roaming free in jungles of tall, wild grass. They spent their first nights sheltering in scrapes, or set about building rudimentary huts.

Hunger. Gnawing hunger, and cold to flense the skin. They had not been prepared for such weather, nor for the forbidding harshness of the terrain. They had not paid sufficient heed to the adamant declarations of the Argentine Government that it could not, and would not, grant self-determination to any group of new immigrants. The *Mimosa*'s human cargo was also lacking the right equipment, not to mention monetary backing, even though a pivotal figure in the history of the settlement, the Rev. Michael D. Jones, had not only paid the costs of hiring the *Mimosa* to replace the *Halton Castle* (the ship initially hired to transport the emigrants), but also the accommodation in Liverpool for the travellers waiting to embark, and lent the venture over £2,500, on the clear understanding that this was a loan and not a gift. As we'll find out, Michael D. Jones' support and largesse would cost him dearly later on, including losing his home to bankruptcy. Similarly, the odds were stacked high against the travellers across the South Atlantic right from the start. It remains something just short of a miracle that they withstood the cold and the panoply of misfortunes which beset them initially to establish themselves, persist, and sometimes thrive in this testing land.

But one can only imagine the depth of their disappointment as they surveyed the chill, low cliff-scape, and beyond it, desert terrain. It transpired that this Promised Land was, in truth, a wind-blasted wasteland, a terrible terra incognita, seemingly entirely useless for the purposes of farming – not that many of the settlers knew one end of a hoe from another, and certainly not how to plough one's own furrow. Many of them came from mining communities such as the one Huw Morgan had left, in places like Mountain Ash. Theirs was the underground world, the place of mandrill and pick, the miner's tools of choice, which were of no use whatsoever here. Little wonder, then, that William Jones sent a letter to his uncle in Bala in November 1865, complaining bitterly that 'the worst things here are the men, the clumsiest and most useless bunch that ever could have come together. Most of them are coal miners and salesmen with no experience of working the land …'

So … Bungling? Certainly. Magnificent? Let's hear the verdict of an elder statesman of Welsh letters, the poet Bobi Jones. Writing in the Welsh-language current affairs monthly *Barn* in 1965, on the occasion of the colony's centenary, he opined:

> The Patagonian celebrations in Wales this year have been rather unreal. Many deceived themselves that the emigration had been a success, that it is wonderful to think that there is an exotic land beyond the southern hemisphere where people preach in Welsh, that there us is some future to Welshness in the shadow of the Andes. That is, we deceive ourselves that the emigration was worthy of note, that it has some historical value, and we inflate the whole thing to seem like a significant element in our national life.

The efforts of these emigrants seeded such myths without effort. They had, after all, come to a barren, inhospitable place, where even the chill winds weren't like the howlers and gusters at home. Here, the wind was all scythes and sickles, cutting through to the chill bone marrow, cutting to the quick. Hyperbole? Perhaps not.

Over the years, people have vied with each other to register just how bleak and testing is this South American terrain; this, at times, deeply unforgiving land. One of the early Welsh settlers grumbled, with good reason, that Patagonia was the last place to be created by God, and he was thus too tired to finish the place properly. Another weary pioneer, noting the way the hot winds of the Pampero blew across the steppes, maintained that 'it was God who created the world, but it was the Devil who created Patagonia, and made it as similar to hell as possible.' The author R. Bryn Williams recalled an English doctor who visited y Wladfa, and was questioned by all and sundry why he had come there in the first place. His answer was, presumably, a tad ironic, because he explained that he had dreamed that he had died, and had arrived at the pearly gates of heaven. Here the gatekeeper Peter declined him entry on the grounds that he was too morally bad to come inside. He then went to the portal to hell, where he was similarly and summarily turned away. Confused by the turn of events, he asked the Devil where he could go now, to which Old Nick peremptorily replied, 'Go to Patagonia'.

Despite their hellish aspects, the empty, wind-whipped topographies have their charms, their undoubted hold on the imagination. The evolutionist Charles Darwin thought the Patagonian plains had a very sterile appearance, covered as they are 'with thorny bushes and a dry-looking grass that will forever remain nearly useless to all of mankind' and, furthermore, thought 'the curse of sterility is on the land', but nevertheless the author of *The Origin of Species* had a fondness for it too. His capacious mind returned there often: 'In calling up images of the past, I find the plains of Patagonia most frequently cross before my eyes. Yet these plains are pronounced by all most wretched and useless. They are only characterized by negative possessions; without habitations, without water, without trees, without mountains, they support merely a few dwarf plants.'

Such descriptions do nothing to dampen the enthusiasm of the increasing number of visitors from Wales, who delight in taking tea and cakes in one of the many Welsh teahouses in Gaiman, or who beat a Nonconformist pilgrim's path to the chapels that still offer silent witness – except on Sundays – to the sinewy path that sustained the Welsh spirit, candles against the dark trials of life which refuse to gutter, despite the keening wind sweeping in across desolate plains.

Not that the Welsh have always taken an interest in y Wladfa. There were periods when out of sight meant out of mind. Those in Wales were accused of shamefully neglecting the colony, especially between the two world wars. It took the centenary celebrations of 1965 to spark interest and forge new links. Since then, there have been regular educational exchanges and scholarships for Argentinian students, dedicated literary competitions at the National Eisteddfod for Patagonians, and a Welsh Government-sponsored scheme, administered by the British Council, to supply teachers from Wales who offer classes in Welsh in the Patagonian communities. The scheme was established by Cymdeithas Cymru–Ariannin (the Wales–

Argentina Society) in 1990. This isn't a very costly scheme, and there are constant, and understandable, grumblings about the tens of thousands it takes to maintain these educational links, with people feeling that much more could be done. In the context of the Welsh Government's overall budget, it is pretty much petty cash, but it's an important international gesture of solidarity.

The flags that fly in the fierce winds of y Wladfa are primarily the blue and white of the Argentine, although Y Ddraig Goch (the Welsh dragon) does flutter its reptilian, pennant wings in places. For the people who live here are no longer Welsh people living in Argentina, but rather, Argentinians with Welsh roots. This can lead to some interesting tensions. When Russell Isaac, an HTV current affairs journalist, was covering the Falklands / Malvinas war in 1982, he found a young soldier-translator, Milton Rhys, working for Mario Benjamin Menéndez, the post-invasion Governor of the Malvinas. The soldier's family was Welsh-Patagonian from the Gaiman, and yet his first encounter with native Welsh people were the Welsh Guards who had entered Port Stanley in full battle dress. It was little wonder that Rhys spoke very emotionally about this experience on the *Byd ar Bedwar* programme, which also featured a Welsh-speaking woman and her Argentine colonel husband. Notably, it was this colonel who managed to secure Isaac's release when he was arrested, along with Simon Winchester from *The Times*, near a naval base at Comodoro Rivadavia.

In the many accounts of y Wladfa, the courage, tenacity and heroic endeavour of the early settlers is always emphasised. Theirs was a struggle to cope with a land greatly at variance to that which they had been promised and, to boot, as one observer put it: 'The venture was ill-informed and ill-planned and jeopardized from the outset by ignorance of the physical and climactic features of the Chubut region'. In the face of such punishing obstacles, they were called upon to be brave and tough, as tough indeed as some of the native trees whose wood is so hard it can blunt the keenest axe blade. Members of the Welsh colony stayed on despite extreme hardship and deprivation, and achieved a great deal – as, for example, when they won awards in Chicago for their wheat, or when they managed the great feat of canalizing the Chubut river and using its waters for irrigation, or ran a railway track across the desert. It suggests a certain stubbornness of character, a solid fibre of determination that still forms the backbone of the communities of the Andes and the flood plains of the lower Chubut river. Something determined to cling on. You can hear it in the desiccated voices of the chapel congregations, holding on to God and singing their praise in notes of pure Welsh.

It was, perhaps, inevitable that I would go to Patagonia myself. I've been what I'd have to describe as a professional Welshman for a long time – the sort who'd pick up John Davies and Marian Delyth's book called *Wales: the 100 Places to See Before You Die* and say, yes, ticked all those off in life's journal. So where else would a man besotted with Welsh culture go? What would be the one-hundred-and-first place? For many Welsh speakers, Patagonia would top the list of overseas destinations, of absolute go-to places. Fancifully, some might see the place as the linguistic equivalent of those seed-banks of endangered plants that are preserved in airtight chambers under Arctic ice, or in cabinets in Kew Gardens: should the language die out in Wales, there'd still be some Welsh speakers left, safe in Argentina.

I've also travelled a great deal through Latin America, and often, it was books that had triggered those journeys. The first such journey was to Mexico, to locate the *cantina* where the Consul gets impossibly pissed in Malcolm Lowry's *Under the Volcano*, and to experiment with mescal, to see whether the cactus-based booze is hallucinogenic if you ingest enough of it. (It is. You'll see insects the size of bears. Believe me.)

To begin with, my knowledge of y Wladfa was scanty. Once, having misbehaved in a Welsh class in secondary school, I'd been punished by having to play the *paith*, the Argentinian prairie, in a class reading of a Saunders Lewis play. Fortunately for me, having suffered years of chronic asthma, I was able to produce an eerily emphysemic whistling sound, which reasonably evoked the wind sweeping down from the *cordilleras*. I'd also read the former Archdruid R. Bryn Williams' many books about the settlement, and, of course, *In Patagonia* by Bruce Chatwin, that great fabulist and fictioneer among travel writers, who made the genre his own for a good while.

Before I set off, I read avidly about the place: the books span the entire six-foot span of my writing desk, teetering and tottering in untidy piles. One book tower contains Geraint Owen's *Crisis in Chubut*, George Chatworth Musters' *At Home With the Patagonians*, and Marcus Tanner's *The Last of the Celts*. Some volumes, such as the *Field Guide to the Birds of Argentina and Uruguay*, take pride of place. Frankly, this is the sort of ornithology porn through which I love to leaf, revelling in the litany of exotic names – festive coquette, sharp-tailed streamcreeper, cinereous tyrant, not to mention Olrog's gull. And the exact drawings by Dario Yzurieta of some of the Patagonian species, such as the Chilean flamingo's wash of pale pink, or the drab browns of the lesser *castanero*, brought out the twitcher in me, gently convulsing at the very thought of spotting a *chimango caracara*, a bird of prey that typically flies in flocks.

But too much of this sort of research can be a bit of a mistake. Books such as Elvey MacDonald rigorously researched *Yr Hirdaith*, and Glyn Williams' *The Desert and the Dream* made me feel inadequate, my knowledge too sketchy, my understanding too thin.

And there was the creeping feeling that not only had someone seen it all before, but that someone had also written about it. One day, I was writing my description of a cliff face near the main road connecting dusty Trelew and high Esquel. I noted that it had the same colour scheme as Neapolitan ice-cream. Then Bruce Chatwin's letters were published, and in that volume, there is a description of what must be the self-same cliffs. Chatwin notes that: 'Sometimes it seems that the Almighty has been playing at making Neapolitan ice-cream', because they are indeed 'strawberry, vanilla and pistachio.' Bruce had beaten me to it; got there first.

So, just as it's difficult to see Paris without Proust somehow getting in the way, or imagining Dublin without seeing it through Joyce's eyes, or at least one of his characters', so too was it hard, during my one long sojourn in Patagonia, to see the place without those other accounts intruding – Eluned Morgan's pellucid prose-poems in books such as *Dringo'r Andes*, the peregrinations of R. Bryn Williams in *Crwydro Patagonia*, or even the fanciful and problematical fictions that make up the settlers' handbook, which drew people here to this wind-scorched patch of earth in the first instance.

Together, these volumes made me question the need for another book about the place, but I was somehow doomed to write one. Patagonia is now under my skin, burrowed there like a chigger, and, besides, writers don't have much choice. The books come to seek us out, demanding to be written. The pages of this one are animated by whisper-fingers of Patagonian wind, flipping and turning its pages, seeking out the story.

Chapter 1

New Found Land

Cambriol

The idea of establishing a specifically 'Welsh' community in another part of the world emerged long before the mid-nineteenth century and its emigrations from Wales to the United States of America, and to Patagonia. As early as the 1610s, Sir William Vaughan, from Golden Grove near Llandeilo, sought to establish a Welsh community called 'Cambriol' in Newfoundland, almost two and a half centuries before the settlement in Chubut. This was one of the first overseas ventures by the Welsh, taking settlers to chill northern climes.

Colony Vaughan

William Vaughan was a polymath and peregrinator, a man of many talents: an Oxford-educated lawyer, a colonial pioneer, a scholar and a poet. After a Grand Tour of France and Italy, he studied for a further degree at the University of Vienna, and on his return to Wales in 1616, he became High Sheriff of Carmarthenshire.

His early adult life was blighted by a freak accident and family tragedy, when his wife Elizabeth died as a result of lightning striking their home. Vaughan could have retired into a shell of grief, but instead he came out fighting. Not that the enduring, deep grief didn't have a profound effect on him – at this testing time, he became utterly sickened by the poverty he saw all around him in Carmarthenshire. He saw an answer, if not the complete answer, in overseas colonization. His often oddball writings comment on the sad state of Wales at the time, and castigate his fellow countrymen for a lack of energy and enthusiasm, while his vision of an energetic overseas colony was perhaps too confident and overambitious right from the start.

Meanwhile, Vaughan railed against a certain fecklessness displayed by the Welsh that was, at least in part, responsible for the desertification of the mountains and the poor crops of their wheat fields. He wrote about a country stricken by poverty:

> Although many strange sicknesses haue diuers times of late yeares afflicted us, yet notwithstanding, the multitudes of people are here so great, that thousands yearly doe perish for want of reliefe. Yea, I haue known in these last deare yeares, that 100 persons haue yearly died in a parish, where the Tithes amounted not to fourscore pounds a yeare, the most part for lacke of food, fire and raiment, the which the poorer sort of that Country stand in greater need of, then the Inhabitants … by reason of their Mountaines and hills, which cause the winter there to be most bitter with stormy winds, raine, or snow, and that for the space of eight monneths …

The answer to this lack of pretty much everything, he averred, lay in creating a colony on a huge, triangular, northern island, set in roiling, churning seas off the east coast of Canada. There is no evidence that Vaughan ever visited Newfoundland to assess it in advance of sending settlers, or to fully consider any mercantile possibilities, unlike, say, Lewis Jones who visited Patagonia three years before the settlers from Wales travelled there in 1865. But the existence of an earlier and established fishery in the area gave Vaughan hope that the settlement would be sustainable, in terms of fish, at least. This was, after all, cod heaven. For, as he put it: 'I saw that God had reserved the Newfoundland for us Britaines'.

The newly-found land had already been claimed for Henry Tudor by the Venetian John Cabot, who had sailed out of Bristol in May 1497. Two months later, this maritime adventurer was steadfastly bound for the far shore of the North Atlantic, in search of the then legendary Northwest Passage through northern Canada to Japan and China. Like Christopher Columbus, who had discovered America five years earlier, Cabot was searching for a sea-route to connect with the Far East, and the fabled treasure houses and chests of India and China.

The Northwest Passage! This was a veritable grail for navigators, and could not be found, or even looked for, without facing real and terrible dangers. As if proof was needed, even as late as 1845, the perilous acres of ice at King William Island trapped Sir John Franklin and the crews of his venturing ships the *Erebus* and the *Terror* in a vice of ice. Not a frozen soul survived.

What Cabot had found was a three-sided island, with a land mass slightly larger than that of Ireland. He also found plentiful fish. Cabot would be followed by many like-minded adventurers and questers, such as Martin Frobisher, not to mention two intrepid Welshmen, Sir Thomas Button from Cardiff and Captain Thomas James of Monmouthshire. They all faced winters of paralyzing cold, complete with the dangers and oppressions of endless ice or enshrouding fog and mist.

But the fabled Northwest Passage wasn't the only reason for taking such risks: it also allowed countries to claim new lands and territories, through force of arms or simple subterfuge, leading to the bitter and bloody disputes between England and France over land in eastern Canada. The new found lands of the north were no exception to such land grabs. And, of course, there were sea grabs, too, areas of ocean to be claimed for their underwater bounty, at point of sword, or by force of arms, if need be.

This period was one of the high water marks of global exploration. Spain had already been busy colonizing the Americas, via the various voyages of Columbus, followed some 75 years later by English settlements in Virginia. Famously, and contemporaneously with William Vaughan's ultimately doomed adventure in Newfoundland, was the voyage of the *Mayflower* in 1620, bringing the Pilgrim Fathers to a new home, and to a new and liberating religious freedom, in Plymouth.

The seas around Newfoundland were bountiful, if treacherous by dint of storm and wild water. From Cabot's time onwards, it was well known that there were plentiful stocks of fish to be had in the cold seas off the island's coast, promising both food and, ultimately, wealth. Commentators averred that 'the sea there is full of fish that can be taken not only with nets but with fishing-baskets'. It suggested that catching cod was as easy as catching a cold.

Little wonder, then, that the seemingly limitless fish stocks of the Grand Banks attracted tough fishermen from Devon, France, Spain – and especially the skilled sailors of the Basque country – not forgetting the redoubtable seamen of Portugal, to cast their nets thereabouts.

Vaughan knew all this and, serendipitously, in 1578 a very favourable report appeared, which he read avidly, much as Hugh Hughes read equivalent reports about Patagonia later on. It was written by one Anthony Parkhurst who, perhaps a little too enthusiastically, described the quality and fecundity of the new found land. It hinted at the value of the forests and, by way of a clincher, suggested that the natives were benign. Later documents would suggest that these North American Indians could be 'ruled wisely', and thus ensure their obedience and furthermore that 'only by establishing a settlement on the island could the poor pagans of the Country be led from their Barbarism to a knowledge of God and thus ensure their salvation'. This, too, adumbrated the descriptions of the Patagonian natives some of the Welsh would read before venturing to South America.

In August 1583, the island of Newfoundland was officially claimed by Sir Humphrey Gilbert on behalf of Queen Elizabeth I, with the aim of encouraging the fishermen to settle the land, but many of these only visited in the summer, and there was also the matter of French boats harrying and harassing the fishing fleets to dissuade those thinking of putting down roots on the island, or challenging them for the fishy wealth of the teeming waters.

James I then authorised merchant adventurers to settle Newfoundland, with a Bristolian, John Guy, taking advantage of this Royal Assent to create a settlement. But an ultra-hard winter in 1613, not to mention unruly settlers, sent him sailing home, tailcoat between his legs. By 1660, only 150 families from England had crossed the Atlantic, so pioneers, and the basic skills needed to pioneer, were in short supply.

Vaughan wasn't among those early enthusiasts who took up King James' early offer of land, but in 1616 he bought himself a substantial tract of Newfoundland. Indeed, he purchased the entire Avalon peninsula south of a line from Caplin Bay (now called Calvert) stretching across to Placentia Bay, which he then christened Cambriol, thus creating a little Wales in the New World. The Avalon peninsula itself was so named 'in imitation of Old Avalon in Somerset wherein Glassenbury stands, the first fruits of Christianity in Britain'. Glastonbury, allegedly the home of the Holy Grail, was a good model for a new pilgrim destination.

Vaughan nursed his desire to establish a foreign colony for a long time, and there are hints of that desire in a book called *The Golden Grove*, which appeared in 1600, purporting to help 'all such as would know how to gouerne themselues, their houses and their country'. The fact that he had at one time entertained the idea of settling far-off, and entirely remote St. Helena island, a tropical, volcanic island in the South Atlantic, suggested a certain impracticality, if not downright fantasy, in his way of thinking.

But Newfoundland, if nothing else, was nearer Britain, and Vaughan was probably seduced by the persuasive flow of pro-Newfoundland propaganda, expressly designed to lure settlers and an influx of investment to its rugged shores and wooded slopes, coincidentally and strategically thwarting the French desire to also own the place. Vaughan's ambitions must have been bolstered, too, by the achievements of his talented Scottish friend, Sir William Alexander, the Earl of Stirling, who had managed to conjure Nova Scotia into being.

In 1617, Vaughan sent some men and women – there is no accurate figure of how many exactly – at his own cost, to the patch of earth he had baptized as Cambriol. It was a land he would later describe as being 'entirely bountiful', although the reality would prove a little more austere and harsh:

> The commodities of the Land are Furres of Beuer, Sables, Blacke Foxes, Marternes, Musk-rats, Otters, and such like skinnes, as also of greater beasts; as Deere, and other wild creatures. To this I adioyne the benefit, which may be made by woods, being pine, birch, spruce, Furre, &c. fit for boords, Masts, barke for tanning, and dying, Charcoales for making of Iron. Out of these woods we may haue pitch, Tarre, Rosen, Turpentine, Frankinscence, and honey out of the hollow trees, as in Muscouy, and heretofore in our owne woods before they were converted to the Iron Mills. There is great store of Mettals, if they be lookt after.

The cost of each passage was probably of the order of ten shillings a head, at a time when the trip to Virginia would have cost five pounds. A bargain. The settlers were taken to the area near Trepassey, which would later become famous as the departure point for Amelia Earhart's plane called *Friendship*, as she became the first woman to fly across the Atlantic. Vaughan soon realized 'that the burden was too great for my weak shoulders'.

On the Grand Banks, and other banks offshore, it was reasonably simple to seek out the fish stocks at any time during the season, but inshore, where most of the English ships worked, a knowledge of the grounds took years to acquire, to be added to in each generation. The inshore fishery was dependent on the cod migrating annually from their offshore feeding and breeding grounds in early summer, and every harbour and inlet had certain peculiarities. The Welsh settlers from the Tywi valley knew nothing of such things. In such circumstances, ignorance equals starvation.

Meanwhile, the Spanish, Portuguese and French concentrated on hauling in the catch from the fishing ground called the Grand Banks, off Newfoundland, where the silvery cod could always be found. The harvest was then salted on board the ships and brought back to Europe to be dried and sold. Even when they fished near shore, these fishermen usually used abundant supplies of salt. The English and Welsh fishermen did not have access to the supplies that were available to the others, and could not salt their fish to the same extent. They were, however, able to develop a system which combined light salting for a short period, followed by thorough washing, and then drying in the open air. The result was the light-salted product for which Newfoundland eventually became famous.

The settlers from Wales certainly had their work cut out. Importantly, the Welsh migrants might not even have been fishermen in the first place: we simply do not know if they had actually left agricultural lives on the farms of the Tywi valley. Nets, salt, tides and swell might well have been entirely mysterious to them.

So, ill-equipped, especially for the severe weather, the Cambriol venture quickly foundered, with the colonists seeking refuge in the harbour of Aquaforte, where they spent the bleak winter months huddled in temporary cabins built by migratory fishermen for summer use. The colony's future had few prospects of outlasting a candle's burning: it was sadly destined for sudden expiration.

Problems with the French

To compound their problems, the other fishermen who had been lured here from all compass points were in no mood to share the fishy spoils, and did their best to interfere with the newcomers' catch. The French, in particular, had designs on claiming land, and they attacked the Welsh pioneers with some ferocity, scaring them with the intention of driving them away. In the face of these extra challenges, in 1618, Vaughan hired the experienced fishing master Richard Whitborne to bring further colonists and provisions to bolster the precarious settlement, and appointed him governor.

Whitborne, a man with brine running in his veins in lieu of blood, had been pretty much born to the sea. He had been a sailor even as a young boy, and had first visited Newfoundland in 1579. He was to become a renowned captain and navigator, winning plaudits for his bravery during the defeat of the Spanish Armada in 1588.

Whitborne did his best to reorganize the colony, beginning by moving it to better quarters in the town of Renews, but, even as he did so, he had to deal with the consequences of one of his own ships being attacked by piratical deserters from Sir Walter Raleigh's Guyana fleet. On another occasion, despite his nautical skills and experience, he was attacked by a French pirate ship and relieved of £860, which, in those days, would have been a king's ransom.

In the end, only half a dozen colonists spent the winter of 1619 at Renews, and they were forced to abandon the settlement completely the following year. Vaughan's own health wasn't sufficiently robust to visit the island during this period, and thus offer encouragement to his own pioneers.

Defiantly, Vaughan retained his property south of Renews, after selling off the Ferryland area to Sir George Calvert, and a plot of land in Fermeuse to Lord Falkland. Calvert built a house on the island, but persistent harrying by the French led to its eventual abandonment, too. There is no real evidence that Vaughan made any further attempts at colonization, though some sources claim he set up a short-lived settlement near Trepassey. A trifle late in the day, Vaughan visited the island for two extended stays, between 1622 and 1625 and 1628 and 1630, although not everyone agrees that he did actually visit the islands in person at all.

Even in 1630, he still had vestigial hope for settling the new found land, and suggested that grants of land might be forthcoming, saying that 'Our noble brother-in-law, Sir Henry Salisbury, with some gentlemen of north Wales, will next Spring proceed to do something in that country which with open arms awaits their coming'. If nothing else, Vaughan managed to make some marks on the island's history. A splendid map of the area was drawn up in 1625 by 'Captaine John Mason, an industrious gent: who spent seven yeares in the Countrey, who was also the second governor of the island'. Cambriola is clearly marked, showing the extent of Vaughan's holdings, and Avalonia is also clearly marked, being the area transferred early on to Calvert and Falkland. The map also shows six Welsh place names, arranged in a semi-circle, namely Brechonia, Cardigan, Pembrok, Cardiffe and Glamorgan. Vaughan's old home, Golden Grove, has its Newfoundland counterpart on the map, too, as well as 'Colchos' and the eponymous 'Vaughan's Cove' nearby.

Just as the establishment of the Welsh colony in Patagonia would later be touted and recounted in scores of books and many a documentary series as a tale of stubbornness, grit and, ultimately, success, Vaughan equally promoted Newfoundland in an unusual book called *The Golden Fleece*, which appeared in 1626. Vaughan was appropriating the apparatus of myth to make himself and the history of his short-lived colony seem more successful.

The Golden Fleece, transported from Cambriol Colchis, by Orpheus Junior, is a long and fantastic prose allegory, dealing with the 'Errours of Religion, the Vices and Decayes of the Kingdome, and lastly the Wayes to get wealth, and to restore Trading' through the colonization of Newfoundland. Colchis was a reference to the mythical land on the Eastern edge of the Black Sea, the departure point for Jason and the Argonauts in the Greek tale. Vaughan was giving the account of the adventure the trappings of a familiar myth, and all its loftiness.

Vaughan divided this eccentric literary outpouring into three parts, namely: an attack on the Church in Rome; an account of the parlous state of the Empire, and a section which purported to show 'how to win money and to renew trade that's the subject of so much complaining'. This latter part was Vaughan's own sales pitch for this northern island:

> Towards the North, the land is more hilly and woody; but the South part, from Renoos, to Trepassa, plaine and champaine euen for 30 miles in extent. It abounds with Deere, as well fallow Deere, as Ellans, which are as bigge as our Oxen. And of all other sorts of wilde Beasts, as here in Europe, Beuers, Hares, &c. The like I may say for Fowle and Fish. I knew one Fowler in a winter, which killed aboue 700 Partridges himselfe at Renoos. But for the

Fish, specially the Cod, which drawes all the chiefe Port townes in Christendome to send thither some ships euery yeare, either to fish, or to buy the same; it is most wonderfull, and almost incredible, vnlesse a man were there present to behold it. Of these, three men at Sea in a Boat, with some on shoare to dresse and dry them, in thirty dayes will kill commonly betwixt fiue and twenty and thirty thousand, worth with the Traine oyle arising from them, one hundred or sixe score pounds. I haue heard of some Countries, commended for their twofold haruest, which here we haue, although in a different kinde: yet both as profitable, I dare say, as theirs so much extolld. There is no such place againe in the world for a poore man to raise his fortunes, comparable to this Plantation, for in one moneths space, with reasonable paines, he may get as much as will pay both Land-lords Rent, Seruants wages, and all Houshold charges, for the whole yeare, and so the rest of his gaine to increase.

Vaughan's *Golden Fleece* was the latest addition to a small but growing shelf of persuasive volumes, such as governor Whitbourne's book about Newfoundland, published six years earlier, and already reprinted three times by the time the *Fleece* was printed. Whitbourne's useful and detailed *Discourse and Discovery of Newfoundland* came complete with 'many reasons to prove how worthy and beneficiall a Plantation may there be made, after a far better manner than it now is. Together with the laying open of certaine enormities and abuses committed by some that trade to that Country, and the meanes laid downe for reformation thereof'. Other books traversed the same terrain, such as John Mason's comprehensive *A briefe discourse of the New-found-land*, which also appeared in 1620. These books sought not only to attract people to settle but, more importantly, encourage people to invest in the overseas ventures.

The allusion to the Golden Fleece says a lot about Vaughan's aim in penning his allegory, evoking as it does Jason and the Argonauts' courage in the face of myriad dangers, from harpies to sirens. Vaughan's attempt to settle a far-off and treacherous place, and the literary account of the endeavours that followed, foreshadows accounts of the later Patagonian adventure, which would similarly be redacted, employing the language of myth.

In the case of y Wladfa in Patagonia, it would generate nothing short of a small library of such accounts and texts, while Vaughan's claimed land would be swallowed up in the fog of history's forgetfulness, the words of his celebrant's poem fading on the sepia-coloured manuscript, the ink fading with the inexorable passage of time.

Chapter 2

From Gwalia to Patagonia: a short history of the settlement

> Rarely has a scheme for colonization been launched in circumstances which were liable sooner or later to generate serious economic and political difficulties. The promoters of the enterprise could, perhaps, have hardly foreseen them. Nevertheless they cannot be entirely exonerated from a sad neglect in not assessing, as correctly as was possible at the time, the actual situation in Patagonia before dispatching 150 of their countrymen to an isolated valley in that immense and practically unexplored land.
>
> Geraint Dyfnallt Owen, *Crisis in Chubut*

On The Move
The past couple of centuries have witnessed huge human migrations across all the peopled continents. Indeed, humanity has always been on the move – following the seasonal paths of animals, seeking better lands, or advantage, or new sources of food and water. In recent centuries, the reasons and compulsions for leaving home and looking for a new one have multiplied and become more complex. The migrants and movers have been searching for *better* lives, or have been on the march for economic reasons, or to escape poverty, war, religious persecution or political oppression. Thus compelled, they have moved in droves, bearing their packs, their parcels, their scant possessions, the numbers swelling so that they were soon travelling in their hundreds and thousands, exchanging village for town, town for city, old country for new.

The Scots and the Irish settled overseas in great numbers, respectively driven by such devastating factors as the Highland Clearances – the enforced, simultaneous eviction of all families living in a given area of Scotland, such as an entire glen – and the Irish famine, which led to the sailings of the appalling armada of coffin ships away from Ireland in the 1830s, leaving a land blighted in the extreme. In fact, Wales, or Gwalia to use an older, archaic name for it – derived from the medieval Latin, Wallia – was a considerable magnet for inward migration, and during the decade just before the First World War, it was second only to the United States of America in drawing in new workers and their families, with an immigration rate of 45 per 10,000. As the irrepressible historian Gwyn Alf Williams puts it in *When Was Wales?*, this tumultuous decade was a time when 'something like 130,000 people – and a mixed, polyglot, buoyant and innovatory people they were – flooded into the coal valleys of south Wales'.

The Call of America
The Welsh emigrations overseas didn't involve quite the same numbers of people as, say, the Irish and the Scots. That isn't to say that the Welsh mainly stayed at home. North America and its myriad opportunities held its attractions for the Welsh, just as it did for their Celtic cousins. The United States, in particular, was the principal emigrant destination, with the coal fields and steel towns of the East ardently keen to utilize those well-developed skills of the Welsh colliers and metalworkers. By the 1850s, there were 30,000 immigrants from Wales in the U.S., and that number would treble within four decades.

This wasn't the first time that the Welsh had turned emigrants. There had long been a trade in peoples across the border into England. But then, between 1660 and 1720, some of the Welsh fled religious persecution by crossing the expanse of Atlantic, such as the group of Baptists led by John Miles, who left Europe bound for Massachusetts while the Quakers, especially a contingent from Meirionnydd, who left with William Penn in 1682, were leaving for what they hoped in their hearts would be a New Wales, a land of freedom, in particular freedom of religious expression. From the 1790s right up until the Great Depression of the 1930s, the Welsh fanned out in increasing numbers across the globe, heading for countries such as the United States, Australia, New Zealand, Canada and South Africa, with a smaller trickle of people choosing to try their luck in an array of places such as Chile, France, Mexico, Russia, Brazil and India.

Dreamers and schemers

The urge to settle elsewhere usually only took one visionary to instill the dream in others. In 1792, a radical Baptist minister called Morgan John Rhys went to the banks of the Blacklick and Connemaugh rivers in Pennsylvania, some 250 miles west of Philadelphia. He was soon trying to persuade fellow Welshmen to follow him, not least when Rhys married the daughter of one Colonel Benjamin Loxley. Loxley and his partner, Benjamin Rush, bought some land together, and in 1795, established a company called the Cambrian Company of Philadelphia. Soon, the new settlements they established were grouped together as 'Cambria', with a main town called Beulah. This attracted migrants like moths to a candle, although the colony would ultimately prove to be short-lived, even though it did manage to send an offshoot to a place called Paddy's Run, near a place now called Shandon in Ohio.

The state of Ohio, especially the counties of Jackson and Gallia, were sufficiently effective magnets for the Welsh that they earned the moniker Little Wales, and had their very own Welsh Calvinist-Methodist synods. In the middle of the nineteenth century in Minnesota, there were sufficient Welsh people to justify the translation of the state constitution on behalf of the inhabitants of places such as Blue Earth and Le Sueur. Some of the Welsh emigrants had left places such as Llanbrynmair in rural Montgomeryshire (with this village being particularly depleted), bound for Ohio, and had bedded down there sufficiently well, and in sufficient numbers, to attract others. Attempts were made elsewhere, also, including one to establish the settlement of Brynffynnon by Samuel Roberts in Tennessee.

In 1857, the Reverend Samuel Roberts, a minister from Montgomery, wrote a series of pamphlets outlining the unfair treatment of tenants and attacking landlords, tithes and church rates. Roberts argued that the only solution to this egregious situation was emigration to the United States. Roberts arranged for William Bebb to establish Brynffynnon. However, the venture was not a success. With Roberts' blessing, 100,000 acres of land were purchased in East Tennessee, and a mercantile company was established in tandem with the purchase.

As the Welsh immigrants across America exchanged dollars for pounds in their pay packets, the new arrivals were also under pressure to assimilate, to abandon their own customs, culture, and indeed, their language, in order to fit in. Admittedly, there were pockets where the Welsh presence was sufficiently strong to keep some sort of Welsh culture alive. But whatever age you were, there was an expectation that you would become an American, often a Young American, with new allegiances within the emerging American industrial culture, and with the English tongue as, ironically enough, the lingua franca.

By now, there was Welsh immigrant activity and energy right across the map of the United States, with winners and losers. William Jones from Llangadfan wanted to set up a colony in Kentucky, but his plan came to naught. Meanwhile, emigrants from the castellated town of Caernarfon in north Wales were setting up shop in Utica, New York State, while, in 1803, settlers from Radnorshire created Radnor Township in Delaware, and there was that failed attempt to create a colony in Tennessee, of course. Many Welsh utopian dreamers and schemers saw their plans fail to properly bear fruit, the visions dimming, the dreams turning to dust.

The germ of an idea

Learning the English language broadened the horizon of opportunity so that the Welsh settlers could fan out to seek work in further flung parts of America. As they had not arrived in great numbers, they tended not to meet and commingle with other Welsh people, so that, a generation on, they had lost pretty much all of the cultural baggage they had brought with them across the Atlantic, and were wearing the bright shiny clothes of New Americans.

This phenomenon irked one man in particular. Michael D. Jones was a Welsh nonconformist minister, tee-totaller and steadfast nationalist. Described by the twentieth-century poet Gwenallt as the most important Welshman of the nineteenth century, and the greatest nationalist after Owain Glyndŵr, Jones originally came from Llanuwchllyn, near Bala. Jones visited America as a young man and didn't like what he saw; the way the country subsumed his fellow Welshmen and women. He would end up railing against this submersion, and coming up with an alternative.

Michael D. Jones simply loved growing up in Wales. His recollections of its craggy mountains and foaming rivers, written down by him in later life with both lyricism and fondness, suggest that a man who would become renowned for his steely, driven and uncompromising character, concealed a more romantic side.

He certainly eulogized the rural way of life. Jones enjoyed eating simple fare, and he also loved fishing and hunting – he wore the basic, unadorned clothes of the countryside. But he also dressed this way because he thought a cleric should wear the same clothes as his flock, and besides, it helped to directly support the rural industries of farming and weaving. The countryside was in his blood. There is one telling story about his turning up late to deliver an evening sermon because he had got lost in the pleasures of hunting woodcock on the way, annoying the congregation that had been waiting for him.

His great love of angling, on the other hand, brought him into direct conflict with some of the landowners, not least Sir Watkin Williams-Wynn of Wynnstay. Jones organized public protests against the appointment of a keeper to patrol his favourite fishing river, the Lliw. In this he succeeded, and the keeper was indeed removed, but Michael D. Jones' father ended up a fishing fly's hair's breadth away from being turfed out of his tenancy as a consequence of his poacher son's agitations.

Michael D. Jones studied in Carmarthen – having already become quite a scholar of Greek and Latin by the time he got there – and at Highbury College in London, before travelling to North America in 1848, where he took up a ministry in Lawrence Street Church, Cincinnati, Ohio, despite having been offered two very substantial English churches in London.

He set sail across the Atlantic at a time of considerable foment and unrest in Continental Europe, not least an uprising in Hungary, which forced a change of government. Later, this event in central Europe was to have signal repercussions for Michael D. Jones' way of thinking.

Jones' sister Mary already lived in the United States, where she was married to Evan Bebb Jones, the cousin of William Bebb, the governor of Ohio, and they were just one part of a much extended Bebb family, as well as a substantial cohort from Llanbrynmair who had settled in the area. A cousin of Michael's, Ezekiel Hughes, was the main instigator of the Welsh settlement at Paddy's Run, Ohio. But Michael D. Jones didn't just go to America for a family visit: he wanted to see how the Welsh fared overseas. He had left a country blighted by poverty, with a recession triggered in part by the end of the Napoleonic War in 1815. Many workers who had moved to the industrial belt of south Wales were forced to return to the rural heartlands as chill economic winds blew over the coalfields and foundries. Church ministers, pivotal in their influence, started to discuss the advantages of emigration in cultural, religious and economic terms. Go west, young man. Go east. Go in any direction.

By Michael D. Jones' assessment, almost all of the rural workers of Montgomeryshire and Meirionethshire lived in abject poverty, their families starving hungry and clad in nothing more than rags. His own mother was evicted from her home when she was 75 years of age because of her son's political convictions, which had again brought him into direct conflict with Sir Watkin Williams-Wynn, who happened to be his mother's landlord. It was against a background of this sort of landlordy dastardliness and dire poverty that Jones stood firm in his belief that rural unfortunates could escape the grip of blighting poverty and venal local politicians by moving to another land. He claimed that as many as 20 per cent of Welsh families were undernourished, and he really wanted to put food in their swollen bellies.

During the eighteen months that he spent in the United States, 26-year-old Jones observed the powerful influence of American society on the language, religion and customs of Welsh emigrants. He watched the Yankee-fication, the absorption and assimilation of his fellow Welshmen and women into the new country and culture with a growing sense of horror, a genuine appalled-ness, and undertook to try to stem the tide. He saw some of his fellow countrymen and women ignored by officials because they couldn't speak English. He noted how their Welshness dwindled and then died like a grape on the vine. The Utopian, yet pragmatic, solution, he felt, would be the establishment of a Welsh settlement, a place where the national characteristics of the emigrants could be fully expressed and allowed to flourish unhindered. Michael D. Jones became immutably convinced that the creation of a second motherland, independent of, and thus protected from, outside influence, was the way ahead. He thus set up a society, Cymdeithas y Brython, to help poor immigrants from Wales, and became its first secretary.

His thinking was influenced by figures such as the eighteenth-century German philosopher Johann Gottfried Herder, who argued that civilization was, at its heart, a tapestry of various cultures, and that each one was unique and valuable. Furthermore, said Herder, each one was defined by, and protected by language, and by the community that used it and, in that sense, had been created by that language.

There were other European ideas at play in the fervid mind, too, not least the influence on Michael D. Jones of the leader of the Hungarian uprising against the Austrian Empire, Lajos Kossuth. The uprising had had a considerable influence on radical thought in Wales, with a crowd of 3,000 attending a public meeting in Bangor to support it, and the freedoms it upheld. In a letter written in 1890, Michael D. Jones described Kossuth as a bright star in the European firmament who had 'ignited in many a soul an undying philosophy that each nation should have the right to govern itself'. Closer to home, the damning, if totally biased, government reports on the state of Welsh education contained in the *Blue Books*, often referred to as Brad y Llyfrau Gleision (the Treachery of the Blue Books), made Jones' blood boil, and he referred to the authors of the three blue, leather-bound volumes as bribed traitors. The *Blue Books*, compiled by three Anglican barristers, laid the blame for what its authors saw as profound failings in the education system in Wales squarely at the door of the Welsh language, which it described as a vast drawback to the country, and 'a manifold barrier to the moral progress and commercial prosperity of its people. It is not easy to over-estimate its evil effects'. The reports, with their sprawling 1,200-page portrayal of an uncivilized and barbaric people wounded that people, and their effects reverberated down many a long year. It has been argued that it was this experience of seeing his country and culture debased, but viewed, crucially, from America, via a long perspective, that made Michael D. Jones things see and feel things more sharply. In this, he was like the nationalist critic and dramatist Saunders Lewis' critical perspective on Wales from the trenches of the First World War or the poet Gwenallt's take on his motherland as seen from, or rather imagined from, the west of Ireland in 1929. Michael D. Jones set out his stall in a letter written in Cincinnati in October 1848:

> Are not our language, our customs, our religion and our morals worth maintaining? And doesn't our history, on this side of the Atlantic, as well as the other side, prove that losing our language is to pretty much to lose the other three in pretty much every circumstance as well?

His first counter-strategy to the Yankee-fication involved the creation of Welsh societies, expressly to create bulwarks to enable the Welsh to shore up their identity. But the bulwarks soon appeared to him to be too flimsy to hold back the huge forces at play. Soon, he was suggesting that the only way to help the Welsh maintain their identity was to create an overseas colony expressly for this purpose. Initially, he suggested bringing people over to America, and this idea received a considerable amount of support, with a charitable society in Utica, New York, offering to pay the cost of bringing fifty new settlers of Michael D. Jones' own choosing across the Atlantic. At the time, he favoured creating a settlement in Wisconsin, which would itself be a bridgehead for pushing further west into the country, and eventually settling in Oregon.

By the time Jones paid his second visit the United States in 1858, the debate about the merits and demerits of creating such a settlement had been raging in the newspapers for nearly a decade. Michael D. Jones could see that support for the notion of such an enterprise had built up a head of steam in America, and thought this could be just the engine to drive the idea forward. He posited that it would only take 100 men, drawn from the ranks of the already experienced pioneers of the United States, to establish a settlement in South America. Vancouver Island in Canada was also mooted as a possible centre for settlement, along with Oregon, while countries in South America were also suggested, such as Paraguay, Brazil and Uruguay. Other suggested destinations included Palestine, New Zealand and Australia, but those were soon overtaken by a much more remote option, namely Patagonia in Argentina. Indeed, at one stage, the dream was to fill the whole of southern Patagonia, all the way down to the deep south, to Cape Horn, on the northern rim of Drake's Passage in Tierra del Fuego.

The Brazilian Experiment

During the 1850s, an attempt had been made to form a Welsh community in Rio Grande do Sul, or Great Southern River, in Brazil. It was led by Thomas Benbow Phillips, who was born in Tregaron in 1829 and moved to Manchester as a young man. He hadn't been in the teeming, smoggy but pulsatingly energetic city very long before he met some entrepreneurial merchants who had useful contacts in Brazil, and who wanted to send people out there to work, producing cotton for their northern English mills. Phillips dutifully went to South America and found that it was a propitious time for immigrants, as the Brazilian Government was in the process of creating a board to oversee the process of attracting newcomers and had authorized a budget of £25,000 to this end.

By September 1850, Phillips had reached the Rio Grande, where he arranged to buy land less than 20 miles from the town of Pelotas. The area was framed by two rivers and was set at the base of a chain of mountains called the Seres de Tepes. Here, Phillips paid a quarter of the money necessary to fund the settlement, while a company called Carruthers & Souza paid the rest of the requisite funds, also agreeing to pay the passage of anyone who wanted to move there. There was coal to hew as well as cotton to sow.

The plan was to sell the land to the new settlers at a price of five shillings an acre, repayable within six years. The company would also provide a year's supply of food, clothing and agricultural tools and supplies. Meanwhile, other companies were competing to find new settlers, with advertisements inducing people to come to places such as Pedro Segundo. In the face of such burgeoning competition, time was not at a premium, so Phillips had to crack the whip. A mere two months after arriving in South America, Thomas Benbow Phillips registered his proposed colony under the name 'Nova Cambria' while, at the same time, the 'Cambro-Brazilian Amalgamated Trades' Emigration Society' was set up, with 100,000 shares made available to would-be investors willing to buy at a cost of three pounds a share. The formula was relatively simple. For each 1,000 shares sold, 200 emigrants would be sent to Brazil to work 50 acres of land per head, with five of those ready for cultivation.

Phillips proceeded apace to build a home for himself, called Pen-y-graig, and dutifully measured out the land parcels, ready for 120 families. He started building the houses for them, with Welsh names such as Tŷ'r Meibion, Pen-y-Twyn, Glandŵr and Tŷ-Gwyn, and by May 1851, the first six parties of Welsh adventurers had arrived, although they weren't great in number, comprising just over forty people. Phillips also set about building a chapel so that the new migrants could offer up the old hymns. Foreshadowing the first contingent of Patagonian settlers over a decade later, the group of Welsh emigrants which left Liverpool on board the *Naiad*, bound for Brazil at the end of May 1851, was soon followed by another group, numbering 25 adults and 11 children, including Phillips' parents, the following August. By the time the *Madonna* brought more settlers at the end of the year, a total of

80 Welsh immigrants had joined the by now 24-year-old Benbow Phillips in Rio Grande do Sul. Two years later, there were 100, drawn from Anglesey and Denbigh as well as coal miners from south Wales towns such as Nant-y-Glo and Bryn Mawr. By this time, a storehouse had been built, from which food was apportioned and distributed on Mondays, with no limit on the amounts, although they were cautioned that, eventually, food would be sold to them rather than given away. Phillips also tried to look after their souls and ensure their religious freedom, bolstering the effect of building a chapel by also distributing testaments and religious pamphlets in Portuguese.

One problem came in the form of a man called Johnson, a former mine manager from Mold. He was employed by the Brazilian Government to look for coal in the nearby mountains, and found it, then attracted five of the Welsh settlers to join him in working the allegedly rich seams of black diamonds. This was the beginning of the end.

By the end of 1854, Phillips was admitting that his grand project had failed, citing the defection of the miners as well as the absence of more agriculturists among the incomers as two reasons for the failure. There were other shortcomings, too, and he listed them. It had been easy to lure old colliers from their smallholdings, but they had next to no idea how to clear land for farming, choosing to stack the timber from the trees they felled, thus instantly losing some of the acreage they had won by their efforts. He also cited a lack of Welsh nationalistic sentiment among the settlers, who didn't stick together solidly as a group without such cultural adhesive.

Later, though, Benbow Phillips would join the Patagonian adventurers, and sailed there on a boat called the *Rush* in 1872, which had brought new settlers from the U.S., many of whom were daunted by the hardships and promptly jumped ship in Montevideo. Benbow's Brazilian adventure provided him with a plethora of experience and experiences which he shared freely, even though not all of his fellow travellers stayed the course. He had been unwilling to travel to Patagonia before 1872 because his wife was ill, and he didn't want her to face the rigours and tests of travel, so he only ventured south after her death. The area he'd helped open up and cultivate in Brazil, meanwhile, became a ready source of wood and dried meat, which was exported to the north of this massive country. He left just before the experiment was found to have worked, with other people being the net beneficiaries of his pioneering endeavours.

California Dreaming

The beginnings proper of the Patagonian venture may be traced to 18 January 1856, when a Welsh society was formed in Camptonville (then called Comptonville and Gold Ridge) in north-eastern Yuba County, California, with the aim of promoting the establishment of an overseas Welsh settlement. At the society's inaugural meeting, Patagonia was suggested for the first time as a possible location for a Welsh settlement, not least because it wasn't under any real government, and in the 'possession of no-one other than a few Indians'.

If you go to Camptonville nowadays, turning off Highway 49, known as the Golden Chain, between Downieville, with its tourist-attracting set of town gallows and Nevada City, there is hardly a hint of the astonishing busyness that made the town boom in the time of the Gold Rush. The heat haze melts the ponderosa pines, and a heavy torpor holds the land in chains. The Lost Nugget Gas Station and Convenience Store pretty much sums up the spirit of the place, and there is certainly no sign of any rush at all, while, presumably, all the gold is well and truly mined out, or panned away. In town, the doors of the original Mayo saloon have swung shut for the very last time. Yet, when the God-fearing Welsh of Camptonville convened to discuss prospects for an overseas settlement, this was a town in a process of dizzying change. This was Boomtown USA, a place of rabid energy and growth. Gold, or, rather GOLD!!! was discovered here in 1850, and the place became known as Gold Ridge.

The Gold Rush, which started in 1849 – hence the first prospectors being dubbed the Forty-Niners – led to an enormous influx of people into the area. By the end of that year, there were 100,000 people in California, and 80,000 of those were suffering from gold fever. Some came by ship, largely city men, described as 'editors, ministers, traders, the briefless lawyer, starving student, the quack, the idler, the harlot, the gambler, the hen-pecked husband, the disgraced ...' Only half of those who arrived went into the mines, with the others staying in the towns or settling the farms. This meant that the other half of the gold fever arrivals made the long, hard journey not to mine, but to begin a new life in a new country which, they reasoned, must become rich and provide magnificent opportunities for all because of the millions being pumped into the economy by the lustrous, much-sought-after metal.

So the Forty-Eighter camp at Camptonville was converted into a Forty-Niner town, five times as large as its predecessor, with a shanty town of tents and lean-tos on the hillside giving way to slightly more solid cabins, stores, saloons and hotels on either side of a one-block downtown, with its single street. Soon, the new town had a new name, becoming Camptonville in 1854 when the first post office opened. The name honours Robert Campton, the town blacksmith.

It was soon a rip-roaring centre of the California Gold Rush, with over fifty saloons and brothels, and even a bowling alley. It was also an important stopping point for parched and hungry travellers coming from the direction of Virginia City, Nevada, via Reno, on what was the main route at the time, the Henness Pass Road, or for those coming from the Donner Pass.

Life here was colourful, to say the least. In his book *Men to Match My Mountains: The Opening of the Far West 1840–1900*, the historian Irving Stone conjures up a place where:

> vigorous young men in red shirts, pants stuffed in their boots, wearing beards and swathes of hair like sheep dogs, constituted an all-male society: hard-working, hard-swearing, hard-drinking, hard-playing; the weaker ones coming down with everything from homesickness through scurvy and dysentery to rheumatism, typhoid, tuberculosis and smallpox. They were buried in their blankets. Doctors, tiring of the unaccustomed physical labour of the mines, had gone back to their practice, charging one ounce of gold per consultation and one dollar for a drop of medicine.

This was the sort of machismo-riven and whisky-swigging society the teetotal Welsh joined, beset on all sides by all manner of temptation. Walking the straight and narrow path wasn't easy once you'd first strayed into a saloon, the moonshine turning your legs to jelly. One William Jones, living in Nevada City, California, was clearly exercised by the dizzying downward spiral in morals and standards, and subsequently penned a letter to a Welsh–American religious journal in 1851, suggesting that 'many fall into temptation after coming to this country. Some were good members of the church at home but here they are wasters. Some, when at home, preached the gospel, but here they feed among the pigs'. He clearly thought some of his fellow migrants had reached the bottom of the trough.

To find evidence of the Welsh who came to Camptonville in the 1850s, one has to go to the town cemetery, which is a veritable haven for rattlesnakes – and I have a complete and utter phobia of snakes. There's a sign telling you what to do if you see one. Even the sign is enough to chill the blood. So every dry-grass rustle and insect whine set my nerves a-jangling. But the beating sun cooking up the rocks is hopefully enough to keep the poisonous serpents hidden away in their dark holes, their rattles silenced by the day's blow-lamp heat.

Among the Klenzendorfs, the Martignones, the Houghtailings and the Horweges are a clutch of Welsh names. There's William Rowlands from Anglesey, and Griffith Roberts. Roberts, born under a bad star in Wales in 1824, died in the Gold Country in 1889 of 'bad whiskey and suicide mixed with Grant powder' (probably a reference to gunpowder; and a reference to John Grant, who was involved in the Gunpowder Plot of 1605). There are jagged-toothed rows of headstones, leaning rickety with age: here a clutch of Lewises, including John Lewis from Anglesey, who died when he was 32 years old, and his wife, Jane Lewis, who survived him by over two decades and died in 1890, aged 77, because of fatty degeneration of the heart. John and Jane are buried with their son Willy, aged three years 10 months and Sarah Griffiths. There lie the Humphreys', namely Humphrey and Maggie, who are buried together with their 11-year-old daughter. They came from all over. The Phillips family drifted from Ohio to die here. The Prices came from Caernarfonshire to California. There's another Williams, a Joseph Jones and a lone Davis headstone. But no rattlers, thankfully.

These long-dead were just some of the Welsh who'd been drawn here by the prospect of gold, and the general advantages of an economy buoyed up by precious metals. In a meeting in the town, a hyper-enthusiastic and animated man called Edwin Cynrig Roberts addressed the extensive crowd. Roberts was a true son of the pioneer age, who had long been fascinated by the ideas of expedition and settlement, not least the fanciful tale of the Welsh-speaking Mandan tribe who inhabited the riparian stretches of the Missouri. A native of Flintshire, whose family had emigrated to Wisconsin in 1847, as a boy, he read books such as *An Enquiry into the Truth of the Tradition Concerning the Discovery by Prince Madog ab Owen Gwynedd, about the Year 1170 and Further Observations on the Discovery of America by Prince Madog*. When Edwin got up to speak in front of the Camptonville crowd, he had a fire in his heart.

> Do you know what, people? I would rather be buried alive whilst speaking Welsh than live until I'm eighty and be buried as a Yankee. There are, here in the West, thirty thousand of us Welsh. Sell your farms, every last one of you, and come with me to Patagonia, travelling as one strong crew, so that nothing can stand in out way. We will go in great number to look for a place where we can establish in both town and country.

Even those who'd barracked him, and asked what on earth such an unshaven and seemingly callow youth could teach them, changed their mocking tune, and soon the crowd was chanting their intention to go to claim their new land. Patagonia. Patagonia, indeed.

The heady and communicable enthusiasm of the gold field congregation was soon fully harnessed to the Patagonian plan, and the fervid atmosphere of the Camptonville meeting was duly noted in the Welsh-language American newspaper, *Y Drych*, which announced in the September 1857 issue that the Californian Welsh contingent was very keen indeed to see Patagonia settled in this way. It would be a place where the Welsh language could be preserved – a linguistic or cultural nature reserve, if you like. Their nonconformist, Protestant religion could be practised there, far from the dominant and domineering pressures of the English language and one of its principal promulgators, the Anglican Church, or the Church of England. As one of the early propagandists for the creation of what might be described as a Little-Wales-at-the-Far-Ends-of-the-Earth, Hugh Hughes suggested, 'Our desire is to have a country where we can govern our internal affairs entirely, without interference in matters worldly and religious by another nation'.

In this, the movement to Patagonia reflected the greater movement of people from village to town, an age-defining journey of hope and aspiration that had certainly been one of the formative forces of industrially-developing Wales, with a population that pretty much doubled from 601,767 to 1,118,914 between the census years of 1801 and 1851. It might also be argued that the first wave of Welsh settlers in South America were actually moving back to the countryside, albeit in a totally different country, one with condors instead of buzzards, armadillos rather than hedgehogs.

The population of rural Wales had to contend with the oppressions of the landowners, who mainly belonged to the Church of England. Their tenants, meanwhile, attended chapel, where the nonconformist ministers preached individual salvation and railed against the culturally alien squires who lorded it over the land. While industrial Wales grew and grew, the countryside faced all manner of hardships beyond the ravages and demands of depopulation. Agriculture was in the doldrums, not least among the hill-farmers who had faced a succession of bad harvests between 1793 and 1801. The economic depression occasioned by the end of the wars against Napoleon similarly blighted life for the lowland farmer. It led to both decline and exodus, with even more people forsaking the land for the huddled terraces of the south-east and sinew-testing employment in mine and foundry, even though many terrace dwellers left the industrial south at the same time. To and fro they went, from country to town and then back again, blown like chaff by the ill winds of economics. Meanwhile, in America, a plan was taking shape ...

Embracing the idea

After the seminal meeting in Camptonville, a circular letter was sent to Welsh newspapers to appeal for support for the idea of the new Patagonian settlement, and Michael D. Jones, sometimes called the 'father' of the settlement, responded by organizing a public meeting in Bala. The meeting, held at the Calvinist Methodist College in August 1856, resulted in the formation of a similar emigration society in Bala. Other societies were formed in Wales over the following months, the most active being in Caernarfon. There, the local literary society, known as Cymdeithas y Bwcis (the book-lovers' society, rather than bookmakers, even though it sounds a bit like a gambling den), used to meet in Engedi chapel.

The 'society' here was pretty diminutive, some six in number, but they included two printers, Evan Jones and Lewis Jones (no relation) who were about to go into business together. They set up, not surprisingly, as E & L Jones, not only printing but publishing too, bringing out a Welsh variation on the satirical *Punch* magazine, *Y Pwnsh Cymraeg*. Another of the stalwarts of the society of half-a-dozen members was the aforementioned

Hugh Hughes, a muscular carpenter, a.k.a. Cadfan Gwynedd. He read a circular letter sent from California, expounding the virtues of the idea of a settlement in Patagonia. It properly fired up his imagination, as Evan Jones explained in a vignette of the man published, much later on, in *Y Genedl Gymreig* in 1922. In this article, Hugh Hughes was described as a man completely drunk and besotted with the idea of y Wladfa. He believed that the Welsh would eventually 'inherit the earth, and the Welsh language, as in Eden, would swallow all the other dialects. He read geography, and his red cheeks would swell as he described the ships of the world, like a drove of cattle swimming, all at anchor in the river Chubut or at Port Madryn …'

Advertising Utopia

The seemingly venal and greedy interference of English-speaking landowners in the lives and livelihoods of Welsh tenant farmers was something people clearly wished to escape from, given half a chance. The internal colonist behaviour of the fat cat landlords was certainly a factor in the minds of some people as they sat down to read the equivalent of today's holiday brochure that was the *Llawlyfr y Wladychfa Gymreig* (*The Welsh Settlers' Handbook*), written by Hugh Hughes. Cadfan, full of uncommon zeal for the new idea, had been avidly reading everything he could find about Patagonia, but he fixed on one account in particular, namely that penned by Captain Fitzroy, who navigated the *Beagle* on her famous voyage with Charles Darwin on board. Fitzroy's account of the expedition's discoveries in Chubut in 1833 gave Hugh Hughes rich material from which to fashion, or indeed, fabricate, his settlers' handbook:

> Part of the west shores of New Bay seemed to be fit for cultivation, being covered with a fine dark soil; and there is abundance of fire-wood. Some small ponds of excellent water were found, over a clayey bed, in which were tracks of cattle. A *guanaco* shot here was superior to any killed elsewhere, as to condition. Many thousands of seals were seen on the rocks, which did not take to the water as soon as disturbed – therefore they could not have been much molested by man.
>
> On the 24th, Lieutenant Wickham discovered the river Chupat, and after waiting for the tide, anchored half a mile within the

entrance. Next day, he went a few miles up it in a boat, and found that, though free from drift-timber, it was shoal and narrow, few places being deeper than six feet at low-water, or wider than a hundred yards. The stream ran down two or three knots an hour. Many tracks of cattle were seen, but none of natives. As the river seemed to be free from sunken trees, and to have but few banks in it, Mr Wickham decided to move the *Liebre* as far up as he could, and then make another excursion in his little two-oared skiff. Between pulling and sailing, the *Liebre* was moved 12 miles up in one day, and was moored in the middle of the stream, lest Indians should be near.

Next morning, Mr. Wickham went in his boat, about eight miles further; but in a direct line, he was then not more than 12 miles from the entrance. Along the banks on each side, as he had advanced, both he and those with him were much struck by the richness of the alluvial land (caused doubtless by the river overflowing its low banks), and by the quantities of drift-timber, which actually looked like the stores in immense timber-yards. Among the drift-wood there were many large and sound trees left several hundred yards from the banks, therefore the periodical floods must be great.

At Mr. Wickham's westernmost point 'the river and the country round had a beautiful appearance, as seen from a rising ground on the south side – an excellent position for a settlement.' From this elevation, the stream was traced to the westward, running with a very serpentine course, through level meadow land, covered with rich herbage. Several herds of wild cattle were seen, and their traces were observed every where in such numbers as to indicate a great abundance of animals.

This all gave Hugh Hughes plenty of good material, plentiful enticements for emigrants to a far-flung place. Roll up, roll up! This was a land cattle blessed but mainly native free, with areas of fine soil, coasts which were a food-rich habitat for tame, and therefore eminently hunt-able seals and whales, which were already proving very profitable to the small fleets of American whalers working off the Falklands. Fitzroy's report was akin to marketing copy written by a famous and widely respected sea-captain. It had to be true. The cattle had to be there, calmly sloshing their way through the high grasses. In among the plentiful blandishments of the *Settlers' Handbook*, there were also some admonishments, some muted notes of caution, urging would-be settlers to ensure they had enough money not only to pay for their passage but also to last a year after their arrival on foreign shores.

Little wonder that the poor read the *Handbook* so avidly. After all, it described a land of plenty, and to chapel-goers who frequented the various Biblical Gerazims, Rehoboths and Pisgahs three times on a Sunday, the chapel was a very real community, and a bastion, too, of culture, and of language in particular: these people clearly knew all about the Promised Land. And they wanted to go there, with all heart. Who wouldn't want to swap a tatterdemalion cottage edged by hard ground for a farm of one's own, to wriggle out from underneath the landowner's jackboot? People such as Michael D. Jones hoped that 30,000 people would feel that way, as this would be a sufficient number to be able to lay claim to a proper swathe of paradisical Patagonia.

Cadfan's marketing slickness in the handbook seemed to work not just on would-be settlers. It was Cadfan, Evan Jones averred, who infected Lewis Jones with the 'sickness of y Wladfa', and insisted that they invite Michael D. Jones to address the society, to pour some more paraffin on the flames of their enthusiasm. Jones duly attended, and expounded the idea of sending pioneers not from Wales, but from America.

Michael D. Jones, despite his pivotal role in driving the idea forward, wasn't the first proselytizer for such a settlement. The Welsh Independents' newsletter, *Y Cenhadwr*, had carried a series of articles in the late 1840s which first proposed such a colony as a way of protecting the language.

Between 1856 and 1859, the movement to establish a Welsh settlement gathered momentum in the United States. It was during this period that Edwin Cynrig Roberts emerged as one of the chief promoters of the campaign, as his appearance in Camptonville underlined.

Argentina recruiting

The horizon of possibility had very much widened in Argentina by this time: it was a country opening up, actively seeking new settlers. An advertisement placed by the Argentine Consulate General in *The Times* on

8 September 1856 announced that 'Notice is hereby given, that the following REGULATIONS as to the COLONIZATION on the coast of Patagonia, and the admission of vessels trading to the Free Ports of Bahia-Blanca and the Rio Negro, have been decreed by the Government of the State of Buenos Aires …' Not only were vessels able to visit the free ports, but there were promises of free land for individuals and families, with up to 100 leagues on offer.

Meanwhile, the proprietors of the Welsh American newspaper *Y Drych* started to promote their own shiny new idea, having bought land for a settlement in Kansas, and, with this purchase, their opposition to the idea of creating a colony in Patagonia grew pretty fervid: they wanted nothing less than to send a wrecking-ball through it, to smash the plan to smithereens.

Cadfan Gwynedd had left Wales for Liverpool, and his enthusiastic lectures, letters to the press and scattergun correspondence with all who expressed an interest in the merits of the Patagonian venture had attracted plenty of devotees who, together, had built up a collective head of steam. It was becoming a real transatlantic push. In Oshkosh, Wisconsin, Edwin Cynrig Roberts had been lecturing about the need for a Patagonian settlement, and encouraging folk to sell their farms and travel to Patagonia in one great contingent, promising that nothing could stand in their way. Another meeting followed in the American town of Berlin. From town to town, from community to community, the idea spread.

Thus, in 1859, it was arranged for a group of Welsh Americans to travel to Patagonia, but the plan did not come to fruition. There were more attempts to create Welsh colonies in the United States. One sprouted briefly in Missouri, with 50 people transplanted there by 1864, but this, too, hardly truly blossomed. It was a race to see who could establish a properly sustainable colony, in North or South America, Kansas or Patagonia.

Despite the antagonism of certain members of the media, there was still a wellspring of support for a South American settlement. Realizing this, Edwin Cynrig Roberts considered emigrating to Patagonia on his own, but he was persuaded at the last moment to travel to Wales in search of others who shared his views. He was a born proselytizer, a persuasive orator, so his powers of persuasion would be more than gainfully employed in Gwalia.

Having arrived in Liverpool, Edwin Roberts contacted Michael D. Jones, who suggested that he travel throughout Wales to promote the Welsh settlement. Roberts also came into contact with the group of individuals who had been gathering frequently in Liverpool to discuss the proposed overseas adventure. Among its members were Hugh Hughes and Lewis Jones, both of whom, as we know, were former members of the society in Caernarfon. Jones' background as a printer had obviously proved extremely useful in disseminating their intentions and attendant information, while Hughes' efforts were seen by historians such as R. Bryn Williams as fundamental to the Patagonian venture: 'Without Cadfan, I do not believe that y Wladfa would have been settled at all'.

In July 1861, this group organized themselves as a society, and Liverpool soon became the focal point of the movement to establish a colony on the far shore of the South Atlantic. The Liverpool Emigration Society thus expressed its desire to establish a Welsh settlement in Patagonia to the Argentine consul in Liverpool, Samuel R. Phibbs. His advice was that a board of trustees should be formed to act as a link between the Society and the Argentine Government.

Five trustees were duly appointed to the board, and they included Michael D. Jones and Captain Love Jones-Parry of Madryn. To fend off any charges of parochialism, the society was quickly restructured as a 'National Committee', which included representatives from several parts of Wales. The propaganda campaign was now up to speed. By the end of 1862, the Committee had published not only the handbook, *Llawlyfr y Wladychfa Gymreig*, but also a fortnightly journal, *Y Ddraig Goch* (*The Red Dragon*), to further its aims, which would help counter the splenetic tirades of some newspapers against the idea of a Patagonian settlement, not least the Welsh-American *Y Drych,* which consistently favoured considering American destinations, arguing against the very idea of y Wladfa with every logic, spin and fact, as newspapers tend to do energetically when they don't like something.

In response to its application for land in Patagonia, the Liverpool Committee received an invitation from the Argentine Government to send representatives to Buenos Aires. In November 1862, Lewis Jones travelled there on behalf of the Society, and he was later joined by Captain Jones-Parry.

Here were two men of very, very different dispositions. Thomas Love Duncombe Jones-Parry, the High Sheriff of Caernarfonshire, was an aristocrat whose inheritance included a castle in a 14,000 acre estate at Madryn, on the Llŷn peninsula. Despite his incredible wealth, he had a reputation for fairness, and seldom increased his tenants' rents. Unlike many landowners, he was able to converse with them in Welsh, and about poetry, which was an unexpected enthusiasm of his. He even had a bardic name, namely Elphin. Elphin may have been born with a silver spoon in his mouth, but the plates at the castle were made of nothing less than solid gold, while the walls of the impressive country pile were hung with Gainsboroughs and Van Dykes. Madryn Castle wasn't his only home, for he also had a residence at St. James's in London, close to the London base of his friend, the Prince of Wales. Jones-Parry lived a louche life, and reputedly once bet £8 million on a horse in the Derby, and lost. Yes, eight million. A fortune in today's money, and an almost impossibly gargantuan sum in the mid-nineteenth century.

Kyffin Williams, in his travel journal, *A Wider Sky*, tells a story about Jones-Parry's wooden leg, which was accidentally scythed off when he was lying in a wheatfield after forcing himself on the milkmaid, the sharp end of poetic justice. Jones-Parry was already an inveterate traveller who had once been imprisoned and sentenced to death in Spain for attacking a Gibraltar border guard with a whip. So, in Buenos Aires, his chosen habitat was the clubs, gambling dens and drinking clinics, and his recreations revolved around sport and pleasure, although his political aspirations made him the right man to liaise with the Argentine authorities. Meanwhile, Lewis Jones' diaries underline his more wholesome interests while travelling, in church and chapel history. Therefore, Jones-Parry and Jones were not, perhaps, the most obvious or ideal travelling companions, especially when they were travelling into the unknown.

After several meetings with government officials in Buenos Aires, the two men travelled to the port of Patagones, a small anchorage protected by a fort overlooking the Rio Negro, before embarking on a voyage along the coast of Patagonia to the mouth of the Chupat River. The area had been surveyed repeatedly, if incompletely, since the first mapping expeditions of the 1780s, and there was much to learn about the profits and perils of the coast. Both men kept detailed notes of their journey, with Jones-Parry comparing what he initially saw to the vineyards on the banks of the Douro in Portugal, noting the deep dark soils and herds of wild sheep and goats.

In fact, the intrepid two misidentified some *guanacos* as wild sheep, which was a minor thing in itself, but might have tipped the balance in favour of emigration should someone be in two minds.

Meanwhile, Lewis Jones, noting the serpentine nature of the river, gave it its Welsh name, Camwy, which mimics the Chubut's meanderings. A salty flavour of the Jones and Parry-Jones mini-expedition can be found in an account by Eluned Morgan in R. Bryn Williams' biography of this fine writer. In it, she points out that travelling the 800 miles that lie between Argentina and Patagonia was a very testing proposition fifty years previously, and that only Fitzroy and Darwin had any idea of the nature of this wild and tempestuous coast. By dint of a combination of diligence and research, the two spies (that is the word she uses) managed to charter an old shell of a schooner, the *Candelaria*, weighing some 25 tons, and persuaded an Argentinian of Welsh descent called Harris to be their guide, quite simply because he claimed to know the way. Things didn't improve when the crew was hired, as they were a ragtag assortment of blackguards and ruffians. En route through uncharted waters, the expedition was nudged perilously close to collapse when the dipsomaniac captain Summers drank himself into such an uncontrolled frenzy that he had to be clapped in chains. The crew was busily plotting mutiny, and storms were churning the waters off Chupat. Things did not augur well. Having surveyed the land – albeit only in the vicinity of the landing point – for about a week, Jones noted the grass growing between the hills, suggesting the land was 'suitable for growing light crops most excellently', while Jones-Parry appreciated the ample anchorages apparent here. These heartening, if challengeable opinions were duly reported back to the Liverpool committee.

The two adventurers then returned to Buenos Aires – after more altercations with the captain, who had gone off on a side-mission to loot a wrecked ship – to finalize the agreement with the Argentine Government on 25 March 1863. Their argument, or rather that of the Emigration Committee, was that Wales was 'a distinct and separate cultural group within the British Isles', and that a number of Welsh people were interested in exploring the conditions under which they could live in Eastern Patagonia.

The representatives of the Emigration Committee had made significant compromises in order to secure this agreement with the Argentine

Government. The Argentine Government, in turn, had not responded positively to their request for independence, and had insisted that the new Welsh settlement should remain under the authority of Buenos Aires and, furthermore, that it should be officially recognized as an Argentine province once its population reached 20,000. Nevertheless, the Committee remained totally convinced that Patagonia was the best location for the settlement, and therefore accepted the terms of the agreement. However, in September 1863, the Committee was informed that the Argentine Congress had refused to ratify their agreement with the government. With the movement on the verge of collapse, the Committee decided to make a request for land in the Chupat valley on the same terms as ordinary immigrants, and Samuel Phibbs was sent to Buenos Aires to negotiate a new agreement.

In October 1864, the Welsh Emigration Society received a letter from the Argentine Minister of the Interior, Guillermo Rawson. Their request for land in the Chupat valley had been granted under the above terms. Furthermore, local autonomy would be ensured, and 25 *cuadras* (about 100 acres) would be given to each family, or to every three adults, and they would receive their deeds within two years. By way of further encouragement, the settlers were exempt from military service for ten years. Hats must have been thrown up in the air. Having waited so long for a positive reply, the members of the Liverpool Committee voted unanimously in favour of accepting the Argentine government's terms. Having secured an agreement for land, the Liverpool Society stepped up its efforts to find people to pioneer the Welsh settlement, with the aim of ensuring an annual flow of between 300 and 500 settlers every year for a decade, as this was their part of the deal with people-hungry Argentina.

In the press and at public meetings throughout Wales, potential emigrants were given favourable reports and promises of new opportunities in Patagonia, with the reports by Love Jones-Parry and Lewis Jones given due prominence, such that when the descriptions were later found to be misleading, admonishing fingers were pointed at the two, but especially in the direction of Jones, who was cast as a dissembler. If he was guilty of any deceit, his crime was simply not realizing that the areas they'd surveyed around Rio Negro were not similar to comparable areas in Chubut and that they were, in fact, extremely different, with the emphasis on 'extreme'.

When Lewis Jones, after his return, started to travel around Wales to sell the venture, he was greeted with tepid waves of antipathy. Little wonder, then, that he got out his embellishing kit and started to extol the virtues of the land. By now, the vegetation he had at first dismissed as 'being quite grassy' had been fertilized in his imagination, so that it was greener, 'enormous', even, and 'its tips were white because of age'. The encouraging register of his sales pitch got higher and higher. The rivers, he said, were as wide near the Andes as they were near the sea. In a lecture he gave at Aberystwyth, Lewis Jones suggested that for every one measure of wheat sown, 45 times that much would be harvested, while the sheep, he promised, weighed 300 pounds each, and to boot, tasted of venison. Hugh Hughes had similarly seemingly swapped veracity for mendacity, as evidenced in a speech he gave at Liverpool's Concert Hall, in which he described the probability of there being not one but two harvests every year, and noted enthusiastically how figs and grapes grew freely and perfectly in the open air. Their enthusiasm was infectious. Between them, they were painting an Edenic picture, a panorama, a Patagonian paradise made up of two parts observation and one part imagination.

What they didn't know was that Guillermo Rawson's plans had whipped up a storm of anti-English, or rather anti-British, sentiment in Argentina, convulsing Congress and igniting the Legislative Assembly with angry talk about the Malvinas / Falkland Islands. These were, and are, the focus of territorial claims and counter-claims by the two countries and are islands close, in relative terms, to Patagonia, not to mention – as we know nowadays – substantial oil reserves under the waves of the South Atlantic. But Rawson, an astute man, knew that Argentina needed to do something about Patagonia, which hadn't been surveyed, and had not therefore been officially claimed by the country. One fast track to a solution would be to ensure settlements under the Argentine flag. This would, he claimed, 'put at rest the question of the somewhat undefined sovereignty over those remote and uncivilized regions'. It might also thwart any plans by Chile, their neighbour to the west, to orchestrate its own gargantuan land grab. The Welsh could be a human shield, or a barrier, to any extension of Chilean national territory.

Rawson even went as far as to start using the Welsh colony as a bargaining chip in starting negotiations with the British over the Falkland Islands. In a meeting with British Minister Thornton in Buenos Aires, he enquired 'whether Her Majesty's Government would not be disposed to take into consideration the possibility of the Islands being ceded to the Argentine Republic', adding that if it were in in his power to forward this, Congress, he was convinced, would put no obstacle in the way of the original contract with the Welsh Committee being carried out.

Only An Ocean Away

Although the organizers of the venture had initial difficulties in finding settlers to make the voyage to Patagonia, plans were made to set sail from Liverpool on 25 April 1865 on a 771-ton ship called the *Halton Castle*. Advertisements were placed in the papers. Passage was available for £12 per adult, reducing to £6 for every child under 12, with babies under the age of one travelling free, with a £1 deposit necessary. The ad suggested that the amount of land available to every settler was pretty certain, but informed potential travellers, in the most tantalizing way, that the other inducements were not, nevertheless suggesting they would include five horses, 10 cattle, 20 sheep, amounts of wheat, a plough suitable for the land, as well as fruit trees for every family. Oddly, in the same year there were proposals to send no fewer than five million, yes, five million, English settlers to Argentina, which made the fledgling Argentine Government very edgy, fearing a complete takeover – not just a land grab of the Malvinas, but of the entire country. This proposal, of course, made complete sense to the greedy architects of the British Empire, who could envisage the whole world map being edged or shaded pink – the colour used to denote its territories – as the Empire's political, economic and, if necessary, military influence grew like Topsy.

The Advance Guard

In March, Edwin Roberts and Lewis Jones, accompanied by Jones' wife, Ellen, set off for Patagonia from Liverpool in order to make preparations for the arrival of the first group of settlers. They sailed from the town of Patagones on 1 June on a veritable ark, bearing 200 sheep, six pigs, 60 chickens, six dogs, half a dozen workhorses and two pairs of oxen. In addition to the livestock, they carried a wagon and two dozen ploughs, 300 sacks of wheat, 20 sacks of potatoes, and 6,000 feet of blanket material. Five hundred cattle had already been sent overland, but these had been stolen by native rustlers.

The advance party had plenty to do – erecting soil enclosures, helping store the wheat in caves in the white coastal cliffs and dealing with insubordinate workers who claimed they weren't being fed enough, even though two sheep were being slaughtered every day. In an act of reasonable chagrin, Lewis Jones left Edwin Roberts behind as he took a boat-load of the lazy, good-for-nothing servants back to Buenos Aires, realizing that there was no point in feeding the indolent.

As the emigrants gathered in Liverpool in April 1865, the Committee was informed that the *Halton Castle* had not returned from her previous voyage, and that she would not be ready in time. Frantic efforts were made to find another ship to make the voyage to Patagonia. In the meantime, the notion of the expedition was under attack in some of the newspapers, especially some of the Welsh papers in America such as *Y Drych*. If they wanted to instil a sense of paranoia among a group of nervous, would-be travellers they need only remind their more jittery readers about what had happened during a recent massacre of pioneers in Minnesota – including several Welshmen – when the unfortunates were variously tortured, dismembered, eviscerated or roasted alive, in ovens.

Temporarily stranded, the erstwhile emigrants kicked their heels and killed time in the port of Liverpool. One of them, Joseph Seth Jones, a twenty-year-old printer with Gwasg Gee in Denbigh, went round the bookshops buying quite an assortment of volumes, including a book on phrenology, *The Persecution of the Protestants in Spain Under Phillip II*, *The London Atlas*, *The Book of Common Prayer* and *The Successful Merchant*. Seth's decision to go to Patagonia had been pretty impromptu, and certainly sudden enough to frighten one of his fellow chapelgoers, who ungrammatically, but decidedly grimly, opined that 'Mr Evans thought it very umproper of you to go and not let them know on Monday night as long as you were at chapel ... Every one as know you seem to be very much surprised at your going so far ... Good bye, poor Jones, perhaps we shall meet in heaven.'

Finally, on 28 May 1865, the wait was over, and the pioneers of the Welsh settlement departed from Liverpool aboard a tea-clipper called the *Mimosa*, destiny-bound. The *Mimosa*, soon to become a sort of Welsh *Mayflower* in the popular imagination, was a relatively light vessel, weighing 447 tons, which had been built in Aberdeen in 1853. She had been hurriedly adapted to carry human cargo, with the installation of three galvanized iron ventilators and planking set along the walls within the bowels of the ship, on which the women and children could sleep, while a rickety ladder led up to the deck. This was far from roomy enough for so many people, not to mention the fact it had no shelter whatsoever from the laser intensity of the equatorial sun. There were three double water closets on the Main Deck, four life buoys, 17 guns – each with bayonets – and a mop. There was, of course, no freezer equipment whatsoever, so all eatables were very perishable, and because no-one knew the length of the voyage, provisions had to last in every sense. So the weekly supplies per person included biscuits, 'not inferior to Navy biscuits', 11 pounds of wheaten flour, one and a half pounds of rice, as well as quantities of tea, sugar, beef, peas, pork, potatoes, a half ounce of mustard, a few pinches of black or white ground pepper and some salt and vinegar. And there was water, of course, carried in over forty 300-gallon casks. Water had to be set in store to last as much as six months, equivalent to three quarts per adult's daily rations, not including water for cooking.

Tickets for the journey promised that each person on board would have room for 10 cubic feet of luggage which could be more than adequately taken up by the goods each traveller was advised to bring, namely: a knife and fork, a tin to raise water, a stash of tea and a tablespoon, towels, a blanket, a plate or two, a cup and saucer, a boiling pot, a quart tin and another tin vessel substantial enough to hold three gallons.

Eventually, with nerves fraying, *hiraeth* for home surely already building, and expectations rising like the tide, it was time to leave the port of Liverpool, to leave Europe, to leave behind a known and familiar way of life. Their motives for going were complex. Seeking a better life, most certainly, but there were other factors, too. The historian D. Leslie Davies argues that a love of country, and a desire to safeguard the Welsh language were certainly alive among some of the simple workers from Mountain Ash and Merthyr who chose to go to Patagonia and that, furthermore, there is evidence to suggest that some of them believed this just as fervently as their leaders. The later waves of settlers might not have been so idealistic, moving to Argentina, more pragmatically, for economic reasons. As another historian,

Gareth Alban Davies puts it, 'The interplay between millenarianism and economic betterment would remain a constant, and provide one of the basic tensions in the foundation and evolution of the Welsh colony in Patagonia'.

First wave

Despite Michael D. Jones' hopes that the settlers would include farmers, seamen, salesmen, craftsmen and so on, the variety of trades and skills they took with them was short on the very necessary skills of agriculture and heavy, rather, on industrial nous. So who were they, these first pioneers? The first contingent, numbering 162 people, included a substantial corpus from what the novelist Gwyn Thomas called the 'riven gulches' of the south-eastern valleys, especially the Cynon Valley. These were men from industrial backgrounds, and only a small handful were farmers like William Jones from Rhiwlas, who had left his smallholding and a smattering of animals behind. Some contemporary reaction to the contingent was more than churlish. In a letter sent to Bala College, one correspondent denigrated 'a hundred and fifty of the dregs of Wales … sent to establish a kingdom at the ends of the earth'.

A third of the settlers came from just two places, namely Liverpool and Mountain Ash, or Aberpennar, which supplied 41 passengers, but many parts of the rest of Wales were represented, too. They came from Bala, Bangor, Bethesda, Bridgend and Brynaman. There were individuals and couples from Anglesey, Aberystwyth, Caernarfon, Abergynolwyn, Tregethin, and Llanfairfechan sharing their hopes and fears with other peregrinators from Ganllwyd, Denbigh, Rhosllanerchrugog, Llandrillo in the vale of Clwyd and the slate country around Ffestiniog, whilst some came from parts of England other than Liverpool, such as nearby Birkenhead, Seacombe and Manchester. On board were not one but three ministers, including a former student of Michael D. Jones, Abraham Matthews, who would become one of the colony's first chroniclers. As if it wasn't nerve-jangling enough an experience, thirty-year-old Watkin William Pritchard Williams' uncle tried to warn him against going by sending a letter in which he flagged up the danger of cannibals: 'Of all the wild, mad schemes that have turned up of late, the wildest and maddest is the Patagonian scheme. I may as well hold my tongue. Therefore I can only hope – hoping against hope – that you will all be successful, comfortable and happy. I also hope that the Indians who will eat you all bodily will suffer a confound indigestion'. The uncle might well have been thinking of *Y Drych*'s horror story of Minnesotan cannibalism when he flagged up these dangers of, or, rather to, the flesh.

The passenger list, the inventory of cannibal fodder, had nothing if not variety. Maurice Humphreys was a cabinet-maker whose wife's family descended from two US Presidents, John Adams and John Quincy Adams. Rhydderch Hughes, a handsome widower, was exchanging the foetid stench of the teeming Manchester slums for great draughts of sea air. There were shoemakers, harmonium players, joiners, carpenters, seamen and servants. A throng, if not necessarily a merry one. One of the children on board suffered from a rare condition, a phthisis which was eating the lower half of his face away. All southbound. All changing their lives profoundly. They sailed with hope in their hearts, concertinaed succinctly in a verse in one of the hymns they sang on board.

> We've found a better land
> In the far South.
> It is Patagonia.
> We will live there in peace
> Without fear of treachery or war,
> With a Welshman on the throne.
> Praise be to God.
> They were sailing to the Promised Land.

Yes, sailing to the Promised Land. The 2,000 settlers who would eventually go to Patagonia were small fry compared with the 100,000 or so who went from Wales to America to seek their fortunes, or, at the very least gainful employment and, it was hoped, acquire some land into the bargain.

With the upping of the anchor in Liverpool Docks, their homes were being consigned to memory, their neighbours too, and indeed, all the familiar tapestries and colours of the Welsh landscape. Unbeknown to them, they were swapping a seasonal palette of countryside hues – oak greens, brackeny russets and purplish birches – for a decidedly greyer, more bleached-out world, at least in the place where they would make landfall. Had they paused to consider such matters, they would have realized that they were leaving a familiar seasonality behind as well, but they knew nothing about the seasons in their new home in South America, any more than they knew, in any meaningful way, what lay ahead – the tests and travails, the difficult and crooked path into the future. There were tears, of course, and children hugged so close to a mother's breast that they almost suffocated from the press of love. The Welsh flag, y Ddraig Goch, the bold red dragon, stood on hind legs, resplendent, as its wings flapped over the mainmast and a Welsh hymn was sung, though subversively set to the tune of 'God save the Queen', with words penned by Edwin Cynrig Roberts. They had 7,000 miles of ocean to cross, and 40 miles of desiccated desert to traverse after that. But first, there was a false start and, because of a blustering storm, they didn't leave until four the next morning. Even then, they lay at anchor in the river Mersey for four days before finally reaching open sea, and then losing sight of land.

An ocean's breadth

The *Mimosa*'s passengers were at sea, or on the ocean, rather, for two months exactly, and with the exception of a couple of storms, their journey was not beset by too much heavy weather, even though the first storm, which caught them just off the coast of Anglesey, almost wrecked them completely, and left even the most hardened sailors in fear that this was it, the day of salty judgement. Even the experienced mate, a Manx man, prophesied they'd all be in hell within five minutes flat. But the captain, Captain Pepperrell, a young, 25-year-old master from Dartmouth in Devon, refused the aid of the local lifeboat, in part, it is believed, because he was carrying goods he hadn't declared. He had captained his first ship only two years earlier, so he wasn't carrying much cargo of personal experience. The *Mimosa* was only his second ever ship, and he was taking her on a very long journey. Even though the weather wasn't harsh or horrible, it was nonetheless a long and difficult voyage, when children such as Elizabeth Solomon, aged 13 months, Catherine Jane Thomas, aged nine years, James Jenkins, aged two and John Davies, 11 months old, all died on board, and were buried at sea. But children were also born, and one marriage was solemnized by the captain. Life's cycle of death and renewal operated even on a ship under sail. The ship's doctor, meanwhile, the Irishman Thomas Greene, was kept frantically busy.

The wind sussurating through the rigging. Whitecaps cresting the waves like catspaws. The horizon like a thin charcoal line, so far out of reach. The stench from the hold, the all too human stench. Immensities of ocean, one moment a deep wine-bottle green, and then a switch to pewter as the clouds close in. Small seabirds, storm petrels flutter by, presaging weather change. The lilt and lift of wave patterns, huge bodies of water in aquamarine flux. Silvery bell sounds, as ropes and maritime paraphernalia only the seamen understand jingle on the masts. The clipper cleaves through the water, carrying its cargo of hope and aspiration. Sometimes the sails billow, proud and white, almost pregnantly, and the vessel picks up speed, scything now through the fathomless waters. On, on and on, across the limitless vast.

Off the coast of Madeira, the captain ordered that the women's hair be shorn, but they refused, arguing that the captain wanted their tresses so he could sell them, even though he was probably only doing so for reasons of hygiene, as the tropical heat started to cook the living quarters, which hadn't been at all salubrious to begin with. Cadfan Gwynedd and Rhydderch Huws faced up to the captain in such a threatening manner that he not only produced a firearm but aimed it at Cadfan's chest, before turning it away and discharging the shot over the waves.

In less dramatic and tense moments, talk on board was of the future, of the land that lay beyond the horizon, their new home. One of the young lads on board, tailor Dafydd Williams from Aberystwyth became a sort of on-board entertainments officer, regaling his fellow travellers with his newly-minted catechism, a new and scabrous set of Ten Commandments, but written from the point of view of an Englishman. It was a lampoon, yes, but also a statement of freedom. The Englishman being pilloried was also the one they were escaping from.

1. Do not be beholden to any governor other than myself.
2. Do not make unto yourself a Welsh Settlement in any glade under the sun, or on the earth below, nor at the bottom of the sea, or under the ground. Do not learn the language your mother speaks, and do not be supportive of your own literature. For I, the Englishman, am a jealous soul, who's been turning the tenants out of their farms for generations, from those who show the least grain of independent spirit; but giving favours sometimes to those who are dragging themselves in crowds through the dust, and who vote as I see fit.

3. Do not complain that the English have overrun your country. Because those who aren't willing to be governed by them are not considered by the English to be innocent.
4. Remember to sanctify the Church of England. You shall work for six days until the marrow of your bones is dry; but on the seventh you will go to the Established Church. On that day, do not go to a single Nonconformist Chapel, neither you, nor your son, not your daughter, nor your servant, nor your maidservant, nor the stranger who is within your walls; because for six days you work to have the means to pay the rent, and the tithes, and the Church tax. That is why Hengist built the Churches and sanctified them.
5. Worship the English adulators wherever they may be, so that they may multiply in the country the English see fit to live themselves.
6. Do not kill 'Dic Sion Dafydd'.
7. Do not make for yourselves a National Eisteddfod
8. Do not take from that which you yourself own.
9. Do not moan that the English treat the Welsh as they want.
10. Do not covet the land of the English, nor the wealth of the English, nor their trade, nor their success nor their majesty, nor anything that belongs to the English.

And then at the end of the catechism came this bold prayer:

> Great Englishman, the one who art in London, I fear your name; in debt is your kingdom; thy will be done in Wales as it is in England. Give us enough labour and banish all weariness, and forgive us because the meagreness of our salaries means we cannot repay our debts; and do not lead us to independence, but rather rid us of Nationalists; because yours is the Britain, and her ability, and wealth, and brilliance for ever and ever. Amen.

This was certainly on-board entertainment with a difference, seaborne satire as the passengers put a brave face on it.

Seth Jones, meanwhile, kept a sporadic diary of the voyage, and it gives an impression of the journey. On the first day, he's taken sick, along with many of his fellow passengers. He's still seasick three days later. When he's finally better, he makes it onto the deck to see four men set out in a boat to bathe in open water. From a distance, the boat looks like a duck at sea. Seth then notes a succession of hot days and an occasion when not one, not two, but three children are baptized off the coast of Brazil. Some days, he drinks half a cup of salt-water before breakfast, on doctor's orders. There are prayer meetings and on-board sermons, and Seth dutifully notes the Biblical passages cited. Porpoise swim alongside. He throws up a yellow-green bile. He is ill on many occasions: his sea legs are at best a trifle wobbly. Some days, he simply stays a-bed. Another day, he witnesses a little girl's burial at sea, the captain reading the service for the burial of the dead at sea, the small box that is her coffin turning into a matchbox as it bobs on the waves before disappearing. The passengers feel the prickle of tropical heat, see trails of bright phosphorescence in the wake of the clipper. On and on and on, as the waves churn and roil: as the *Mimosa* cleaves steadfastly through the water. There are sightings of jagged-toothed sharks, and a flying fish lands on deck, its long, wing-like fins splaying out as it gasps. They pass through the millpond waters of the Doldrums, that belt of calm winds lying north of the equator between the ranges of the northern and southern trade winds. Humidity peaks, stifling those on deck, let alone those miserable creatures sweltering and sweating in the foetid cabin spaces where the stench, by now, is palpable, cloying, dense.

All these things he notes with due diligence, but Seth the diarist mainly feels sick: many of his travelling companions are ill as well, constipated from the salt meat diet, scurvy breaking out despite the daily doses of lime and lemon juice, bringing with it lethargy, open sores and painful gums. Seth prepares an account of his illness to recount to the doctor: 'I went to bed soon after Tea-time on Saturday night, and felt myself very cold, and as for hours before I got warm, – was very ill through the night, yesterday and last night, – felt tremendous pains in my belly, and each pain seemed to be an opposition to the other, which caused, as I thought, I don't know whether it did so or not, my body to be extremely loose'. Luckily, Seth didn't have to suffer a loose body for much longer. After following the coast of Brazil, and having entered the enormous mouth of the River Plate, the Rio de La Plata, the captain had ordered the mainsails be raised, increasing speed, and the sense of journey's end came, if not within sight, then within reach.

There was soon chattery talk of land being sighted, the passengers now perking up, bright as parakeets, buoyed up by excitement, and soon their hearts must have lifted slightly when 19-year-old William Jenkins sighted land from the top of the mast, as they were skirting the great hump of land that is the Valdés peninsula. Soon they were sailing into New Bay, and into their new lives. Seth saw a little boat set off for shore, the sun shining despite its being winter. Lewis Jones' subsequent speech to them lifted the spirits, not least his inventory of goods, property and livestock that had been amassed or built, including 16 houses and a storehouse containing three tons of bread, 300 sacks of wheat, not to mention rice, pumpkins, sugar, oats, barley, coffee, spades and rakes, with many animals ready to transport to Chubut ahead of them. It was like a man on a desert island finding a supermarket. Except the supermarket was a mirage.

So, finally, the settlers had arrived at Bahia Nueva or New Bay, a relatively sheltered sea inlet (because all shelter in Patagonia is relative and tentative, owing to the keen-ness and variety of the erosive wind). New Bay is not a huge patch of brine, measuring some 40 miles long and 20 miles wide, with its mouth, where it kisses the wild, open sea, measuring eight miles across. But it does offer safe anchorage away from the vicissitudes of open ocean.

Edwin and the servants, who had between them managed to get water from a well by now, were in the process of clearing a path through the thorn-scrub over the hill when they saw the boat in the distance. They rushed to the beach, where Edwin raised the Welsh flag on a pole he had already set in place for the purpose, and fired off some rounds from his gun. This was it. Arrival. One woman pointed from the side of the ship at the man with the flag and the gun, who was pretty much the entire welcoming party, and announced that he, with all certainty, would be her husband, and this would, eventually come to pass.

The journey-wearied, sea-bleary passengers of the *Mimosa* thus first set foot on Patagonian soil on 28 July 1865. Edwin Cynrig Roberts had this to say about the emotional effect of the weary contingent making landfall in a strange continent:

> The day of the test has arrived. Strong winds of disappointment blow, tender-hearted mothers with their tears flowing having to make a bed

on the naked beach. The men were busily carrying furniture to the land with the sea to their waists as they meet the boats and heap them here and there, and the mothers try and arrange some sort of shelter among the furniture.

The rim of grey hills which provided a backdrop to these scenes of desperate drama did not exactly proclaim comfort, solace or abundance. As Abraham Matthews described it, the land around the port that would eventually be named Porth Madryn, then Puerto Madryn, was sandy and stony. 'There is neither a valley, nor a river, nor a stream, nor any source of water anywhere. The land is poor and rough and covered with small bushes'. In this, he was echoing the assessment of the whole of Patagonia by Benjamin Franklin Bourne, who in *The Captive in Patagonia* said that:

> Patagonia more than answered the descriptions of geographers – bleak, barren, desolate beyond description or conception … The soil is of a light, sandy character and bears nothing worthy of the name of a tree. Low bushes or underwood are tolerably abundant, and in the valleys, a coarse, wiry grass grows abundantly. Streams of water are rare.

The new arrivals were soon making their own assessments of the terrain and the situation. The jagged dentition of the sullen ranks of cliffs, viewed in a dead and deadening light, seemed foreboding. The pewter, ice-cold sea extended as a dull sheet behind them, chill and unyielding.

Night came on quickly, smothering their dreams about utopia before they had even properly started. The settlers found shelter by building simple cabins to withstand the winter blasts. They had, in one very important sense, arrived too late. By this stage, they had lost the planting season, which extended in the area from May to June, so they would have to go a whole year without any chance of a harvest. Their hearts must have weighed them down, so heavily, indeed that they must have threatened to burst when they breasted the nearest hill and saw the desiccated, unyielding, torn land that opened up before them.

Dafydd Williams, the scabrous satirist of Aberystwyth, went off on a solo wander and was never seen alive again. Yet Lewis Jones had good news to report when he gave them a lecture about the plenitude of materials and natural wealth in the area. On the Valdés peninsula, he promised black marble worth five pounds a ton, and many wild horses cantered there, derived from stock the Spanish had originally brought over. Near the river bar, he argued, there were banks of valuable shingle and shells, worth two pounds a ton, not to mention an abundance of *guano*, or bird droppings, worth five pounds a ton. It was a promissory note of small fortunes to be made by those willing to work for them.

But that lay in the far-off future. For now, the settlers had to cope with life in the fridge. Their clothes were inadequate, their blankets threadbare. As Abraham Matthews put it in *Hanes y Wladfa Gymreig yn Patagonia*, 'Soon it was evident that Puerto Madryn was not fit for human settlement due the lack of fresh water'. A newspaper article that appeared in the *Liverpool Mercury* in January 1866, probably based on one of ship doctor Thomas Green's letters home, catalogued the trials and the tribulations of those who found themselves in New Bay, wind-whipped and winter-battered, and finding the only shelter in:

> a long wooden shed not large enough to accommodate all, and men and women had to sleep, partitioned off, how they could, the rest shifting as best they might. The food had to be cooked out of doors, which was constantly covered by clouds of sand, penetrating even their clothes. The water was scarce and bad, and had to be carried over two miles from a stagnant pond formed by recent rains, and was of a whitish colour from the marly nature of the soil and, moreover, was full of animaculae.

The country he describes is nothing more than level plains as far as the eye can reach, covered with low stunted bushes much resembling the furze of, say, Wessex, or the coastal heathlands of Pembrokeshire. 'The game,' the doctor's brother continues, 'is not much of any kind: some *guanacos*, foxes, etc. The birds are a species of emu, wild duck, etc., all hard to get on account of the level nature of the country … They were obliged to kill a horse for food; and he tells me he was very glad to eat seagulls and owls, and he says he killed a fox, but had the good fortune not to partake of its flesh'.

The burying starts early

Promise. Dread. The settlers must have jittered with a dizzy mix of both, not least when events such as the burial of young Mary Ann Jones took place, a month before her 16-month-old sister died as well, causing their father, W. R. Jones, to curse the place. As the diarist Seth Jones put it, 'the burying started early in the history of y Wladfa'. There were, in fact, 26 deaths in the colony during the first five years. Grim burials and a thin, insistent and seeping rain, sweeping wanly over a lunar, dust-blown landscape. It was enough to break even the most stalwart spirit, and break it completely at that. But there was a birth, too, when Mary Elizabeth Humphreys entered the world, taking her first, great liquid gasp of air. She was the first child born to the colonists, which led to a series of small hills being named after her, and christened Bryniau Meri, Mary's Hills. Others followed, with 43 births up until 1870 bringing their own hope and promise. And the settlers started to make sense of the layout of the terrain, and using landmarks, such as three willows which grew in the Chubut valley, with Tair Helygen being visible from a distance. As some started to get to know and study the land, others chose to depart, to desert the desert, as it were, with five leaving for Buenos Aires as early as the end of 1865.

Overland

The rest of the *Mimosa*'s passengers remained in New Bay for a few weeks before travelling another 30 or 40 miles to the Chupat valley, the place that was to become their new home. The men who undertook the journey – a rag-tag and bobtail assortment of settlers, and certainly not the experienced labourers and farmers that Minister Rawson had been promised, had to cope with parched land, a scarcity of water and thus with raging thirsts, while the women and children were taken to sea in a schooner called the *Mary Helen*, where they suffered their own kinds of hardships. In their naivety, they all expected the rain to fall as it did on the brackeny hills and terraced towns of home, and even though it was wet winter when they arrived, it was a different rain that fell, and on a far more parched earth. *Mae'r tir yn sych.* The land is dry. *Mae'r tir mor sych.* The land is so very dry.

Tending the livestock wasn't an easy task for the former coal miners but others turned their hands to thorn clearance to great effect, clearing great swathes of tough brush for planting. But when the *Mimosa* left the Bay, its sails breasting out towards deep ocean, they must have each felt very alone, the chill winds scything across the shelter-less beach. The sibilant hiss of cold waves washing over a pebble beach, must have added a miserable soundtrack to their inner despair.

But at least they had money – thin bundles of Welsh Patagonian currency – although this would have offered scant consolation. It was the early equivalent of Monopoly money. Before they left Liverpool, they had privately printed bundles of paper money in various denominations; in pounds, and notes of ten shillings and five shillings. Each one enjoyed an official blue stamp along with the signature of Thomas Ellis, Treasurer to y Wladfa, on the pound note, and that of Lewis Jones on the others, in the same way as the Governor of the Bank of England attaches his name to the promise of a modern ten-pound note. It was intended that such notes be used in exchange for food or labour, but in the absence of the former, the currency was soon devalued, and eventually became nothing more than a worthless paper curio.

Hardship aplenty

In the early days of the settlement, food was extremely scarce. On one occasion, they staved off starvation by boiling a fox for food. On another, they shot a circling kite and one of the men tore off its head with his bare teeth, and vampired every drop of its blood, completely draining its limp body.

This was not the land of milk and honey they'd been promised. There was no honey, no milk and where on earth were the wild cattle, the tall grasses, the fine soil, the beautiful countryside admired in the *Settlers' Handbook*? Instead, this was Bleaksville, Patagonia – cold, low cliffs, forbidding terrain, a desert full of thorns like razor wire. It certainly wasn't the country they'd been reading about – part Nirvana, part Shangri-La, a utopian version of the green land they'd left very far behind.

Unbeknown to them, they had arrived in a place that was even more dystopian than they knew, as the country had just embarked on a long and expensive war, in concert and collaboration with its neighbours Brazil and Uruguay against Paraguay, a war which would be a huge drain on the national purse. Lawlessness also swept through the land, with some of the criminal elements eventually drifting through the lands being hard-scrabbled by the Welsh. There were even rumoured government plans to move 200 prostitutes from the nascent cities of Argentina to Chubut, bringing a mix of moral turpitude and fleshy temptation to upset the three-times-on-a-Sunday chapel-going folk. Who already had enough on their plate, or, rather, *not enough* on their plate.

The *Mimosa*'s cargo of settlers had already ventured very far, and already suffered a great deal, and now they had to contend with seeing their dreams smashed to smithereens. But the practical exigencies would not have allowed them much time for bitter introspection, as food and water had to be sought, as well as temporary shelter.

Later, a deacon, in a chapel in Bala said categorically that life for the early emigrants was worse than had they been transported to Australia as convicts:

> Surely, there has been nothing so foolish since the day of the South Sea Bubble to the present hour. It is high time to put a stop to the work of a man who goes about the country to induce simple-minded people to go to such a wretched place. Those who are there would have been better off if they had been transported by the government to Botany Bay.

There are conflicting versions of how the settlers found themselves shelter, with one version of events describing how they hewed themselves simple caves in the soft limestone rock of the sea-cliffs. Others maintain that they built rudimentary cabins, keeping out of the wind and cold in that way.

Meanwhile, the proposed site for the settlement lay some 40 miles away, and to get there was a new challenge. Edwin Roberts rose to it, and took eighteen young men with him. Each carried a gun, complete with bayonet, ten pounds of hard biscuit – sufficient to last a four or five day trek – along with a single horse. One of the trekkers brought along a wheelbarrow to lessen his burden, but the wheels sank in the sand, so it was abandoned after just a couple of miles. They were beset by problems on the trek, not least when the vessels containing water were found to be broken, so that some of the more desperate men drank sea water and suffered badly as a consequence. There was an odoriferous meeting with a skunk, which they baptised *drewgi*, or stink-dog. They moved on, confusing dust devils for smoke from Indian camps, with many of the men edging towards so much exhaustion that fifteen of them gave up the ghost and had to be left to rest while Edwin and two others pressed on, and managed to find water for their companions. The party walked on, to Llyn Halen Mawr, or Big Salt Lake, and then they finally got to the river, and followed its course until they arrived at what was to be their first real home. They called it Trofa Unnos, as befitting a place for a single night's stay. Nearby stood an old fort, or a fortified hamlet, which had been built by Henry Libanus Jones, a Welsh seaman and merchant, who had earlier set up shop trying to capture and sell the wild cattle that reputedly lived in the area. Soon, the hamlet would be named Caer Antur, the Venture Fort or Adventure Fort, as the other settlers congregated here, and started to find a rhythm to their days.

Daily routine around the fort saw the Red Dragon flag being raised in the morning and lowered at night in a place which Edwin Roberts called Brythonfa, his own name for the settlement. Other people had their own ideas, later on, including Kymrovania, Y Fro Wen, or the white place, and Kymrovia, which won its place in some newspapers at home. When he wasn't leading such expeditions, Edwin dreamed of establishing a Welsh army and daydreamed up some uniforms, even, with rabbit-skin hats decorated with a ribbon of scarlet thread; what the well dressed militiaman is wearing this season.

The new settlement at Rawson was established in September 1865. It was named by the Welsh in honour of Guillermo Rawson, Interior Minister and a sterling ally of the community. It lay on a shingle spit four miles from the mouth of the Chubut river, where the water was deep enough for light craft to navigate, and there was a supply of fresh drinking water, too. Rawson himself gave support in many ways, such as finding a monthly allowance of £200 to buy provisions, and a separate grant for purchasing livestock. He also earmarked £200 to compensate the native Indians for any tribal lands ceded to the Welsh. Rawson was a godsend, and naming the township after him was entirely natural.

The old fort, Yr Hen Amddiffynfa, at the heart of the settlement, measured 100 square yards, and within its walls stood three small houses. At each corner of the fort there was a lookout post, and the small site was enclosed by a defensive moat. Yr Hen Amddiffynfa acted as a nexus for the first wave of buildings. They had to be sturdy enough to withstand floods, as proved by a flash flood that washed away the earliest dwellings in 1865. Initially, these were nothing more than the most primitive huts, made of clay and willow, with old boxes acting as furniture. In the blighted terrain, wood for building was in very short supply, other than the very occasional trees that grew along the riverbanks. Later, these primitive accommodations would be upgraded by using ostrich feathers as some kind of window glass, while old barrels that had been washed up on the shore were used as rudimentary tables.

But despite the material deprivations, there was still room to attend to spiritual sustenance. The settlers did manage to hold their first religious service in a storage shed, with a big box for a pulpit, and the small congregation seated on grain sacks to listen to the Reverend Abraham Mathews preach on a very appropriate subject, namely 'Israel yn yr Anialwch' or 'Israel in the Desert'.

A visit by a British warship, the *Triton*, in 1866, resulted in a pretty scathing report on the plight of these new Patagonians, suggesting they had fallen foul of a snake oil salesman, because 'the prospectus circulated in Wales, in the Welsh language, was calculated to deceive persons desirous of emigrating, by holding out advantages to do so which were not subsequently realized'. It also suggested that Interior Minister Rawson had been duped, noting that he was very disappointed by the impoverished skills bank of the newcomers.

Some of the early setbacks were orchestrated by nature. Harvests were poor to non-existent, and by June 1867, the cost of subsidizing the colony was such that the Argentine Government considered cutting its losses and moving all the Welsh to the province of Santa Fe. The settlers, now both starving and desperate, were quite willing to decamp, and they set about slaughtering their animals and moving to New Bay to duly make the move to Santa Fé. But protracted negotiations, and the need to replenish the stash of government food supplies, sent them back to Chubut, and back to the land. And even when the harvests improved, they were a long, long way from any market, and the cost of moving goods was prohibitive in the extreme, as was the cost of importing necessities without a proper connection to the sea routes. But the Welsh finally took charge of the situation, not least with the establishment of the Cwmni Masnachol y Camwy / Compañía Mercantil del Chubut / Chubut Mercantile Company, which held its first meeting in April 1885, with the intention of renting, and eventually buying, a trading vessel of their own.

Spreading the news

In 1868, mass media took off in the colony, with the first publication of *Y Brut*, a monthly newspaper edited by R. J. Berwyn, containing 25 handwritten pages, which was paid for not in money but with paper, as the cost of a subscription was a dozen pages of writing paper. The method of circulation was cost-effective in the extreme, as each reader had to undertake to hand on his or her copy to the next subscriber. The first issue contained, among other things, a letter from Michael D. Jones and a useful article about seal hunting. By this time Rawson had its own school, adapted from the cabin of a shipwreck, where 30 barefoot pupils sat on rows of seats rudely carved from willow. They only had three slates between them, so children would use any old flat stone on which to learn to write. One of the pupils was Eluned Morgan, who went on to become one of y Wladfa's finest writers, proof of the calibre of the education even in a school with only the most rudimentary facilities.

R. J. Berwyn was one of the early teachers on a grand salary of £15 for six months, payable in cash or in kind. He wrote a handbook in Welsh, which was published in 1878, the first Welsh book to appear from South America.

The testing conditions at Rawson prompted many to try their luck elsewhere, causing the population to dwindle. One of the settlers headed back to Wales, his tail between his legs. In 1869, the monthly supplies from Buenos Aires were suspended for twenty months, leaving the Welsh unutterably marooned. Visitors even came from Australia to assess the prospects in Patagonia, but one of those, Evan Ellis Jones, could only express his complete dismay, asking where were the good and fertile valleys he had read about, and opining that it was a terrible thing that folk had been encouraged to break up their homes to travel to such a place as Chubut. In a letter to the newspapers, Ellis Jones expressly forbade people from Australia to follow him, so strongly did he feel about what seemed to him to be a serious deception.

In the early 1870s, there was Indian trouble. One Saturday night, a commotion was heard on the southern side of the river, and in the morning, it was discovered that many cattle and horses had disappeared. A posse of a dozen men, each equipped with two horses, was dispatched to get the animals back. After hours of tracking, they came upon one of the cattle tied to a bush. There was an armed altercation between the two parties.

And pressure now came from a new direction, with the news, broadcast by Michael D. Jones, that new colonists were eager to move to Patagonia from the United States. Food was already scarce, so, in Argentina – especially in government – some shrill alarm bells rang: a colony that could barely maintain itself could scarcely be expected to absorb and feed a new influx. Pressure was put on the British Emigration Commission in London to produce an advertisement cautioning against moving to Patagonia. There was even talk of abandoning the Chubut colony altogether, rebuffed in part by a flurry of letters pointing out the steady progress made in terms of farming, the exploration of new territories and the success of the new irrigation schemes. Lewis Jones added a confident, if not strident, voice to the clamour for the colony to be allowed more time to develop, and appealed for more new settlers, not fewer. 'I am confident that the valley of the Chubut will never again be deserted, though it is left to ourselves to decide whether we or some other people will be the inhabitants ... If Welsh emigrants do not come here soon, others will ere too long.' Michael D. Jones, writing from Wales, suggested that 'to stop emigration would be to damage the colony. What is needed is more emigrants with more capital and more labour to work the canal'.

Campaigns to attract new blood from America bore fruit with a small vessel called the *Rush* arriving in 1873 and the *Spark* delivering 33 further adventurers from Pennsylvania in 1874, even as another contingent, numbering 49 people, arrived from Wales. And so, by the end of 1874, the population had grown to 273. The following year, the settlers were granted official title to the land by the Argentine government, which settled nerves, and served to attract even more Welsh people to these harsh lands in South America.

The next wave of immigrants was substantial, not least because chill economic winds were blowing through the coalfield of south Wales. No fewer than 500 people from the Rhondda valleys and places such as Aberdare chose to travel to Chubut between 1875 and 1876 to escape the deprivations of the Depression at home. They were probably buoyed up by the news of the success of the wheat harvest of 1873. At the same time, more land was being allocated to each arriving settler, and the first steam-powered thresher was delivered.

Thus, by 1876, the population numbered 690, with 135 of these being second-generation Welsh and 35 being non-Welsh settlers. The colony was beginning to demonstrate some sort of sustainability, with exports of wheat, butter and even sealskins, now that some of them had taken to hunting the animals along the coast. All these brought in receipts totalling £7,000. But this was also the year the Congress passed the Colonization Law, which stipulated that Justices of the Peace and municipal bodies should be elected locally. Lewis Jones, among many, railed against this, saying, 'The Government undoubtedly aims at crushing our Britishism and making *gauchos* of us. We are what the *London World* called "splendidly stubborn" on the point, and we will struggle on, come what may.'

Y Drych in the US, which consistently raged fiercely against all matters Patagonian, and had, of course, even warned about the danger of Patagonian cannibals, turned the arc lamp of its scrutiny and scorn onto articles in the Australian Welsh paper, *Yr Ymwelydd*, designed to woo hardy migrants from Australia to move to South America. One such dampener was the response in *Y Drych* to a report penned by the Rev. D. S. Davies after his eight month-long visit to Chubut:

> It is a pity that by this the Welsh in Australia should be misled about the true situation in the Camwy valley. Instead of publishing this sort of trash, the editor would perform a greater service to his fellow nation by chronicling the heartbreaking stories that have recently come out of y Wladfa. It is only too easy to conjure up Paradise on paper, which is precisely what the Rev. D. S. Davies has done, but it is quite another matter to encourage men to break up their homes in Australia or the United States, and migrate to somewhere far less promising. If it is a hard life in the mines of Australia, then going to Patagonia will be nothing less than 'jumping out of the frying pan into the fire'.

Another *Drych* correspondent, hiding behind be sobriquet The Josakeed, railed against what he saw as incontrovertible facts about y Wladfa, mainly about the desertified terrain which would, he averred, be a graveyard for a language.

> Rather than a pleasant spot to nurture the Welsh language it is, rather, a cemetery wherein will be buried, so very quickly, every memory of her, and where Spanish will flourish on her grave … In Patagonia, it will be necessary to learn three languages – Welsh as the language of religion, Spanish as a political tongue and English as the medium of trade. And is this something they'll continue to do into future generations? It is not. Only a very small number will be able to afford to give their children English lessons. And then they'll be confined to the narrow and Papist world of the Spanish nation.

But the picture wasn't all bleak. With the recent wave of new arrivals had come new energies. The availability of labour meant that a pipe dream, if you pardon the pun, of creating a system of irrigating canals, could be realized. This led to nothing short of an agricultural revolution, turning parched earth into productive land, and fuelled the expansion of the colony and many of its early successes. This was achieved in spite of the country's government, which had passed a decree demonstrating its commitment to provide the necessary equipment for the construction of dams in Chubut, but on the condition that the settlers themselves worked for nothing to build them: a kind offer, quickly and summarily refused! Perhaps the greatest triumph of this period came in the shape and quality of Benjamin Brunt's award-winning wheat, grown on his smallholding called Argoed, which garnered first prize in Chicago in 1889 – and this despite being up against 40 other competitors – and put the still miniscule colony on the world map. The following year, Brunt again submitted his wheat to the competition, and this time won against no fewer than 38 other countries. The reputation of the Welsh when it came to irrigation led to Australian states such as New South Wales and Victoria offering them various inducements to move there later on. The quality of the wheat, meanwhile, was sufficiently impressive to persuade Ernest Scott, in a report about y Wladfa to the British Government in 1902, to describe the grain as being of the best possible quality, 'comparing easily with the best wheat of Manitoba'.

One of the most inspiring of the early pioneers was a quiet man who wouldn't say boo to an Andean goose, namely John Daniel Evans. Evans was born in Mountain Ash, and was three years of age when he sailed to Patagonia aboard the *Mimosa* in 1865 with his family. He was raised on the family farms in the Glyn Du area, near Trerawson. He became well-known as the leader of a number of expeditions in search of new land in Patagonia, earning him the nickname 'El Baqueano', which means 'masterful guide', because of his thorough knowledge of the prairie and its pathways. A diminutive man in terms of stature, with lots of humility, he was nevertheless a sterling adventurer who had the gift of leading other men. In 1882, he took a quartet with him to explore the southern stretches of Patagonia, and later that year, took three companions to search for gold in the catchment of Afon Fach, the Little River.

In November 1883, he took four men on a tragic expedition in the direction of the Andes, again in search of gold, without any real knowledge of the dangers ahead, the jagged dentitions of high mountain ranges, the rivers to cross, not to mention the marauding presence of natives who were themselves being hunted by other white men. To avoid their deadly predations, Evans had to employ native cunning himself: at one point he set the eighteen or so horses they had to walk in the waters of a river for some 25 miles to avoid leaving any hoof-prints. This bought the Welsh posse enough time to reach Dol y Plu and Hirlam Edwin. But at some point, they became afraid. They turned for home, riding day and night. The hooves of the horses bled. Two of the men had to be tied into their saddles. Suddenly, at a place now called Valle de los Mártires – the Valley of the Martyrs – they were attacked by a vicious, marauding band from Chile. Three were killed with spears, their bodies slit open, their skeletons hacked out and their bones scattered, their severed sex organs stuffed into their mouths.

Miraculously, John D. Evans escaped. He spurred his horse, Malacara, across a twenty-foot wide ravine and down a steep scree slope. They made the 200 miles back to the lower valley in 40 hours. The horse swiftly became an equine legend, up there with Red Rum, Trigger and Silver.

The following year, another band of 29 pioneers, armed with Remingtons and thereafter nicknamed *los Rifleros*, or the riflemen, sought a new place of settlement in the Andes, crossing the huge expanses of scrub and wind-parched terrain. Once again, Evans was the man who led them, finding water and following tracks. Among their number was Colonel Fontana, the Governor of Chubut, who was amazed at the shooting skills of the Welsh contingent, who numbered 20 men. They blended with the *gauchos*, rode hard and showed plenty of true grit.

On their way toward the mountains, the men visited the place where Evans' companions had been murdered, now called Dyffryn y Merthyron, the Valley of Martyrs, where they raised a mound of rocks by way of creating a grave, and held a simple service.

On they went, climbing a rocky cliff that is called Craig Goch nowadays, and eventually beheld a fertile valley, set among snow-crowned mountains, which made them all mute with its beauty and promise. It moved one of the company, Richard Jones, to exclaim 'O! dyma gwm hyfryd'. Here was indeed a beautiful valley, Cwm Hyfryd, and thus was a new home for the Welsh duly baptised, even though for a short while, Dyffryn y Mefus (Strawberry Valley) was also in the frame.

In September 1888, 29 men travelled the self-same 400 miles from the lower Camwy valley to the high reaches of the Andes, under the leadership of John Murray Thomas, a.k.a. the Stanley of Patagonia, but with John Daniel Evans once again at the vanguard, as the most experienced of scouts.

Three years later, he led a group of four families, as well as some single men, into the mountains, leaving on 27 August and arriving on 21 November 1891. It was a veritable caravanserai, with overtones of the pioneering wagon trains that crossed America, with bullock carts, four wagons, 100 cattle, an array of horses and mares as well as boxes containing pigs and chickens which were attached to the sides of the wagons. There was a sort of found poem in their progress, although some of the names remain somewhat untranslatable, such as Gaiman, Ceg y Ffos (The Ditch Mouth) and Hen Eglwys (the Old Church). On they went, via Rio Chico, Gwersyll Tair Cainc (Three Branch Camp), Pen y Bryn (Top of the Hill) and Dyffryn William, (William's Vale). Determinedly on, through Dyffryn Coediog (the Wooded Vale). Passing Paso de Indios, Top yr Hafn, Nant y Cran, Tromen Wfgo, Caltrawna, Cwm Llechi (Slate Valley), Langew, Gwrw Siriol, Sacamata and Tafarn Bedw (Beech Inn). Mike Pearson, the director and co-author of theatre group Brith Gof's work, *Patagonia: Breuddwyd yn yr Anialwch*, wrote this haunting advice for such trekkers: 'However arduous the journey, however unyielding the wagon springs, always take a mirror. For it shows you where you are not, looking back from a world where no sweat bleaches your hat band, where no dust etches your skin, where no relentless roar deafens your ears …'

Given the jaggedness, harshness and sterility of the terrain, the going was never going to be easy, mirrors or not. Axles broke, the bullock cart overturned, but the intrepid travellers nevertheless managed to cross the arid wastes unscathed, with even a new baby being born on the way.

Change was also on the way. It only takes one official to challenge the status quo, to completely upset the apple cart. Governor Luiz Jorge Fontana, a staunch supporter of the Welsh, was recalled to the capital to be replaced by a Señor Eugenio Tello, who altered the relationship between the officials and the colonists at a stroke. Tello ordered all young men over eighteen to join the National Guard, and decreed that Sunday was a day for military drills, which flew in the face of staunch Welsh chapel-going. He also interfered with the management of the canals, arguing that the government should regulate their use as they owned the river, even if the canal system was private.

It was a testing time for the colony's diplomatic spirit. Soon, the Welsh turned a tad sullen, somewhat broken and cowed, not least when Tello's successor seemed to be deliberately inciting a spirit of revolt when he instituted military parades on the Sabbath and asked for a garrison to be suddenly stationed in Gaiman, originally called Pentre Sydyn, or Sudden Village, reflecting the way houses quickly mushroomed on the river banks. The plan to militarize the settlement and conduct drills on a Sunday was insulting both to Welsh Sabbatarianism and pacifism in a breath. The dastardly official also wanted Welsh masters in schools to be replaced by Argentine teachers, thus denationalizing some of the education about Welsh language and culture, stripping it away by this re-staffing.

A delegation from Chubut went to London to express their very serious misgivings about the changes that were being foisted on them, almost at gunpoint. Bringing troops into the area would mean that 'life and property will not be safe, and the honour of women will be at the mercy of a licentious half-caste soldiery composed of assassins and the sweepings of jails. The Welsh, whether they wish it or not, will be driven into making reprisals and Chupat will then become an Argentinean Cuba'. Change, in so many guises, sometimes uniformed, was seemingly inexorable.

Waves of incomers kept on coming, with the period between 1880 and 1887 being particularly busy with new arrivals. Patagonia, despite its local difficulties, remained a migrant magnet.

A hint of insurrection

One Sunday in January 1899, things in the colony took a definite turn for the worse, when Governor O'Donnell – who would later be pilloried as the 'Nero of Chubut' – dispatched policemen to Trelew, where the chairman and secretary of the self-styled Colonial Council were told to leave their chapel devotions. They were accused of high treason, for having sent Llwyd ap Iwan and Thomas Benbow Phillips to England on their behalf, the two being castigated as troublemaking emissaries. At the Foreign Office, the men had presented a scathing and trenchant criticism of the Argentine administration of, and in, Chubut, sparing no scorn whatsoever for the plan to bring in the soldiers. The two Welshmen made their case for secession in London at a time when some of the papers in Buenos Aires were suggesting ejecting the Welsh from Chubut. Little wonder the police arrived.

The charges were soon proved to be trumped up, and the men were released, but not in time to stop a new nervousness flickering though the corridors of power in London. What were the Welsh Patagonians up to? Which side were they on? The Argentine Ambassador, in the usual placatory diplomatic mode, underlined the fact that the Welsh were 'good Argentine citizens', although the *Liverpool Mercury* was in no such mood, choosing to fan the flames of controversy with its headline 'Strong Repressive Measures' above an op-ed attack on the plans to militarize Chubut. 'There can be nothing in the state of the colony itself calling for this step, which is manifestly calculated to serve the double purpose of overawing the colonists and of emphasizing the Argentine decision to hold possession of the district against possible British (or American) intervention'. Meanwhile, a cannon-like comment boomed out from the unexpected direction of genteel Monmouth in Wales, where retired Vice-Admiral Brent railed against the treatment of his fellow Welshmen and stated, boldly, that 'if her Majesty's Government can stand between the Welsh and the Argentine Government, or become their protectors, it would be a merciful and humane work … I am wondering whether it would be possible to obtain the valley of the Chupat and the surrounding country as a Welsh Republic owing fealty to the Argentine Government'. When the man formerly in charge of the British squadron in the south-eastern waters of America started taking a republican line, it was proof of a very new kind of gunboat diplomacy! And the Vice-Admiral wasn't alone in his pro-Welsh-in-Chubut stance. In the House of Commons, the Welsh MPs set up a pro-Chubut, cross-party committee and asked for a meeting with Sir John Broderick, the Under-Secretary of Foreign Affairs, when three MPs were joined by none other than Llwyd ap Iwan and Thomas Benbow Phillips. Arguments that Patagonia wasn't, in fact, Argentine territory, and that Britain could assert sovereignty over the place, were soon dismantled by Foreign Office lawyers. But it was a pressure-cooker situation, with the heat really turned up, at a time when Italian colonization in Chubut was proceeding apace, with the newcomers granted 200,000 acres of land. The rule of law was also breaking down, as evidenced by the case of John Morley, a farmer in Trelew, who lost all his stock of cattle and sheep to a notorious villain called Benjamin Artiles. When Morley appealed to the authorities for help, some dismissed the theft as an 'insignificant act'. Cattle rustling grew to be a source of vexation, and underlined a rift between the settlers and the sympathies of the officialdom that presided over them.

The 1890s also brought a dose of gold fever to the area, and in 1892, the Welsh Patagonian Goldfield Syndicate was established to sieve and sift the areas around Corcovado, Tecka and Mica. They found they could recover 24 grams from 14 pounds of excavated material, but there was never the sort of return that made miners and panners dizzy with discovery in California. Even so, other companies followed, ready to chance their arm, such as the Rio Corintos Gold Mine and the Phoenix Mining Company. These made little profit, although they did help open up areas in the Andes to other forms of development.

Immigration dwindles

The chill economic winds that blew through the south Wales coalfields from 1904 to 1912 provoked others to venture to the New World to seek fortune, or, at the very least escape certain penury. It was a time when typhoid claimed many a life. But in addition to the deprivations of illness, there were internal pressures as the make-up and mixture of people in Chubut changed at an accelerated pace. In 1890, the Welsh numbered 2,500 while there were about 100 Argentine officials, and by 1896, the process of Hispanification reached a high-water mark with the passing of a law insisting that schooling, as we know, should be through the medium of Spanish. Just four years later, a substantial influx of Italians poured into the area, and with the colony now divided into two townships, namely Rawson and Gaiman, there were opportunities for growth in officialdom and bureaucracy at precisely the same time that the Welshness of the area was being diluted. 1904 saw the death of Lewis Jones, one of y Wladfa's principal architects – as early surveyor, proselytizer, first administrator, railway promoter and developer, and head of Trelew as a municipality – which recognized his great contribution by naming the town after him, 'tre' meaning town in Welsh, thus creating Lewis-town, and enshrining his great contribution to the state of Chubut. Farming the dust. Settling the desert.

The Welsh settlers had indeed tamed a desert, and farmed what had first seemed like unfarmable land. In the 1860s, only 62 hectares of land were under the plough, but by the end of the century, 5,500 hectares were given over to crops. The stock of cattle, too, grew exponentially during the next three decades, from 60 to almost 50,000, sheep from 800 to 108,000, horses from 40 to 16,895 and pigs from 6 to 1,151. And land value increased by dint of the irrigation canals, the advent of the railways, the co-operative company and the absence or rents, taxes and tithes: thus land was worth 800 per cent more in 1895 than it had been ten years earlier. By this year, the number of chapels had grown, too, from one in 1865 – Moriah in Trelew – to no fewer than 17 in 1895, representing four denominations, namely Independents, Baptists, Wesleyans and the Church of England, when the population had grown to just over 3,000.

News gets around. The success of the area attracted new settlers. The Welsh were no longer alone in Patagonia, and the solid Welsh identity of Chubut started to erode, especially with the dwindling immigration from the home country. The contingent that arrived with the *Orita* in 1911 was the last substantial contingent of immigrants from Wales, numbering 113 people, who set sail from Liverpool in November 1911, as war clouds gathered over Europe. There could have been many reasons for the reduction in numbers, not least the sinking of the *Titanic* six months later, which would have surely rocked people's faith in the safety of sea travel, specially as this mighty vessel was proclaimed as being unsinkable.

The First World War had repercussions in Argentina, too, with a fall in the price of wheat and alfalfa, and a subsequent flu epidemic stopped people travelling in many parts of the world. Nevertheless, there were 23,000 people living in Chubut by 1915, a half-century after the first settlement, and many of these were foreign immigrants, if we allow the idea that the Welsh were no longer foreigners by now, but were assimilating as full Argentine citizens. Indeed, a visitor to Chubut in this period suggested that one could see the changes in people's physical features and physiognomies between one generation of Welsh settlers and the next, 'with red-faced, open-eyed, straight-backed boys, each with a bright-coloured handkerchief around his neck and the *guanaco*-wool poncho hanging from his shoulders … the latter who are Patagonian-born seem to be part of their horses, but the elders, however excellent long practice has made them, never attain the proficiency of their sons'. Intermarriage helped explain these changes, at least in part, 'and so the efforts of the forefathers who fared overseas to found a new home shall be made null and void', especially as, the visitor noted, 'the average Argentine girl is rather apt to make roast meat of the hearts of Welsh youth'. A poet writing at the turn of the century described one of these young Argentineans, roaming the land like a *gaucho*, on the back of mare that can run like the wind.

> He is a Welshman of blood and kindred,
> But he speaks a rough Spanish;
> He boasts that he has no taste
> For his mother tongue on his lip.

The age of the car

Even more dramatic that the changing appearance of the Welsh – and in rivalry to the *gaucho*'s speedy mare – was the advent of a newfangled travel machine, the Model T Ford, which ushered in the age of the motor car in a part of the world which had, up until then, very few roads on which to drive. But the days of the horse, and horse-drawn agricultural equipment, were numbered, as the car – and especially the *chata* or Ford pick-up – came to be seen as a symbol of both status and progress. Add to that the arrival of electricity and electric light, and one could see that the modern age was sending its most dazzling and effective advanced guard. In 1950, the last of the original travellers on the *Mimosa*, Rhondda man Daniel Harries, had passed way. Things were changing. One age was giving way to another.

The irony of having escaped American assimilation only to drown in these new waves of intermarriage wasn't lost on the Welsh. But they had other things to lose, too, not least the fertile plains they had created with the help of canalized water. They had also colonized new areas, with those doughty travellers led by John Daniel Evans having crossed the parched plains to find lush land on the Andean slopes in Cwm Hyfryd, the Beautiful Valley. But there were not near enough new immigrants to shore up new colonies, despite efforts to establish two, one to the south of Chubut between Lake Colwapi and the coast, and the other some 100 miles west of Rawson. Wherever the Welsh went, of course, the new immigrants were heading there, too. The stream of emigrants from Wales had by now turned into a miserable trickle, and was in danger of drying up entirely, thanks particularly to the British government policy of encouraging people to seek their fortunes elsewhere, suggesting countries such as South Africa, Canada and Australia. In 1902, Canada managed to lure 234 Welsh settlers *from* Patagonia, who travelled on the *Orissa* to acquire land set aside for them in Saltcoats, Manitoba.

Soon, the Welsh settlers of Chubut were in the minority, with only a third of the 12,000 people in the lower Chubut valley being Welsh. Their success was part of the problem, as were government initiatives to boost economic growth. The Spanish came in numbers. The Italians came in further droves, not to mention considerable numbers of Argentine nationals and smaller influxes of people from Chile.

The next fifty years or so would see many of the institutions created in the Welsh settlement riven by dispute and ongoing arguments, the Co-operative Society being just one of them. The utopian unity of the community, as dreamed of by Michael D. Jones, was in danger of dissipating, changing into a dystopian future. Connections with Wales dwindled year by year, decade by decade, until the centenary celebrations in 1965 rebuilt bridges and rekindled interest both in Wales and in Patagonia. As Fernando Coronato told Marcus Tanner, author of *The Last of the Celts*, the celebrations wrought great change. 'A great many people came here from Wales and interest revived. In the last 15 years there has been more and more. But no one thinks Welsh will ever again be a spoken language in the street. It's all about a search for identity.'

The veteran politician Dafydd Wigley, now Lord Wigley, recalled his 1965 visit to y Wladfa in an article for *Ninnau*, the newspaper of the North American Welsh:

> I was sitting in a cold, empty carriage on the London Underground almost 50 years ago, riveted by the booklet. It was a prospectus for the centenary celebrations of the Welsh community in the Patagonian state of Chubut, Argentina. I had been working with the Ford Motor Company for less than a year after leaving university. My annual salary was only £800 and the trip would cost £300. I was only entitled to 15 days holiday a year – and the trip would take more than that! When I asked my bank manager for a loan, and my line manager for more holiday, both were so taken aback that they agreed! I went off to Patagonia in October 1965 – the experience of a lifetime.
>
> I was amongst the youngest of the 70 who flew out in a Comet aircraft built in Flintshire, where Airbuses are currently constructed. If the centenary celebration barely made a footnote in London newspapers, it was headline news in Argentina. We were given a tremendous welcome, with the Argentine Government giving a million dollars' worth of support in today's money. They even printed a special postage stamp to celebrate the centenary. Our first stop, Buenos Aires, had a string of receptions, then we flew down to Trelew, the original Welsh settlement, by 1965 a city of some 20,000 people, today with over 100,000 inhabitants.
>
> As our plane landed at Trelew airstrip, we were encircled by a huge crowd. We came down the steps to be bear-hugged by hundreds of tearful, joyous people. They didn't know us from Adam, but gathered to welcome us – and the fact that Wales was at last recognising, with pride, the epic history of this remarkable Welsh settlement.

So was it a success, this overseas settlement? Dafydd Tudur maintains that the settlement of y Wladfa was:

Beyond doubt, a bold and courageous enterprise that could easily have resulted in disaster. Bearing in mind the harsh circumstances that the settlers endured, their success in turning an arid and desolate region of Patagonia into arable land, and in fact that the Welsh language was still spoken in the Chupat valley at the turn of the twenty-first century, the venture may be considered a remarkable triumph over adversity. However, when considering the original aims of its promoters, it is difficult to consider the Welsh Settlement in Patagonia as anything but a failure.

Failure? In some senses, yes, but unlike the hapless colonists of Cambriol, y Wladfa still exists, with young children learning Welsh and congregations still going to chapel. For a Welsh speaker such as myself, the pleasurably shocking experience of hearing Welsh words – plump, warm and fully-rounded – on the sun-dessicated lips of a farmer standing on the banks of a Chubut canal, or coming from the crinkled mouth of a former nurse as we take tea together in the high Andes, is nothing short of remarkable. This, one reminds oneself, whilst quietly pinching the skin, is, after all, South America, and this is the language taught me by my mother. Every verb, it seems, offers evidence of the backbreakingly hard work that went into the taming of this land, to farming the parched earth. Each Welsh noun seems to bear testament to the tenacity, *y dygnwch*, of the early settlers who, resolutely and unbowed, faced up to the corrosive winds scything in over the plains. And each sentence, carried on an invisible but still detectable undertow of Spanish sense and Spanish syntax seems to carry, in its lilt and flow, an echo of the shape of the land they left behind – the hills of green and gentle undulation they exchanged for some pretty harsh terrain. Those settlers didn't keep their old identity – that would have been impossible, and somewhat pointless – but they did remember where they came from, bringing an old language into a new land and managing, by dint of stubbornness and steely resourcefulness, to keep it. So the Welsh became a part of Argentina, and very proudly so, but managed to remember, honour and cherish the past, to protect it within the stockade of language, if you like. Most of the conversations recorded in this book were conversations in Welsh, and every time I heard the language uttered on this unfamiliar continent I was always slightly startled. Those words, that used to be heard under oak shadow, or spoken in the tight concertinas of terraced homes in Mountain Ash and the farming homes of Llandrillo, now spoken under a testing sun, in a world of spiky grey grasses. To hear the words for cream cakes, moist and warm, in Esquel … *cacennau hufen*. The very taste of home, a mere ocean's breadth away.

Chapter 3

The Great Emptiness

The great Argentine poet and fabulist Jorge Luis Borges once suggested: 'You will find nothing there. There is nothing in Patagonia. That's why [W. H.] Hudson liked it. You will notice there are no people in his books'. Hudson, a great naturalist, was probably more interested in wildlife than humanity – that was his job, after all – yet Borges has a point. You can travel for a very, very long time in Patagonia and not see a soul, or any evidence of people and their activities. Like Montana, or Nepal, it is a place of big skies overhead, enlarging the sense of distance and space way up high into the stratosphere. And thus, it can underline, quietly and persuasively, the great, essential human loneliness, all of us dwarfed by the world, marooned in it.

This emptiness troubled people, and the first bona fide classic of Argentine literature, the seventh president of Argentina Domingo Sarmiento's book *Facundo: Civilization and Barbarity* (1845), expresses anxiety about how the Republic can control such an enormous territory:

> The enormity of country that extends toward the two extremes is quite without any populace; she has rivers that are navigable, but they have not seen any craft – even the most frail variety venture – along their reaches. It is the very length and breadth of the Republic that vexes it; surrounded on all sides by desert which sinks into her very innards; loneliness, a country without habitation and without people, here are the indefinable boundaries between one state and the next.

At the beginning of theatre company Brith Gof's *Patagonia: Breuddwyd yn yr Anialwch*, there's a reference to the French philosopher and critic Jean

Baudrillard, who wrote a newspaper essay in which he found 'on every side nothingness, wasteland, sterile horizons, infinite vistas'. Brith Gof's script responds by saying 'Baudrillard is right. There is no seduction here. No half-hidden, no half-exposed. No objects of desire. No-one to call you by name. No one to look you in the eye. No-one to see you from over there. No trees with the promise of shade. No verticals at all, just an endless horizontal. The only possible shot is the pan. As easy to lose your mind as lose your way'.

Losing your mind under a big sky, in a place of essential human loneliness. This is true of some aspects of Patagonia, certainly. In his book, *Pethau Patagonia*, Fred Green recalls a time when he and his family lived at Rhyd yr Indiaid, and the desperate loneliness that would beset him on the *paith* (prairie). He recalls not hearing a word of Welsh or Spanish for weeks on end, and notes how a letter from the lower valley could take a month to reach him in the winter, and even then, he would have to ride for nearly a day to claim it before getting the chance to read it. For those in need of regular company, he noted, the idea of having to earn a living by dealing with such loneliness would be nothing short of painfully cruel. Green knew of many a soul who tried to live on the *paith* but they suffered from such biting *hiraeth* – that aching, Welsh nostalgia – for chapel, community and company, that they would be forced to move back to the valley and its distractions and comforts.

The enforced isolationism of the place was seen by the English press as one of the most insurmountable obstacles facing the Welsh colonists as they strove to bed down in the desert lands, far from the teeming terraced houses of their homeland, of their motherland. In 1869, countryside magazine *The Field* reported the opinion of W. Perkins, the Argentine Immigration Secretary, that 'the Welsh colony is a failure because it was from the commencement a great mistake … The poor Welshmen were settled in Patagonia, out of reach of civilization and with no market for their produce … had North Americans been settled there, the result might have been different, but with the Welsh settlers, the change from their thickly populated native land to such dreary isolation unnerved them'.

One of the few signs of modernity set among the nothingness and the vast emptiness was the occasional simple store, equipped with a stove to offset the chill outside, on which a traveller could cook a bit of meat on his journey. Some of the native Indians would purchase a litre of wine at such places, and this could lead to arguments and quarrels in the tiny kitchen. Fred Green saw an altercation which led to a man being fatally stabbed right in front of his eyes. But gradually, he became inured to the effects of loneliness, especially as he learned to 'follow the tracks of animals across the land, and noticing everything that went by or did not go by, noting the signs of the weather and finding myself able to predict the behaviour of animals. My mother was of the same disposition as she was especially clear-eyed and she could spot a puma in the far, far distance. That is also true for my eldest son, as he now lives out there, continuing the work started by his grandfather over eighty years ago'.

The Welsh painter Sir Kyffin Williams, a man with an accomplished eye for colour, thought Dyffryn Camwy to be a cream and yellow land, as both the scrub bushes and the cactus that grew in the desert lands had small yellow flowers, and the birds in the orchards and gardens such as the *urraca* and *benteveo* flashed yellow as they flitted from tree to tree. Furthermore, 'the parched land on which no grass could grow was yellow ochre, and the cliffs to the north and south a uniform cream'. Kyffin also noted the colors of the 'cockscomb outcrops of red, pink and yellow rock that sprout in the landscape, reminding one of Arizona or Nevada', and when he reached Cwm Hyfryd in the Andes – where he made 200 drawings – he delighted in the way the sky became blue-black at evening, making the land appear vivid gold by comparison, and in the searing reds of the Chilean flame trees growing high above on the shores of the upland lakes.

There are other colours, too, of course, especially as you traverse the huge swathes of unpopulated land between the Chubut valley and the *cordilleras* of the Andes and the stark, regal mountains beyond. There are slate greys, pewters and low shrubs turned bonsai by the wind, in hues of the dullest lead. But the river brings with it a flow of colour, the bankside vegetation a bright Hooker's Green in places, the hue fresh-squiggled from the artist's tube.

For Kyffin Williams, the experience of visiting Patagonia was a transformative one, a veritable series of little epiphanies, one following on swiftly after the other, such that the cumulative effect was that he 'started to work, and images appeared on my canvas that were very different from any I had previously painted'. As Paul Joyner describes it in *Gwladfa Kyffin / Kyffin in Patagonia*, the difference came both in the form of high colouring and the clarity of his compositions. Before visiting y Wladfa, he was fully absorbed with studying Wales, and one could clearly see the influence of others on his work, for instance, the *impasto* of the Post-Impressionists, the defined shapes of the Camden Town School, the pure paint of Cedric Morris. He had not yet been released to explore colour and texture with an innovative sparkle. Y Wladfa was to Kyffin 'as Morocco was to Delacroix, or Venice to Turner. Each artist found something which deeply resonated with the spirit and introduced a fresh use of colour alongside beautifully crafted images', according to Joyner.

The Patagonian works amply show this expanded range of colour and texture. In the portrait *Father and son above Trevelin,* the clouds lour overhead in swirls of octopus ink, while the vegetation through which they pass is rendered deep with ochre, mustard and gold. A pen and ink depiction of cattle being driven through Cwm Hyfryd is full of verve and vibrancy, the muscle power of the animals competing with the authority of the *gaucho* leading them. A watercolour of a *guanaco*, demure and shy, is full of lovely russets and rusts, while some of the landscapes, such as *Los Altares* and *Lle Cul,* are like the colours of a woman's make-up box, puff powder pinks, lipstick corals and blusher beige. Elsewhere, a willow, ablaze with orange, animates in a wind that seems to want to blow its leaves off and toss them all the way to Peru.

Crossing the *paith* had its delights for Eluned Haf Wigley, too. Eluned caught the Patagonia bug from her politician father, Dafydd, and spent months out there helping the teachers in the school of Gaiman to learn Welsh and English, and she became fascinated by the brutal history of Argentina, the Tehuelche and the *desaparecidos* during the *dictatura*. For her, there was a surreal quality to the terrain. It was, she said, 'Like being in a painting by Salvador Dalí. The flat, wide, land shining golden in the sun of late summer, which is a small spot in the blue sweep of sky, not to mention Los Altares – the altars – huge chunks of red and bronze rock, which are like mere pimples by comparison with their bigger brethren. And there are the Andes, like giants on the horizon …'

Living in the lonely places
When I met Alwina Hughes de Thomas, a sprightly octogenarian, in her neat, uncluttered flat in the Belgrano district of Buenos Aires, she reminisced

enthusiastically about her upbringing out there in the emptiness, where her parents farmed sheep and some cattle and horses. Every two or three months, they would venture out to civilization to buy some goods before retreating back again. 'We'd go to Esquel, in a Ford motor, taking an hour or two to reach the town, where we'd visit *Nain* and *Taid*. We would do this maybe every three months or so, but for the rest of the time, we'd be out on the camp. We'd have to buy flour and sugar, and everything we needed for bread.'

Alwina was born in Esquel on 8 October 1928 to Lotty Roberts and Emrys Hughes, but spent the majority of her childhood near Tecka, in the heart of the Patagonian steppes, or 'camp' as she calls it in Welsh: a word, as she explains which has been subsumed or appropriated from the Spanish 'campo', for countryside. She recalls days of happy childhood wandering the camp, as the children went searching for ostrich eggs. Discovery was a bonanza, as each nest might contain as many as 12 eggs, with each and every one equivalent to a dozen hens' eggs. When she or one of her siblings, Caeron, Ivor or Elgar, found them, their mother made 'tortillas with potatoes and onions all bound with those ostrich eggs, oh, we had those many, many times. Mother could feed us all with a tortilla made with a single egg. Imagine that!' Some people put the eggs to other uses, such as using them as shampoo. Alwina recalls that:

> Sometimes, there were little ostriches everywhere. My father liked hunting partridge, and if we went from Esquel to the valley, he would stop to hunt them. He didn't hunt hares, but he would shoot foxes and skunks because they would eat our chickens. It was lonely. It made me very shy and I wasn't used to seeing many people at all. When it was time to go to school, Mama would come with us to Esquel and Dada would stay in the *camp* to look after the animals. We would walk up to the top of the hill where the Freemans lived, and that's where we lived, in a place called Bryn Amlwg.
>
> I had to live in Esquel to go to school when I was seven. The school year in those days lasted from September to May. I walked to school every day, starting at eight and finishing at midday. I didn't have very much Spanish when I started, because until then, we'd spoken only Welsh at home.

Alwina stayed in school until sixth grade, or year seven in UK terms, being the beginning of secondary schooling, but there wasn't a secondary school in Esquel at the time, so:

> … my mother took me to St David's, the English boarding school in Trelew: there were some fifty pupils there in all. I couldn't speak a word of English, and when my mother left me, I cried as if it was the end of the world. I had five- and six-year-olds teaching me, and I was 15. When I was 17 or 18, I went back to the *camp*, doing housework, tending flowers and looking after the chickens.

Out in the *camp*

In his autobiography, *Llwch*, Elvey MacDonald tells how his grandfather, John James Jones, enjoyed nothing more than adventuring in the *camp*, hunting over the great flatlands on his white horse, Blanco, in the company of his two hunting dogs, Ray and Kaiser, and the speedy bitch, Paloma, who could run like the Patagonian wind. Elvey's mother remembers them returning at day's end loaded with *guanaco* meat, or weighed down with ostriches, hares and ostrich eggs, ready for the feast. When winter came, or when rain or flood inundated the grasslands in the lower valley, John James Jones would take his horses out to the camp, safe in the knowledge that they'd be able to graze there, and survive.

Businessman Eos Griffiths, a bright-spirited man I had the good fortune to meet in Trelew, and with whom I spent some entertaining time is a Welshman who married a Patagonian, and has travelled a great deal across the *camp*, the Patagonian steppes.

> Once, I was hitch-hiking towards Esquel, somewhere near Dol y Plu, and was at a crossroads when a girl on horseback came towards me, obviously meeting someone off a bus. She was early, because time doesn't mean much here – *mañana* will do. She started to talk to me, and had to ask which way Esquel was. She had no idea where the town was, nor Trelew. But she'd been given orders to meet someone after a journey. The strongest thing the people who live in the middle of the *paith* have is the odour of horses and a knife, the weapon everyone carries. Everyone uses

a knife, which keeps order. It makes you think it's dangerous to talk to anyone, so that you don't start arguing with people.

At night, Eos recalls, one might only have the stars for company.

> You can be very lonely. *Gauchos* sleep on animal skins as they drive sheep from an area of denuded pasture to better grazing ground, pasturage, carrying *mate* [tea] with them. They say – even though I've not seen them – that in the middle of Patagonia there are people who live in caves, keeping a few sheep.

Patagonia isn't an easily-defined area on a map even today, in this era of pinpoint satellite imagery, as it straddles two countries, Argentina and Chile. Bruce Chatwin's biographer, Nicholas Shakespeare, suggests that it is defined in part by its soil. 'You know you're in Patagonia when you see *rodados patagonicos*, the basalt pebbles left behind by glaciers, and *jarilla*, the low shrub that is its dominant flora'.

Jarilla is certainly one of the most predominant plant species, a hardy bush that grows up to two metres in height and is found in Argentina from Mendoza to Chubut. There are two kinds: *jarilla hembra* (*Larrea divaricata*) and *jarilla crespa* (*Larrea nítida*). Both are woody bushes of similar appearance, generally windblown. They grow at a distance from each other, and in the areas in between, other undergrowth and herbaceous species grow. The original inhabitants used this plant as an anti-inflammatory medicine as well as a healing agent and a hallucinogenic.

Patagonia may also be defined by its climate. The wind which blows with terrific force from October to March made writer Antoine de Saint-Exupéry's plane fly backwards instead of forwards. It can also be defined by its effect on the people who live there, some of them hunchbacked by years of attrition and blast by the endless, scouring wind. The loneliness blows through this land mass, too, leaving some of its sparsely scattered inhabitants living in solitary confinement, despite the huge spaces.

Yet, the emptinesses and vastnesses of Patagonia have a way of imprinting themselves in the minds of people. Charles Darwin, detailing the voyage of the *Beagle*, found that in calling up images of the past, the plains of Patagonia frequently crossed before his eyes, even though 'they are pronounced with all wretched and useless':

They can be described only by negative characters; without habitations, without water, without trees, without mountains, they support only a few dwarf plants. Why, then, and the case is not peculiar to myself, have these arid wastes taken so firm a hold of my memory? Why have not the still more level, the greener and more fertile Pampas, which are serviceable to mankind, produced an equal impression? I can scarcely analyse these feelings; but it must be partly owing to the free scope given to the imagination. The plains of Patagonia are boundless, for they are scarcely passable, and hence unknown; they bear the stamp of having thus lasted, as they are now, for ages, and there appears no limit to their duration through future time. If, as the ancients supposed, the flat earth was surrounded by an impassable breadth of water, or by deserts heated to an intolerable excess, who would not look at these last boundaries to man's knowledge with deep but ill-defined sensations?

The naturalist W. H. Hudson felt that Darwin's perplexity had much to do with the powerful effect of nature on man, the observer, in these empty places. It was better to look for nothing at all than to search for the specific, to open oneself up to feeling the place. If one did this, then the secret of the persistence of the Patagonian images would be understood along with 'their frequent recurrence in the minds of many who have visited that grey, monotonous, and, in one sense, eminently uninteresting region. It is not the effect of the unknown, it is not imagination; it is that nature in these desolate scenes ... moves us more deeply than in others'.

Hudson found tranquillity and solace here, away from human voice and presence.

One day while listening to the silence, it occurred to my mind to wonder what the effect would be if I were to shout aloud. This seemed at the time a horrible suggestion of fancy, 'a lawless and uncertain thought' which almost made me shudder, and I was anxious to dismiss it quickly from my mind. But during these solitary days it was a rare thing for any thoughts to cross my mind; animal forces did not cross my vision or bird-voices assail my hearing more rarely. In that novel state of mind I was in, thought had become impossible ... I had become incapable of reflection: my mind had suddenly transformed itself from a thinking machine into a machine for some unknown other purpose. To think was like setting in motion an engine in my brain; and there was something there which bade me be still, and I was forced to obey. My state was one of suspense and watchfulness: yet I had no expectation of a meeting with adventure, and felt as free of apprehension as I feel now when sitting in a room in London ... I was powerless to wonder at, or speculate about it; the state seemed familiar rather than strange, and although accompanied by a strong feeling of elation, I did not know it – did not know that something had come between me and my intellect – until I lost it and returned to my former self – to thinking, and the old insipid existence.

This suggests that, to Hudson, Patagonia was very different from places with great biodiversity (not that he would have used that term back then), where the sheer, riotous plenitude of life – the birdsong, singing colours, the hubbub and tendrilly growth, the shows of both camouflage stealth and mating display – all busily underlined the superabundance of animal life and served to engage all the senses at once. This was in contrast to the colour palette and empty sound world of the Patagonian steppes:

In Patagonia, the monotony of the plains, or expanse of low hills, the universal unrelieved greyness of everything, and the absence of animal forms and objects new to the eye, leave the mind open and free to receive an impression of nature as a whole. It has a look of antiquity, of desolation, of eternal peace, of a desert that has been a desert from old and will continue a desert for ever; and we know that its only human inhabitants are a few wandering savages – who live by hunting as their progenitors have done for thousands of years.

This emptiness, exaggerated and deepened by an absence of trees, which are bent double by the gusting winds, starts at the coast, and it would have been one of the landscape features, or lack of features, that would have tested the first Welsh pioneers. But the land wasn't empty. This wasn't a desert of sand, like the giant Empty Quarter in Abu Dhabi. This was a desert of thorns growing on the sand. There was, indeed the Crown of Thorns, more low shrub than regal growth, but with deep, determined roots and tough, snaggy thorns that are as lacerating as sewing needles – if you're planning on sewing something like leather, that is. Then there was Celyn y Bryniau, growing as one seemingly endless, squat hedge, its leaves yellow, its leaves bitter as wormwood to the taste. It came in very useful, as it produced an amplitude of smoke when burned, and could be used to signal across the Patagonian vasts. There was *picijin,* a grey thorny shrub, which fruited berries in season, its fruit slightly more luscious than the beans of the Crown of Thorns, which were said to be little better for slaking a thirst than sucking stones.

When that doyen of travel writers, Paul Theroux, arrived in Patagonia, he felt he was nowhere.

> But the surprising thing of all was that I was still in the world – I had been travelling south for months. The landscape had a gaunt expression, but I could not deny that it had readable features and that I existed in it. This was a discovery – the look of it. I thought: Nowhere is a place. Down there, the Patagonian valley deepened to grey rock, wearing its aeons' stripes and split by floods. Ahead, there was a succession of hills, whittled and fissured by the wind, which now sang in the bushes. The bushes shook with this song. They stiffened again and were silent. The sky was clear blue. A puff of cloud, white as a quince flower, carried a small shadow from town, or from the South Pole. I saw it approach. It rippled across the bushes and passed over me, a brief chill, and then it went rucking east. There were no voices here. There was this, what I saw; and though beyond it there were mountains and glaciers and albatrosses and Indians, there was nothing here to speak of, nothing to delay me further. Only the Patagonian paradox: tiny blossoms in vast space; to be here it helped to be a miniaturist, or else interested in enormous empty spaces. There was no intermediate zone of study. Either the enormity of the desert or the sight of a tiny flower. In Patagonia, you had to choose between the tiny or the vast.

Some travellers viewed the landscape in a gentle version of Cinemascope, allowing themselves a quiet hymn of rhapsody to the quiet enormity of the place. In *Crwydro Patagonia*, R. Bryn Williams, the former archdruid and pre-eminent historian of y Wladfa, describes a train journey across the monotonous plains which lasted from nine in the morning until eight at night.

> The expanse of the place is stunning, only huge grassy levels which extends like a sea from end to end, with only the occasional cottage, or here and there a cluster of lonely trees … And you see the breeze running its fingers through the silky grasses … I saw the occasional *gaucho* in his colourful clothes on a handsome horse prancing across these expanses like a gentleman. The expanse and the loneliness and the beautiful tranquillity of it all pulled gently at the heartstrings.

Habitat of the *guanaco*

There are animals out on the *paith*, too. Wild relatives of the llama, *guanacos* are humpless camels that inhabit the arid and semi-arid habitats of South America, as well as the Andean forests of Tierra del Fuego. These hyper-tough animals range from southern Chile to southern Peru, up to elevations of 14,500 feet. Indeed, their last remaining stronghold is the Patagonian steppe. In order to survive in harsh, dry climates, *guanacos* have a remarkable ability to conserve water and, like other camels, can obtain moisture from the plants they eat.

Most *guanacos* live in herds composed of family groups or 'bachelor' males and females, but some males are solitary. They graze on grasses, leaves and buds, and, as the largest native herbivore in Patagonia, they played a key role in structuring native vegetation communities. Their quivery, sensitive lips help them select tender food among thorny and woody vegetation, and their softly padded feet do not damage the soil and vegetation as the hard hooves of livestock do.

Guanacos have been reduced by nearly 95 per cent of their original number, which may have been as much as 50 million, bringing to mind the huge herds of bison of North America, hunted to the very edge of extinction by hunters who didn't even keep the meat. In South America, meanwhile, early explorers described long-distance migrations by huge herds, but now *guanacos* are mostly confined by fences, livestock, and hunting. Nevertheless, conservationists have discovered three substantial wild sites where thousands of *guanacos* still make seasonal migrations. Protecting these migrations will simultaneously conserve the last large intact highland areas of South America, which can properly be called *guanaco* country.

Chapter 4

Terra Gigantica

The Welsh left a small country, the merest spot or dab on the world atlas, for a gigantic place. The region of Patagonia, at 400,000 square miles, is about the same size as many single countries – Venezuela, for example – or three times the size of Italy, and could swallow Wales whole and not spit out the pips. Patagonia's population is miniscule, with no cities of any real size, and the few towns clinging like limpets to the coast or hugging the banks of the rivers that cut and dissect their way from the Andes to the sea.

Not only was the new home of the Welsh set within a very substantial tract of scrubland and arid, wind-scorched plains, but it was also a stalking ground for legendary giants, too, a *regio gigantum* as it was marked on maps of the New World. Not that the Welsh were unacquainted with giants – they had their own already, striding through tall tales in their literature. They had Bendigeidfran, the giant king of Britain, who features in the *Mabinogion*, that shimmering collection of some of the finest European folk takes, and their Bibles had their giants too. In the Book of Numbers, for instance, when Moses sent his spies to scout the Promised Land so that the children of Israel could enter it, the spies reported seeing beings there who were giants, so large, indeed, that regular sized men appeared as 'grasshoppers' before them.

There were very different giants waiting for the Welsh in Patagonia, though, some giving name to the place itself. The first outsize creatures had been sighted by a man called Antonio Pigafetta, a diarist and fellow traveller to the explorer Magellan as he circumnavigated the globe. Pigafetta was, in many ways, the wellspring of myths and misconceptions about Patagonia for, as the Colombian novelist Gabriel Garcia Márquez noted, his lists of the fanciful were abundant in the extreme, and 'contained the seeds of our present novels'. The litany of exotica, a literally marvellous bestiary in Pigafetta's zoo of the mind, included 'hogs with navels on their haunches, clawless birds whose hens laid eggs on the backs of their mates, and others still, resembling tongue-less pelicans, with beaks like spoons', not to mention a 'misbegotten creature with the head and ears of a mule, a camel's body, the legs of a deer and the whinny of a horse'. It was this sort of ultra-dependable observer who told the world about the Patagonian giant.

In September 1521 the ultra-imaginative Pigafetta spotted a very, very tall man near a place called San Julian:

> One day, without anyone expecting it, we saw a giant, who was on the shore of the sea, quite naked, and was dancing and leaping, and singing, and whilst singing he put the sand and the dust on his head. Our captain sent one of his men towards him, whom he charged to sing and leap like the other to reassure him, and show him friendship. This he did, and immediately the sailor led this giant to a little island where the captain was waiting for him; and when he was before us he began to be astonished, and to be afraid, and he raised one finger on high, thinking that we came from heaven. He was so tall that the tallest of us only came up to his waist.

His height wasn't the only peculiarity, because the man's face was brightly painted a startling red and yellow. He had two hearts boldly emblazoned on his cheeks, while his almost bald pate was painted white, as if showing the skull beneath the skin. The dancing giant was clad in fur clothes, which were more than adequately sewn and tailored, while his feet were shod in thick fur boots, which made his feet seem even bigger. He was a massively exotic sight to the sailors, but this was nothing to the way he looked to himself when shown his reflection in the mirror. It was the captain of the vessel who baptized the giant and, by dint of this, his race:

> The captain named this kind of people Pataghom on account of their large feet. They have no houses, but have huts made of the skins of animals with which they clothe themselves, and go hither and thither with these huts of theirs, as the gypsies do;

they live on raw meat, and eat a certain sweet root, which they call Capac. These two giants that we had in the ship ate a large basketful of biscuit, and rats without skinning them, and they drank half a bucket of water at each time.

It struck the ever resourceful Magellan that these giants would make excellent souvenir gifts for Charles V of Spain and his Queen Empress, so he tricked them both into wearing manacles. Too late to spot the ruse, they puffed and bellowed and blew. Indeed, as Pigafetta put it, they veritably foamed 'like bulls, crying out very loudly the word "Setebos", that is to say, the great devil, that he should help them'. There was a great fuss, followed by a fight, and in time, when the giants were properly pinioned, they were baptized. But these outsize giants, meant as gifts for the king and queen, never made it to Spain. Both died on the way. It is said they died of heartbreak.

One hundred years later, in *The World Encompassed*, the first detailed account of Sir Francis Drake's circumnavigation, the author, Drake's nephew, who had the same name as his uncle, wrote:

> Magellane was not altogether deceived, in naming them Giants; for they generally differ from the common sort of men, both in stature, bigness, and strength of body, as also in the hideousnesse of their voice: but yet they are nothing so monstrous, or giantlike as they were reported; there being some English men as tall as the highest of any that we could see, but peradventure, the Spaniards did not thinke, that ever any English man would come thither, to reprove them; and thereupon might presume the more boldly to lie: the name Pentagones, Five cubits viz. 7. Foote and halfe, describing the full height (if not some what more) of the highest of them. But this is certaine, that the Spanish cruelties there used [referring to Magellan's hostage taking], have made them more monstrous, in minde and manners, then they are in body; and more inhospitable, to deale with any strangers, that shall come thereafter.

Other explorers had their sightings, too, and therefore plenty of tall tales to tell. The story was certainly read by William Shakespeare, and the giant's tale transmutes into some parts of *The Tempest*, feeding into the portrait of Caliban, the sub-human son of the malevolent witch, Sycorax. It may also be that the Irish satirist Jonathan Swift had the Patagonian Indians, the Tehuelche, in mind when he conjured up the amiable but outsized inhabitants of Brobdingnag in *Gulliver's Travels*. And there were other literary outcomes to Patagonian gigantism too, for some of the wildlife was pretty big, with enormous seabirds off the coast, such as the albatrosses, which were so big they were perfect targets, especially for one Captain Shelvocke, an English privateer in the eighteenth century, who saw one, shot one and in so doing gave Coleridge a memorable ancient mariner to write about:

> The heavens were perpetually hid from us by gloomy dismal clouds ... one would think it impossible that any living thing could subsist in so rigid a climate; and, indeed, we had not one sight of one fish of any kind ... nor one sea-bird, except a disconsolable black albitross, hovering about us as if he had lost himself, till Hatley (my second Captain) observing, in one of his melancholy fits, that this bird was always hovering near us, imagined, from his colour, that it might be some ill omen ... and after some fruitless attempts, at length, shot the Albitross, not doubting perhaps that we should have a fair wind after it.

Huge birds, huge distances, huge people. Patagonia had them all.

The poet Lord Byron's grandfather, Captain Thomas Byron, was one of those who adopted, and thus promoted, the term *patagones* to describe the giant natives and, in his case, a woman he encountered was so substantial she measured twice his height. Captain Byron had been shipwrecked on a wild southern coast, and was thus the latest of the explorer breed to encounter the Big Feet: 'Thomas Cavendish had measured the imprint of one of their feet and found it be eighteen inches long'. Byron, on tip-toes, could just reach the top of the head of one of the Patagonians.

In European descriptions of the Patagonian natives, their middle stature seemed to be about eight feet: 'their extreme, nine and upwards', as one of Byron's officers wrote. The giants, with time, seemed to be getting more gigantic; their feet, in successive reports, even bigger, in an explorers' version of Chinese whispers.

In the 1700s, the myth of the Patagonian Indians was still very much alive and very much entertaining European readers. Horace Walpole, the English historian and gothic novelist, published *An Account of the Giants Lately Discovered: In a Letter to a Friend in the Country* following the return to Britain in 1766 of Captain John Byron, who had circumnavigated the world in the *HMS Dolphin*. Word leaked that the crew had seen nine-foot giants in South America. Byron's docking in May of that year and the publication of Walpole's short book in July suggests the rapidity with which rumours passed swiftly and exaggeratedly along the London grapevine. In his 31-page pamphlet, Walpole satirizes the whole idea, and facetiously suggests that a limited number of the giant women could be imported in a crazy eugenic experiment 'for the Sake of mending our Breed'. The official account of Byron's voyage, appearing in 1773, finally debunks the myth, but not without respecting the Patagonians' vertical features:

> When we came within a little distance from the shore, we saw, as near as I can guess, about five hundred people, some on foot, but the greater part on horseback ... [O]ne of them, who afterwards appeared to be a Chief, came towards me: he was of a gigantic stature, and seemed to realize the tales of monsters in a human shape ... [I]f I may judge of his height by the proportion of his stature to my own, it could not be much less than seven feet. Mr. Cumming [one of Byron's officers] came up with the tobacco [a gift], and I could not but smile at his astonishment which I saw expressed in his countenance, upon perceiving himself, though six feet two inches high, become a pigmy among giants; for these people may indeed more properly be called giants than tall men ... the shortest of whom were at least four inches taller.

By the eighteenth century, travellers, such as the Catholic missionary Thomas Falkner, was writing in his *A Description of Patagonia* that although the Tehuelches – by now consistently known as Patagons in Europe – were impressive in size, he himself had encountered human bones that well-nigh dwarfed them:

> On the banks of the river Carcarania, or Tercero, about three or four leagues before it enters into the Parana, are found great numbers of bones, of an extraordinary bigness, which seem human. There are some greater and some less, as if they were of persons of different ages. I have seen thigh-bones, ribs, breast-bones and pieces of skulls. I have also seen teeth, and particularly some grinders which were three inches in diameter at the base. These bones (as I have been informed) are likewise found on the banks of the Rivers Parana and Paraguay … The Indian historian, Garcilasso de la Vega Inga, makes mention of these bones in Peru, and tells us that the Indians have a tradition, that giants formerly lived in these countries, and were destroyed by God for the crime of sodomy.

A Description of Patagonia was to be found on the shelves of the ship's library on board the *Beagle*, so Charles Darwin must have read it. He was, therefore, probably on the lookout for giants. When he reaches Cape Gregory, he finds people who fit the description, giants who were, moreover, able to speak both Spanish and English because of previous encounters with whalers and sealers. The faces of these giants were painted, their physiques striking:

> We had an interview … with the so-called gigantic Patagonians, who gave us a cordial reception. Their height appears greater than it really is, from their large *guanaco* mantles, their long flowing hair, and general figure: on an average their height is about six feet, with some men taller and only a few shorter; and the women are also tall; altogether they are certainly the tallest race which we anywhere saw.

A half century later, the redoubtable and adventurous Lady Florence Dixie ventured to Patagonia, simply because it was 'an outlandish place and so far away'. After a few months of hard travel, with no small measure of tribulation, she too finally chanced upon some giants, but found them not quite the sort of size she'd expected. They weren't dwarves but neither did they dwarf:

I was struck, not so much by their height, as by their extraordinary development of chest and muscle. As regards their stature, I do not think the average height of the men exceeded six feet, and as my husband stands six foot two inches, I had a favourable opportunity for forming the accurate estimate. One or two there were, certainly, who towered far above him, but these were exceptions.

The Tehuelche the Welsh would meet would not be giants, even though they were a much taller race. Their encounters would be remarkable, however, not for the difference in height between the imported Celts and the wind-bronzed horsemen of the plain, but rather for the mutually beneficial relationship between them. This would be so very different from that between most new pioneers or colonists and the native populations, who would often be chased from the land, or much worse.

Chapter 5

The Welsh and the Tehuelche

The Tehuelche the Welsh encountered were seasonal visitors to the Chubut valley, spending July, August and September around its riverine reaches, then fanning out to other locations inland.

The Welsh, unlike so many people who can be described as colonists – to use that problematic and loaded word – generally had a benign and sympathetic attitude to the native tribes they encountered, in this case, mainly the Tehuelche (there were other, fiercer tribes who wandered through from time to time). This was almost the antithesis of what happened elsewhere, such as the attempted mass eradications of North America, or the tribal displacements of Africa. The Welsh were, of course, far from the first inhabitants of Patagonia. For centuries, these indigenous tribes had lived on the Patagonian plains, speaking their own language and practising their own customs.

The organisers of the Patagonian venture were fully aware of the existence of these tribes prior to the departure of the first group of Welsh settlers for Patagonia, though they knew very little about them in detail. In the late 1850s, Michael D. Jones emphasized that the indigenous Patagonians should be treated fairly, and recognized as the rightful owners of the land. He referred in particular to William Penn's exemplary treatment of Native Americans in Pennsylvania during the late seventeenth century. In 1683, Penn made a treaty with the North Americans tribes, in which they vowed not to use force against each other. Michael D. Jones argued that the Welsh should treat the native Patagonians in the same way.

The Welsh weren't entirely phlegmatic and confident about their early dealings with the Tehuelche. Nervousness about the Indians often flickered through the first settler contingent, and led to the appointment of a Defence Officer, the self-styled 'Captain' Edwin Cynrig Roberts, who tried to mould the young men of the colony into a defensive militia force, Y Fyddin Gymreig. Jittery paranoia led to the settlers' council agreeing that they would summarily kill any indigenous folk who ventured to the lower Chubut valley, lest they tell others about them. But their fears were ill-founded, and in general, the newcomers and the natives came to mutually beneficial accommodations with each other. Indeed, just four months after the arrival of the *Mimosa*, a letter arrived from a *cacique*, a Tehuelche tribal leader. It read:

> I am the *cacique* of a tribe of Indians to whom belong the plains of the Chupat. We hunt between Patagones and the Chupat, near the coast of the sea in winter, and in the summer in the interior, where at that season the sun sets … Now I say that the plains between Chupat and Rio Negro are ours, but that we never sold them. Our fathers sold the plains of Bahia Blanca and Patagones but nothing more.
>
> I have a Treaty of Peace with Patagones, but that does not touch on selling lands. I know very well that you have negotiated with the Government to colonize Chupat, but you ought also to negotiate with us, who are the owners of the lands … Mr Aguirre (the Government Official at Patagones) has read a letter of the Governor to me in which I am told to leave you to increase in numbers, and not to do anything to you, and also to speak to the other *caciques* so that they should not molest you. I promise to do all in my power for you.

The *cacique* was true to his word and, two years after the Welsh had landed, relationships were already good enough for the two peoples to host a sporting competition, a sort of first Patagonian Olympic Games, in which the Welsh proved themselves to be better shots, and the Tehuelche better horsemen. Relations between them was usually more than cordial. Indeed, when the so-called 'Indian troubles' broke out in 1868, and the Argentine Government distributed rifles and bullets among the Welsh for their own protection – not to mention instructing them in the organization of militia units – the guns were employed for nothing more than hunting and the Indians were left in peace. The fact that no anti-Indian defences were built in Chubut – or were even considered necessary – at a time when bloody massacres were being perpetrated by native Indians in nearby Bahia Blanca, underlined the bonds of trust and mutual understanding that bound the Welsh newcomers with those who had long lived in these lands.

One of the first proper encounters between the new immigrants and the indigenous people happened in 1870, when three Welshmen joined three Tehuelche, who had initially visited them for purposes of trade, on a journey to meet their chief. The Welsh wanted to ask the chief for guides to take them to Patagones, going overland. To give a sense of the hostility and difficulty of the terrain they had to cross on this mission, one need only list the litany of places they reached, such as: Hirlam Uffernol (Hellish Journey), which later changed its name to the only slightly milder Hirlam Ffyrnig (Fierce Journey), Bana Beiddio (Daring Peaks) and Ceunant Cethin (Severe Ravine). They had to travel 50 miles, with not a single drop or even a sign of water until they reached a spring known as Gangan by the Tehuelche. This the Welsh baptized as Ffynnon Allwedd, the Well of Keys, or Key Well. When they reached the chief, he pointed out that continuing the journey and crossing the plains to Patagones in high summer was just impossible. It had been a long and punishing journey, but it did give the Welsh a useful insight into the way the natives travelled across the land, and found food where it wouldn't necessarily be apparent.

The Tehuelche were one of the two principal tribes that inhabited a huge swathe of a land that would become Patagonia, between the Colorado river to the north and the Strait of Magellan to the south. One of South America's most ancient indigenous societies, they called themselves Tzonecka or Chonek, but were described by the fiercer Araukanians as Teheulche, which meant southerners. These 'southerners' were themselves divided into northern and southern branches. Each branch, or division, had its own dialect and modes of transport; the northerners were classified as horse nomads, the southerners got around on foot. Collectively, the Tehuelche became famous in European literature for their great stature and physical strength and the fact they hunted on foot, with only the strongest runners catching their prey, which mode of hunting was said to account for their height as a tribe. And as we know, their feet were a bit of a talking point, in book after book after book.

Little is known of the original pre-horse culture of the Tehuelche, but their socio-economic organization probably resembled that of the a tribe called the Ona in Tierra del Fuego. The introduction of the horse in the early eighteenth century transformed the subsistence patterns and social organization of the Tehuelche. They began to exploit the brush-covered steppes and pampas of Patagonia much as the first nation tribes of North America travelled and harvested the Great Plains. They lived mainly on *guanaco* and ostrich or rhea meat (a bird similar to the ostrich, the rhea is largest bird in South America), as well as some plant food, but the Tehuelche practised no sedentary agriculture. These were nomads, always on the move, always moving on. For warmth, *guanaco* skins were stretched and shaped to become mantles. Draped in these furs, they could withstand the punishing weather and Patagonian chill.

The Pampean hunters quickly grew in numbers, and their bands conglomerated; the individual Tehuelche bands numbered as many as 500 members. Inevitably, these mounted bands not only hunted, but found themselves engaged in war and, gradually, the successful war leader replaced the kinship leader in importance.

The Tehuelche were eventually defeated and culturally assimilated by the European settlers who brought their own ways and own beliefs, which they tried to foist on the natives. They believed in the spirits of the bush and in a supreme being who had created the world but did not intervene in its working. In *Y Wladfa*, R. Bryn Williams explains how one of their gods was a force for good called Pilan, although others, such as the ethnologists Johannes Wilbert and Karin Simoneau, gathered versions which said this self-same god's name was Kóoch. Whichever was the case, Williams redacted one of the prettiest traditional tales, or myths, which told how this god once landed on a mountain and touched his foot upon one of the slopes, which caused life to flow over it as plant growth and animal life. Another myth suggests that all life was created in the dark cauldron of a cave. The Tehuelche tended to ignore this god, simply because he was benign. But that was most certainly not the case with the evil god Gualichu. They had to pay attention to this god, who wasn't a single deity but rather a legion of them, a pelting storm of howling demons. It was believed that they were responsible for all damage and loss, for every single disease and every misfortune. It was believed that the Gualichu lived deep in a tangle of thorns, and the Indians would leave offerings to them, anything from food to scraps of colourful fabric, much as the pagan Welsh often tied ribbons to trees to appease their Celtic deities. If these dark Tehuelche devils managed to inveigle their way inside a person, it would result in sickness, and then the shaman was summoned to try to expel the Gualichu in a ceremony of illness-expunging dance.

It was also believed that the bad spirits would sometimes skulk around the tents under cover of the night. At such times, the entire tribe would rouse from their slumbers and yell at them like banshees in order to drive them away. The Tehuelche shied away from the woodlands and forests that blanketed the slopes of the Andes and the *cordilleras* because they believed that the demons lived in numbers in there. They would often hear their cries emanating from such wooded fastnesses, even though, in all likelihood, it was nothing more than the sound of ice cracking and splintering before chunks went careering down the mountain slopes.

It was also believed that one of these demons caused death, and when someone died, their fellow tribespeople would try to get away from the spot as fast as possible, lest they be tainted, or be caught by the demon. They would only pause long enough to bury the dead in a seated position, with any arms and scant possessions buried alongside, while their dogs and horses were slaughtered even as any grieving women tore their nails across their faces until they were raked with blood.

To another demon was ascribed the power or blight of causing illness, and in H. Hesketh Pritchard's book, *Through the Heart of Patagonia*, there's an account of how he sighted an Indian on a sturdy horse, with a young girl riding another horse behind him, both of them racing along furiously, whooping and hollering fit to burst. While the Indian was mantled warmly in his *tziripa*, the young girl was entirely naked, despite the chill of the weather and the whip of the wind. Pritchard thought at first that the girl had been abducted, but he was later to discover that the man was, in fact, her father, and he was using the cold to drive out a demon who had caused his daughter to become ill.

While the Welsh believed in the cosmology contained in the book of Genesis, with the world being methodically conjured or fashioned into being over seven days and seven nights, the Tehuelche's version was very different. Their shamans cured sickness with assistance from spirits, and even thought their god, too, said 'Let there be light' as one of their other myths explains:

The creator of the world has always existed. In the beginning he lived engulfed in dense and dark clouds over there where the sky meets the sea. Contemplating the formidable solitude that surrounded him, the creator broke down crying. He cried for a very long time, so long that it is impossible to say how long it actually was.

From his tears formed the primordial sea, called *arrok*. It was nature's first element. The name of this eternal and all-powerful divinity is Kóoch. When he realized that the water issuing from his eyes was steadily increasing, he stopped weeping and sighed very deeply. His breath caused the wind which dissipated the dark clouds and let the sun shine forth, just as nowadays daylight follows night on the distant horizon.

Missionary positions

For some of the Welsh, as indeed for the earlier Spanish settlers, these native demons and gods were nothing more than graven idols. The Indians had souls that could be and must be saved. At the beginning of 1874, Michael D. Jones was working to establish a Mission to the Indians in Patagonia, and he had already obtained backing from churches in Llandderfel and Glyndyfrdwy. By April of the same year, the Reverend David Lloyd Jones was sailing upon the *Hipparchus*, southern-bound, and ready to embrace the full challenge of being a missionary, knowing he was expected to learn both Spanish and Tehuelche, and aware of the hardships ahead. He left on 16 April 1874. The previous day, Michael D. Jones noted in his diary that he had helped the new missionary, along with Abraham Matthews, to become Freemasons in a meeting in the Bala, and that they owed him three pounds and three shillings into the bargain. Jones wanted ministers in Patagonia to be Freemasons. The exact reasons are hidden in the usual folds of masonic mystery, along with the meaning of their symbols and with their clandestine organisational structure. Meanwhile Cymdeithas Genhadol Patagonia (The Patagonian Missionary Society) was established in Denbigh, with the industrious publisher Thomas Gee as treasurer, who also assumed some of the society's debt, as their fundraising efforts weren't that effective.

In Patagonia, on the other hand, things were going swimmingly. Rev. Lloyd Jones' work initially seemed to be going very smoothly indeed. One of the early reports describes his reception in Port Madryn. The Indian chief who came to meet him there gave him a vessel of water as a mark of respect, much as a disciple would, and said how happy he and the fellow tribe members were that he had come among them to make them Christians.

The report went on to explain how many Indian children were learning Welsh, and that even some of the chief's own children were visiting the minister to receive religious instruction and education. But despite Lloyd Jones building a whopping big house, with rooms substantial enough to accommodate the children of the Tehuelche, and another suitable for their schooling, his mission turned out to be impossible. The Tehuelche were not disposed to leaving their children in the valley, in one place, for any length of time: these were in essence, after all, a nomadic people who didn't put down roots too readily. And, in truth, they were perhaps less interested in Jesus Christ than they were in the power of Welsh singing, which they found to be euphonious in the extreme.

The historian R. Bryn Williams recalled Tehuelche people attending chapel in Trelew when he was a child, their leader getting to his feet to thank the congregation for their singing. Later, the leader, Nahuelpan (which means lion's head), sent his own son, Gregorio Nahuelquir, to a government school, where he learned Welsh and started to be a regular attendee of chapel services, learning hymns and singing them with gusto.

The war against the native Indians

While the Welsh found trading and more general dealings with the Tehuelche almost symbiotically advantageous, other Europeans struck a far more aggressive attitude. Thomas Holdich, sent by the British in 1902 to help arbitrate in the border dispute between Chile and Argentina, was happy enough to use the native Indians as guides even though he also said that wiping them out, their being 'so many sub-humans and savages' would be a welcome act. Francis Latzina, who wrote a Spanish language emigrants' handbook in the 1880s, similarly delighted in the fact that 'thousands of leagues of land have been snatched from the savage' so that 'the scourge of civilization and the prosperity of the Argentine Republic was done away with'.

But actions speak louder than words, especially if they involve the chatter of gunfire. In October 1878, the Argentine Congress backed an offensive to rout the indigenous people from the territories they held, and the efficiency of the Remington quick-firing rifle turned their attacking words into lethal bullets. There was concern that displaced people would attack the Welsh by way of retaliation, while the British Minister in Buenos Aires at the time, Clare Ford, alerted the authorities to the 'painful impression that would be caused in England were any disaster to befall it'. General Roca, the suitably belligerent Minister of War, and principal architect of the war, sneakily suggested that exterminating them might usefully include Welsh in the same breath, this *dying* breath. Roca was a fervid Argentinian: even his middle name was Argentino, although he became most commonly known by his nickname, 'The Silver Fox'.

The vulpine Roca was as huge a champion of new immigrations – which could, of course swamp the Welsh – as he was of the subjugation of the Indian tribes. He wanted nothing less than government control over all of the national territory, and safe havens for any new arrivals to the nascent Republic. As he stated, adamantly: 'Let us offer a solid guarantee for their lives and property to those who bring their capital and their brawny arms to the work of fertilizing these regions, and we shall soon see multitudes of men of all countries and races pour into them, and new states arise to the greater power and greatness of the Republic'. These new states would, of course include the state of Chubut. But in order for the floodgates to open, to allow in those multitudes of men, the native tribes had to be eliminated. The criticism of such a course of brutal action was muted at best, with many secretly believing that material progress and civilization would indeed follow this eradication. Some voices spoke out, of course, such as the Bishop of the Falkland Islands, who denounced the government by saying, bluntly, that 'the white man wants the land and the native of the soil must die'.

The Argentine stance on the native Indians was nothing less than morally repugnant. 'Indian hunters', such as one called Mr Bond, were initially paid a pound for every pair of ears they handed in. But because some of the hunters turned out to be insufficiently barbarous, or simply too compassionate to always kill their victims – choosing instead to just cut off the ears – they changed the rules. The hunters then had to hand in proof more positive of the kill, such as the testicles, the heart, the breasts or vital organs.

The Welsh, for their part, wrote a protest letter, albeit a mild one, signed by all the settlers, to Colonel Villegas, one of the commanders in charge of the military campaign. It expressed the hope that he could 'show them every compassion', and said that the Welsh believed 'that small native communities in the region will be a continual assistance to push new settlements into the interior, as has been their trade to us here. We hope therefore, that you will see possible, while understanding your military obligations in accordance with your wisdom, to leave your old native neighbours in their homes while they remain as peaceful and harmless as has been their custom'. The Welsh, meanwhile, were accused – in a telegram from another army man, General Winter, who was also hunting down their neighbours – of selling them arms. This was staunchly denied in the newspapers.

Indigenous friends

The Welsh had undoubtedly befriended the Tehuelche, who returned the compliment by sharing their skills in hunting and in reading the land, as well as trading pelts and feathers they had gathered on the pampas.

As the Tehuelche survived in this harsh land by dint of hunting, it was little wonder that they believed that paradise, called Karrontken, was an animal abundance, located in the sky, among the corral of the stars. It was a place where rheas and plump *guanacos* abounded, and the hunters lived a happy life, without any trace of sorrow.

It's been estimated that, at one time, as many as 1,500 people were involved in a system of barter and exchange with the Welsh, and that this added up to half the value of all the produce of Chubut at the time. The benign symbiosis between the Welsh and their nomadic neighbours didn't please everybody. In a letter from the British Envoy Extraordinary and Minister Plenipotentiary to the Argentine Republic, the Hon. Edmund Monson, to Earl Granville in 1884, it was suggested that:

> there is no doubt that the success of the Welshmen in establishing friendly commercial relations with the neighbouring Indian tribes, effected by the pursuance of a policy of humanity and honest dealing, has been resented by the Argentinians ... The example afforded by the Welsh colony of the possibility of humanizing them (the Indians) by fair treatment has only aroused the jealousy and vindictiveness of those who preach and practise the sanguinary doctrine of wholesale, indiscriminate massacre.

At about the same time as this letter was written, a confidential report by Commander Fullerton of H.M.S. *Algerine* suggested that some of the Indian tribes who were well disposed toward the Welsh were duped into travelling to Chubut under false pretences, then forced on board a steamer against their wishes. Thence they were taken to Buenos Aires, where the women and men were forced into domestic servitude, while the men were distributed to work on the coast. This impossibly callous treatment of their friends in Chubut ignited the ire of the Welsh, who objected vociferously, thereby exacerbating the tensions between them and Argentine officials, as if the Welsh attitude to self-government wasn't enough to ratchet up the tension.

In terms of appearance, the Tehuelche were characterised by their dark complexion and black hair. They were usually clean-shaven, and they would often paint their faces and bodies to protect their skin from the sun. The men wore a *chiripa* – a piece of cloth that was tied around the waist. The women covered themselves with a mantle made from the skins of wild animals and tied with ostrich ligament. It was worn with the fur on the inside, and the outside painted red.

The Tehuelche not only hunted the plains but lived there too, thus children were born in open country. Various rituals were attendant on the birth. When a baby was born, a calf or a cow – but sometimes a colt – would be slaughtered, and the stomach removed. The child would be placed within the steaming cavity. Should the animal cry out during this ceremony, it was believed that this child would grow up to become a skilled and dependable huntsman.

Mr James Nicols, originally from Ffestiniog in north Wales was a privileged eyewitness to one of the tribal feasts called the *camaruco*, and recounted the story to R. Bryn Williams. Nicols recalled the Tehuelche coming down the valley when he was a child. They wore only *chiripas*, and paint on their faces. Afraid of their appearance, James hid under the bed, along with the other children. Yet despite this early and fearful experience, Nicols found himself living among the Tehuelche in the Andes later in life.

One day, the tribal leader, Nahuelpan, invited James Nicols to the *camaruco* ceremony as a sign of gratitude to him for helping the chief by writing letters. It was quite a gathering. Tribal groups came from all over, and encamped under a full moon, with only the tinkling sound of cow bells to displace the silence. Then, at daybreak, bright horns sounded out, to be joined by a bleating chorus of other native bugles, made of rams' horns. The gathered tribes-people then rode their horses towards a circle of stones into which a young man – his clothes and horse decorated with bells – rode, dragging a young bull. This was then tied to a large stone in the middle of the circle. Each member of the tribe walked up to the bull in turn and placed a palm on its forehead, believing that all their sins would pass into the heart of the animal by dint of this devotion.

The bull's steaming heart was then extracted, and the young horseman would take it away, to be cast into a bush of thorns some distance hence. The rest of the bull would be quartered, roasted and eaten, although the liver would be eaten raw.

As the people, now sated on bull meat, sat around, they might have pondered, or recounted, the story of how fire was first acquired. In their myth, it was said, only the armadillo, the skunk and the pampas cat used to possess fire. The three of them were friends and liked nothing better than roasting and braising meat on their fire. Then, as luck would have it, Elal, the resourceful hero of many a Tehuelche myth, was skulking around, and could smell smoke, but couldn't understand where it was coming from, or who produced it, realizing that they must also be in possession of fire, and Elal didn't know of any such person.

Elal then chanced upon skunk, who smelled richly of fire, and Elal accused him of possessing the secret of fire, but skunk denied it. So Elal said he was going to look around, to find their leader. In the case of the three friends, the leader was the armadillo and when Elal caught up with him he was making a small, covered-up fire, but despite such evidence, denied he had any flames to share. Elal tried to call his bluff and begged for a little bit of fire – just the merest ember, please – arguing that the people were doomed to eat raw meat without it. But the armadillo was stubborn and refused point blank to yield even the merest bright flicker.

So Elal became angry, and gave the armadillo a mighty boot so that the animal went flying. Then Elal espied the fire, made from the charcoal of *califate* wood. He took the fire, leaving the armadillo without warmth or light, and took it to the people so they could eat roast meat. Not satisfied with just taking fire, Elal also punished the armadillo by cutting its thick hide, which accounts for the grooves scored on the animal's back. The armadillo left the pampas, never to return, and, in turn, the skunk and the wildcat left. Nowadays, in the absence of good hunks of roast meat, the armadillo is resigned to eating small fruit, while the skunk, bereft of fire, feasts on cockroaches, and raw ones at that.

Hitting the bottle
On the second day of the ceremony, the men would give their knives and weapons to the youngest girls to hide in the ground, before the men drank themselves stupid, pulling each others' hair and fighting maniacally for long, crazy hours. H. Hesketh Pritchard, who noted that there were only five tribes' worth of Tehuelche left by 1900, said that it was 'the culture of the bottle' that did for them. Alcohol may have played some small part in their dwindling and demise, but the lion's share of the blame for the eradication of the native Indians can be laid squarely at the door of the genocidal general, Roca.

Huntsmen of the plains
Until the early nineteenth century, the Tehuelche used dogs to hunt. From that time, however, they began using horses. Plenty of food could be collected by hunting on the Patagonian plains, and they would rely heavily on the *guanaco* and the rhea. The implements that were most widely used for hunting were the bow and arrow, and the *boleadores*, or *bolas*. This was a weapon which had three stone balls tied to three leather cords. When thrown, the weight of the balls would tie the cord around the legs of the animal and capture it.

The Welsh settlers had little experience of hunting when they arrived in Patagonia. They were, after all, coal miners and the like. The Tehuelche trained them to ride wild horses and showed them how to use the *bolas*. By mastering these techniques, the Welsh could hunt *guanaco* and rhea in order to ensure a sufficient supply of fresh meat. Had the Tehuelche not been prepared to share their hunting methods, the fate of the early Welsh settlers would possibly have been different.

One of the colonists who later upped sticks and headed for Regina, Saskatchewan, W. E. Davies, remembered with fondness his father's relationship with the Tehuelche.

> The Indians taught us to hunt with the *bolas* and the lasso. My father was expert with both, and then there was this other one – a short one, about a yard long. They used to get rabbits and partridges and anything like that. You'd see a partridge in a tree, and it would just take its head clean off!

Not every Welshman was as expert with the *bolas* as W. E. Davies' dad. In his diaries, Michael D. Jones' son, the Bala-born geographer, surveyor and indefatigable explorer of Patagonia, Llwyd ap Iwan, recounts a comedic episode worthy of an early Buster Keaton film.

> Picking up many ostrich eggs – many omelettes and pancakes followed. Richard Jones, Pantymarch, had a long shot at a *guanaco* and wounded it in the shoulder. The sergeant, who was riding a mule and leading a spare horse, chased it, and succeeded in turning it towards us. As it happened to be in advance of the party, I made an attempt to *bolear* it. My *bolas* caught it round the neck and the animal came thundering down upon me in his endeavour to disentangle itself from the *bolas*. I dismounted to plunge a knife into its breast and as I did so, one of the balls, still revolving around its neck, caught me in the forehead and sent me reeling. Just then, Percy Wharton came up, turning his *bolas* slowly round his head, and as I knew him to be a novice in this art, I cleared out of the way as quickly as my bigger head would allow me, lest his *bolas* catch me instead of the *guanaco*. Anyway, it was soon captured – an old lean buck, released to finish its days in peace and liberty.

While the Welsh developed skills as agriculturalists, winning awards for their wheat in the Chicago World Fair, the Tehuelche demonstrated their horse-prowess to the world. Horses, as we know, were very important to the native way of life, and were named according to their colours, or because of their resemblance to other creatures they saw around them. A black horse was simply *negro* – black – but a slightly lighter one might be the colour of darkness, or shadow, thus *oscuro*; a grey-black animal was *lobuno*, the colour of a wolf, while a piebald was *overo*. A mount with a little bit of white on the tail was *rabicano*, so a piebald that had some white on the tail was *overo rabicano*, while a white-maned horse was *ruano*. A horse with a white spot on its nose was *picolanco*, and others were described as *gateado*, after the wild cats that lurked in high and rocky places.

Because of the Tehuelche's skills on horseback, the Argentine Government invited a party of them to represent the country at the St Louis World Fair in 1904. However, the trip didn't go all that smoothly, as the Tehuelche disliked Baller, the local commissioner in charge of the show team, and that antipathy extended to his son as well. This didn't bode well, as the latter was the man appointed to look after them on their travels. They didn't co-operate with him at all, and he was given just four men to take with him to Missouri. The first, Coloko, was good at felling ostrich with *bolas*, the second, Loco, rode a horse like the wind and probably rode it madly; the third, Casmino, together with another elderly man, excelled at nothing whatsoever. The Tehuelche who were staying at home laughed at Baller's choice, saying he had picked the most inept and useless horsemen, not to mention the ugliest women, to accompany him, yet the group returned from the States trailing glory, having won the prizes for lassoing, beating all the South American *gauchos* and the American cowboys who were competing against them.

The relationship between R. J. Berwyn, one of the first Welsh settlers, and the Tehuelche, is illustrative of the way the two very different peoples learn to cohabit in the same harsh, unforgiving territory. They got on so well that one of the native elders took Berwyn's name for himself. In their company, he learnt how to hunt anything from hares through ostriches to *guanacos*. Indeed, should something happen to the sheep, cattle or horses on the *paith*, it was only by these hunting skills, sharpening an aptitude for killing native game and birds, that the Welsh could survive.

Learning to hunt successfully was typical of R. J. Berwyn, who was a resourceful pioneer, not least when he set up school, using specially stretched and dried ox-skin as a blackboard, then writing on it with lumps of charcoal. Berwyn himself didn't own a horse, so he would have to borrow one to go hunting, but he was a skilful hunter, so he could easily negotiate the loan of an animal in exchange for a share of the spoils. His skills were augmented further when he learned how to use the *bolas* with consummate skill.

Trading partners

Trade was an important aspect of the relationship between the Welsh and the Tehuelche. When visiting the Camwy valley, the Tehuelche would offer ponchos from both sides of the Andes, along with the skins of wild animals, *quillangos* – blankets made of *guanaco* and rhea skins – as well as the principal item, ostrich feathers. These were extremely valuable, and three tons of feathers could be worth as much as 100 tons of wheat. These were given to the Welsh in exchange for bread, butter, milk and alcohol, although the Welsh religious leaders took a dim view of any trade in booze, not that alcohol was unknown in the colony. The indigenous people would also be given, or paid in cassava flour, rice, sugar, tobacco and yerba tea, not to mention soap and clothes. They also made bedclothes, petticoats and children's costumes for the Welsh settlers, while the Tehuelche's skills in smithery and other craft produced *boleadores,* buckles and knives to trade. The Welsh had a reputation for fairness in business, unlike some of the other settlers who had traded historically with the Indians. The Tehuelche were very, very fond of the settlers' bread, and they would often go from house to house to plead with them to exchange bread for meat. Indeed, the word *bara* (Welsh for bread) was widely used by the native Patagonians, one of the first words to be assimilated into their own language

As a result of these visits, many of the Tehuelche learned some Welsh, and there is a record of their descendants competing in the annual eisteddfod in Trelew.

There has been some dispute about whether or not the settlers traded alcohol with the natives, an allegation that wounded Michael D. Jones to the quick, and which R. Bryn Williams categorically denied in his canonical history, *Y Wladfa*. It was after all a declaredly teetotal community. In 1889, for instance, it was decided that no drinks licences should be issued, and that drinks could not be consumed in places where they were sold wholesale, with a fine for anyone who did. But questions still persist, as alcohol was imported into the colony, and if the teetotal Welsh weren't drinking it, who was?

A dying breed

As early as the 1880s, observers such as Michael D. Jones could foresee the extinction of the Tehuelche tribe. He argued that only by conforming with the European methods of settlement would they would have any hope of survival: 'We believe that they face nothing but extinction, unless they give up their nomadic life, and settle in some particular place; lead a civilized life; and focus on rearing livestock and farming the land. Surely, that is their only hope of deliverance. If only the Welsh settlers could persuade them to do that.' In fact, over the following years, the Tehuelche not only adopted these methods of settlement, but were gradually assimilated into the culture and newfangled ways of the European settlers. Today, only a small cluster of the old Tehuelche tribe continues to practise the old customs in Patagonia, and these are often Indians who choose to describe themselves as such.

In his book, *Pethau Patagonia*, Fred Green writes very tenderly about the Tehuelche, describing them as affable, gracious, generous and always happy to help. They were especially kind to their children, and seldom ever scolded them, while Green was at pains to stress that in all these respects they were at odds with the Araucanian Indians, with their reputation for violence. The Tehuelche's main fault, Green suggests, is a curiosity bordering on covetousness for the property of others, so that a gift given to one would create a demand for gifts for everyone in the vicinity. Part of the problem was that they had no sense of personal property, in the main because they shared things openly and freely with each other, and expected everybody else to be the same. 'They would walk into houses unannounced, and love bread above all things. *Bara* was expectedly the first Welsh word they learnt, and they loved it so much they were happy to trade a horse for a loaf'.

The Welsh sometimes brought up some of the Indian children as their own. Fred Green's grandmother fostered a few young boys – and taught them Welsh – and when his mother was small, one of these carried her, as a young girl, to school on his back.

When they saw that the Welsh were in need of food and horses, they were only too happy to help, according to Fred Green, and very willing to share their horses and hunting time. Green goes as far as to suggest that the friendship with the Tehuelche was the greatest blessing the Welsh were given in y Wladfa. Not that the Welsh would have appreciated the native pastime of playing with a *viscacha*, being a conventionally cute animal about midway in size between a squirrel and a rabbit. They would skin the animal alive and then let it loose in a thorn thicket and then take bets on how long it would last. It was a bloody game, and there were never any real winners.

Musters

One of the most daring feats of Patagonian exploration was achieved by George Chaworth Musters in 1869 and 1870, when he travelled between Punta Arenas and Patagones. Once he'd reached north of Rio Santa Cruz, he moved across the land in the company of a group of Tehuelche, thus becoming the only major explorer to spend time with this native tribe. It's a classic account, although not without its problems, as ethnographer Fernanda Peñaloza has pointed out. Musters, read critically and as a contested history, reveals 'how evasive and oblique is a world that has been imaginarily and nostalgically recovered', especially in light of the uncritical use twentieth-century anthropologists have made of this nineteenth-century text. At the end of a paper on the subject called *The Ethnographic Imagination and the Tehuelches*, Peñaloza asks, 'Would it be better to ignore completely Musters' ventriloquism and confine the elusive world of the Tehuelches to absolute oblivion?' I'm going to answer by allowing Musters to be the ventriloquist for just a wee while longer …

Musters' account is alive with telling and vivid details about Tehuelche life. He saw them walk effortlessly for 40 miles in about twelve hours, without food. They could abstain from food for two or three days without complaint. They were strong of arm, and could throw ostrich *bolas* over 70 yards. Men's beards, moustaches and eyebrows were all carefully removed by using little silver tweezers. Musters tells us a Tehuelche man is not allowed to look at his father-in-law when he is talking to him. And the finest trait in their character, Musters avers, is 'their love for their wives and children; matrimonial disputes are rare, and wife-beating unknown; and the intense grief with which the loss of a wife is mourned is certainly not "civilized" for the widower will destroy all his stock and burn all his possessions …'

Museum piece

There's one story that seems to throw the iniquitous relationship between the Argentinians and the Tehuelche into savage relief. It concerns Inakayal, who was a *cacique*, one of their leaders. He was captured in 1884 by the Argentinian army during the euphemistically-titled 'Conquest of the Desert', a military campaign directed by the Argentinian Government to occupy Patagonia and subdue the indigenous inhabitants, where the word 'subdue' could easily be replaced by 'wipe out', depending on who was telling the story.

The captured Inakayal, weighted down by chains, was transferred to a prison in the Buenos Aires province. His hospitality to the prominent explorer and academic Francisco Moreno during the explorer's 1880 expedition to Patagonia was recalled after Inakayal's surrender, which was covered by the press. Moreno argued with the government on his behalf to spare Inakayal time in military prison. In exchange, Moreno studied him for anthropology. Along with others in his clan, Inakayal was studied for his resemblance to 'prehistoric man'.

In 1885, Inakayal was brought to the Museo de La Plata to be studied by anthropologists because he was a 'rare' specimen of his 'race', and because he refused to relinquish his identity and culture. In effect, he became a living museum exhibit, a war souvenir put on public display along with other members of the tribe. He was to languish there for three long years and then, on 24 September 1888, Inakayal passed away. But he was not buried, and his bones, brain, scalp and death mask became part of the collection of the Museo de La Plata.

The Tehuelche people and indigenous organisations later requested the restitution of the remains of Inakayal and of other chiefs, but to no avail. By 1990, the pressure was such that the National Senator for Chubut, Solari Yrigoyen, presented draft legislation aimed at allowing the return of Inakayal's remains to his homeland. A year later, the Argentinian National Congress adopted Law 23,940, which granted the return. In April 1994, his remains were finally returned to Tecka, in the province of Chubut. Here, the remains were deposited in a mausoleum, the Argentine flag was placed over the urn, and it was covered in stones in the style of indigenous tombs. The entire ceremony was followed by over 2,500 people. The mausoleum is now considered a sacred place.

In the mid-2000s, the *Grupo Universitario de Investigación en Antropología Social* was established. It proposed to the Museo de La Plata that it should organize and classify all the human remains in their collection. In 2001, the National Congress adopted a new law establishing that the remains of aboriginal people who are part of museums and/or public or private collections should be made available to indigenous peoples. Five years later, a researcher identified the scalp of Inakayal. It transpired that only his bones had, in fact, been returned.

The researchers also found two brains preserved in formaldehyde, and contended that one was the brain of Inakayal. This led to the indigenous organizations and the Secretary for Culture of Chubut submitting new requests for restitution. The museum, however, refused, arguing that it could not find out which brain was Inakayal's because DNA identification was inefficient on tissue saturated with formaldehyde. The wrangling over Inakayal's body parts continued, and in 2007 GUIAS identified Inakayal's brain by comparing observations made by a scientist in 1906.

But even now, Inakayal's brain and scalp are still preserved in jars in the Museo de La Plata, in complete violation of the law. It's like the case of the Elgin Marbles, where Greece and Britain have tussled over ownership of these classical sculptures, but with a real human being at its heart: a man who was one of the last, proud indigenous chiefs to resist the genocidal gunmen of the Argentine army as they ranged across the plains, slaughtering without stop.

Chapter 6

Puerto Madryn

Waiting at Trelew bus station – which has a reputation for the adeptness of its pickpockets – for the connection for Puerto Madryn, I am fortunate to meet two ladies who are also travelling there. Morfudd Slaymaker, from Lampeter, and her friend, Elma Phillips, are heading for exactly the same place as me – the coastal location at New Bay where the Welsh first landed, that first chill winter. They turn out to be most excellent companions. Morfudd, a former teacher of home economics in Lampeter Comprehensive, and mother of the stand-up comic and film critic Gary Slaymaker, is clearly in love with y Wladfa, and enjoys showing her companion around, and I am also the net beneficiary of this enthusiasm. Meanwhile, Elma, from the village of Cellan, near Lampeter, who used to teach history in Tregaron Secondary School, enjoys telling me what I should and should not include in my book. Apparently, she doesn't know I've written the occasional volume before this one, and Morfudd later enjoys ribbing her on this point when they return to Wales. Yet her suggestions were spot on.

Morfudd has family connections with y Wladfa, as her grandfather's sister Ada married one William Jones from Cwmaman, who came out to Patagonia at the same time as John Caerenig Evans in 1875, to look for work. They travelled on a ship called the *Masculini*. Also, Gabriel Restucha, the present mayor of Gaiman, is related to Morfudd, as he's the great great-grandson of Ada and William. One of their sons, Tom, became a blacksmith, known as Tom y Gof. This whole Gaiman family line is sometimes referred to as 'Tongos', a corruption of Tom y Gof.

The caves in Punta Cuevas, where historian Fernando Coronato suggests the Welsh stored food, are nothing more than scrapes in the friable clayey rock called *tosca*: there was no adequate supply of fresh water, other than a pond which gathered run-off, some three miles north. Yet, claims Coronato, 'within these hollows, [Edwin Cynrig Roberts] built some of the 16 crude wooden huts which were finished after the arrival of the colonists'. Other historians aren't quite so convinced, arguing that the number, location and measurements don't agree with those of eyewitnesses. Whichever is the case, the caves have now been designated a historical monument, and there is a visitor centre where tourists' comments think it a good place for the 'fine view', and to 'appreciate the struggle'.

The struggle is enshrined in other monuments to the Welsh, too, such as the sculpture by the famous Argentine sculptor Luis Perlotti, who also designed the Tehuelche Native monument in the city. Both were unveiled as part of the 1965 centenary celebrations, and there is also a granite cenotaph listing the names of all of the passengers on the *Mimosa*.

You may not immediately think of Puerto Madryn (named after Captain Love Parry-Jones' estate on the Llŷn peninsula) as a go-to tourist destination, yet this dusty, slightly jaded Patagonian resort is the most popular in the region – not that there are many contenders for the title. Think Skegness on the edge of the Kalahari. Harsh and desiccated in the arc-lamp heat of summer, in the winter, whipping winds keen over the dried landscape as if wailing for the souls of all lost tourists. Yet, by sheer hard work and determination, the place has become a resort with all the associated amenities, even if the wind blows dust in the face of any sun-worshipper who picks a spot on the beach. The sea isn't ever really suitable for swimming – there are fierce riptides here, and the South Atlantic waves are often stirred up and slightly forbidding. A relatively thin strip of beachfront apartments hug the shore of this town, where 60,000 souls live. Yet the pace of life here is calm and measured, and the beach has its fair scattering of families setting up windbreaks and casual seating, settling in for the day.

Many of the tourists who come here do so for a whale of a time, specifically southern right whales, along with a range of other wildlife, such as the Magellanic penguins at Punta Tomba. These incredibly hardy birds spend six months at sea in the waters of the South Atlantic Ocean. They return to the rookery or nesting area where they were born each spring – which means September in the southern hemisphere – to meet up with their mates and breed. Following an elaborate courtship ritual, eggs are laid – two in a good season – and the parents take turns sitting on the nest over the 42-day incubation period. The male goes foraging for two weeks, returns, and then the female goes foraging for about the same amount of time. Once the chicks hatch, parents alternate, one day foraging, one day guarding the nest. They are fierce defenders of their young, protecting them from numerous predators that feed on eggs and chicks, including birds – *skuas*, southern giant petrels, and gulls – and hungry land critters like that fabled trio of armadillos, skunks, and foxes.

The presence of penguins and whales allow this part of Patagonia to rival African big game – elephants, rhinos, giraffes and the like – in terms of wildlife spectacle. Killer whales, or orcas, torpedo through the chill waters, their black and white bodies dappling, dissolving the shapes of their sleek, lethal bodies. They are hyper-alert to the possibility of there being a sea lion pup to dine on. They will sometimes go as far as to strand themselves by hurtling onshore, skidding along the beach as they try to catch their prey. Seals – slinkily and sleekly aquanautic – twist and veer after shoals of fish. And there are penguins, too, arguably named from the Welsh *pen gwyn* (white head), but this may be a bit far-fetched, like comparing Puerto Madryn with St Tropez, say.

The whales arrive here in the winter months, just as the Welsh did, to breed and play their ebullient underwater games, fanning out their great tails, delighting nature enthusiasts with their friendliness, or fearlessness, which allow close observation of these leviathans. Many of the whale-watching boats head for the Carlos Ameghino Isthmus, the piece of land that joins the peninsula to the continent. Its narrowest area measures six kilometres. At this point, the two gulfs can be seen, namely San José (to the north) and Nuevo (to the south).

Like other right whales, the southern right whale is readily distinguished from others by the callosities on its head – caused by large colonies of whale lice – its broad back without a dorsal fin, and a long, arching mouth that begins above the eye. The mouth contains some 260 plates, or horn-like sheets, originally called '*baleen*', from which the Spanish name *ballena* derives. Approximately 10,000 southern right whales are spread throughout the southern part of the southern hemisphere. They are big, big mammals. An adult female weighs an average 52 tons, with the largest being 88 tons in weight.

Nowadays, calf mortality among the whales causes concern. One possibly significant contributor to the rising rate has alarmed scientists – since at least 1996, kelp gulls off the coast of Patagonia have been observed attacking and feeding on live right whales. The kelp gull uses its powerful beak to peck a hole in the whale's skin, right down to the blubber, often leaving the whales with large open sores. This predatory behaviour, primarily targeted at mothers and calves, means the whales are spending up to a third of their time and energy performing evasive manoeuvres. Therefore, mothers spend less time nursing, and the calves are thinner and weaker as a result. Researchers speculate that, many years ago, waste from fish processing plants allowed the gull populations to soar. Their resulting overpopulation, combined with reduced waste output, have caused the gulls to seek out this alternative food source.

Meanwhile, Morfudd, Elma and I find our own food source, a splendid seafood restaurant where the succulent bounty of the sea is washed down with a light red wine which has more than a hint of wild raspberries about it. We're already settling into this South American Skegness. The taxi driver who brought us into town said his *taid* spoke Welsh and said so with pride. The conversation over lunch is bright with laughter. The plate of discarded crustacean shells piles ever higher. This place, windswept and on the very rim of the Atlantic, can very swiftly feel like a little bit of home.

Chapter 7

Trelew (Lewis Jones-town)

> Trelew, tre lwyd,
> Digon o faw, a dim bwyd
> (Trelew, a grey town, / Plenty of dirt, and no food)
>
> (Local ditty)

Beyond the oldest chapel in Trelew, in some flooded fields, parties of yellow-billed pintail and red shoveler ducks are dabbling among the rushes, while a harrier of some kind quarters the edges, looking for a small bird to snatch, a feathery vol au vent.

I am standing with a local architect, Franklin John Humphreys, a member of Moriah's committee, and we are looking at the grave of two seminal figures of the settlement, namely Abraham Mathews and Lewis Jones. It seems appropriate that they should lie side by side. Mathews was the first preacher of y Wladfa, and wrote a book about his experiences, while Lewis Jones – the printer and visionary – gave his name to Trelew. This chapel, however was built before Trelew, and stood in the middle of a farm in the days when it was the farmers themselves who made the bricks, as there is plentiful clay locally, and sufficient wood to 'cook' them. This chapel was hand-built.

Humphreys is currently working on some local design projects, including the Ysgol Hendre project on land donated by the municipality of Trelew. He grew up speaking Welsh to both grandmothers, *Nain* Hughes and *Nain* Humphreys, on a farm near Moriah. *Hen Dad-cu*, great-grandfather, Williams came from Oneida near New York, and *Hen Fam-gu* also hailed from the United States, the south-east in her case, from Georgia. *Taid* – grandfather – Humphreys came from Blaenau Ffestiniog, moving to South America when he was six years old, when the family decamped, not to Patagonia but, rather to Santa Fe in the north of Argentina. 'When I went to study architecture at the university in La Plata, I returned to find that *Nain Mam*, my maternal grandmother, had died. At home, Dada spoke Spanish and Mama spoke Welsh to us, because Dada said that when you speak Spanish, no-one should be able to discern that you're not a native speaker, and when you speak Welsh, the same should be true.'

Señor Humphreys points out some of the salient features of the chapel. 'The architecture of Moriah is very simple. The windows, doors and stairs have the same style as similar places in Wales, but chapels here have zinc roofs, unlike the slate roofs of Welsh ones. No services are held here any more, just the occasional *cymanfa ganu*, or maybe a service connected with Gŵyl y Glaniad, the festival that commemorates the Welsh landing. Franklin John recalls:

> I used to go to Sunday school at ten in the morning, leaving the carriage in front of the chapel, then the afternoon service at six o'clock, with all the hymn-singing in Welsh. Moriah was full then, with many Welsh people living on the farms, tending cattle and growing grass. They were also learning the Bible, in Welsh of course. My son arranges things in the chapel and he's arranged things on the eisteddfod stage, too. I was chair of the eisteddfod until last year. My eldest son lives in Norwich, England, and my daughter lives near the chapel with her family. I'm a widower.

Moriah was the first chapel in town but by now, of course, there are more chapels in Trelew. The Welsh liked building these simple Christian witness boxes in the Wladfa just as they did back home. Moriah was inaugurated in 1880 as an Independent chapel, followed by the Calvinist Methodist Tabernacle a year later.

There's an apocryphal story about a Welshman who's left stranded on a desert island and when, after many years, he's finally discovered, his rescuers find that he had built not one but two chapels. When they ask him why he's built them both, he points at the first and says: 'That's the one I go to,' then he scornfully points at the other and says, 'and that's the one I don't go to'.

Chapel rivalry was pretty much a staple of Welsh village life, and the tradition continued in y Wladfa. People might leave one chapel for another in a huff, or on a point of principle. The historian Elvey MacDonald's grandfather, John James Jones, was a member of Trelew Council and one of the founders of Moriah chapel. He was a prominent and hardworking deacon, that is until the minister was caught having an affair with the organist, at which point Jones left the chapel and started attending services in Tabernacl. So you always needed that second chapel, especially as a place grew in size.

Franklin John tells me that:

> Trelew is a town that hasn't grown properly – it's developed without any real planning, and the government is currently trying to tackle the issue of growth. It has a nice centre but it's grown too big and too ugly. I'm disappointed by some areas of Trelew. From the centre to the north and the east, the place has grown unhealthily. There are many people without work. The town grew a great deal when there was a factory making clothes here, but now there are too many Chinese imports, and our factory has declined, and people were made redundant.

An early visitor to Trelew, Gaylord Simpson, noted the stark contrast between the evolving town and the landscape beyond.

> The contrast is amazing. There is this narrow band of arable land, a bare hairline on the map of Patagonia, and then at its edges, with no transition, begins a howling desert. Two minutes' walk from Trelew or Gaiman, on the northern side of the valley, is enough to pass from pleasant country scenes to a dry land of pebbles, sand, and thorns. The steep valley walls rise abruptly from the river bottom. They are in most places absolutely barren cliffs and slopes of dazzling volcanic ash, slippery clay, or glistening gypsum.
>
> The value of change is amusingly illustrated by the fact that when the citizens of fortunate Trelew take an afternoon off for a picnic, they do not as a rule go to some shady grove along the river. The

favorite picnic ground is a place called El Castillo (The Castle), a round hill with castellated, in places vertical, sides, which is on the desert side of the valley margin and hence a desolate spot for an outing. This locality, incidentally, has more serious claims to fame than as a picnic site for the élite of Trelew. From its own slopes and those of the main valley wall near it have come many remains of fossil whales of the early Miocene, some twenty-five or thirty million years old.

It is one of the many anomalies of Patagonia that not only here, but still farther from the sea, still higher in elevation, and in still drier parts of the desert are found remains of whales, of penguins, and of many kinds of sea shell. Over almost all of what are now the high plateaus of this region the sea once roared. It is ironic and maddening to be travelling through the hinterland, parched and hungry, with 'water, water …' nowhere, or perhaps only a few tepid drops in a tin canteen to drink, and to come across the shells of oysters a foot in diameter. How one's mouth waters! One oyster, just one, would be a succulent feast for a king. But it is no use. As Mark Twain would say, they are dead now. One could almost curse the name of Hatcher, the great American explorer, for whom these now long-defunct oyster dinners are named …

When the distinguished Welsh artist Kyffin Williams first sighted Trelew from the air, it did not lift his spirits anymore than it did Gaylord Simpson's, as the country looked as if it had died far back in the geological past.

Hundreds of miles of desert scrub passed below the plane, and only seldom did there appear to be any tracks or signs of habitation. When we landed on an arid field outside Trelew, I had somehow failed to notice the valley and the meandering Chubut. I felt immeasurably depressed.

On landing, Kyffin got out of the plane and stepped into a bitter wind that seemed to blow from every quarter. It was not an auspicious start, even though the place, its dry landscapes and hardy people, did gain his affection and admiration over time.

There was also the matter of dead dogs and animals. Over the course of driving a mile through town, Kyffin counted the bodies of three dogs and two cows. It hasn't changed much now, as a lack of fences, coupled with many stray animals, not to mention big trucks passing through at some speed, means that you'll often see canine corpses at the side of the road, mummified by the sun and wind, their teeth grimly bared.

As Franklin John and I saunter on to view some other graves, in the fields beyond the hedge some *teros* – southern lapwings – are screeching and putting up quite a racket. There was a belief that should the *tero* fly around the house, calling loudly as it did so, it foretold or presaged an accident, although some people dismissed this as just a hunter's fancy, as the bird could more prosaically be blamed for alarming other birds such as wild ducks, thus spoiling the gun's chances.

We stand at the grave of Franklin John Humphreys' great-grandfather Dafydd Williams, who died here in 1886 and his wife, Charlotte Green, who died two years later when she was 44 years of age. 'Williams Oneida had plenty of money and he charted ships to bring machinery for the farms from the United States to y Wladfa'.

The plover are still wailing plaintively, their cries melding with the sound of the wind susurrating among the weeping willows down on the riverbanks. These self-same trees commonly appear as designs on the headstones, speaking simply of sorrow and loss. The original settlers who came on the *Mimosa* are signalled by a special symbol on the gravestone of people such as Lewis Jones, John Williams of Dolwyddelan and Captain Jones of Porthmadog.

Humphreys and I next talk about the wind. It's a shaping presence here, no doubt about that.

> Wind blows hard here, with the prevailing winds from the west and south-west often gusting at 11 knots, although blasts from the north can be just as strong. Trelew had some natural advantages, being at the halfway point between Rawson and Gaiman, where a gap in the valley bluffs allowed the train to travel along the very gentlest of inclines. It was also plumb centre in the middle of the wheat-growing area, so it had valuable goods and the means to get them to market. There was talk of calling it Trefel, the town

of Bell, after the engineer who helped build the railway, but those in favour of this were soon outvoted, although it was also called Llanfair for a brief while.

Before we leave the chapel, there's just enough time to read a poem written about the place by Donald Thomas. Its sentiments are clear.

> As long as Patagonian skies lie blue – celestial,
> And the southern sea,
> Stormy and limpid;
> As long as the snow lies on the mountains
> And the Chupat river is slow and sinuous,
> The ground is furrowed that the pioneer joined,
> And there is a drop of Celtic blood
> In an Argentine heart,
> There will be somebody capable
> In Moriah's chapel
> Of singing old hymns in Welsh.

We finish reading, then close the doors quietly, lest we disturb the mice.

Eisteddfod time

I am lucky to be in Trelew when the eisteddfod is on. I love a good eisteddfod, and the National Eisteddfod in Wales is very close to my heart: after all I met my wife, Sarah, at the one in Denbigh in 2001. One of the first people I meet in the Trelew version is Virginia Sosa, from Montevideo, in Uruguay. She was ill for quite some time and, idly scanning the airwaves, chanced upon Chris Needs' show on BBC Radio Wales, where the upbeat DJ occasionally peppered his chat with Welsh phrases. Virginia became interested in the language and decided to learn it, doing so via the internet. I am the first Welsh speaker she's met, and this is her first conversation. When I sit down to take her through the one book of grammar she possesses, her pronunciation is faultless, and soon we are on the final page. It's a memorable start to the proceedings.

The first Trelew eisteddfod was held in 1876 in a room in Betsi Hughes' house, near Moriah. As Moloch Hughes puts it, in his book *Ar Lannau'r Camwy*:

> The railway company owned some wooden houses near the lake, raised in a hurry to shelter those rail-workers who had arrived on the *Vesta*. The first proper Trelew Eisteddfod was held in a wide room in one of these on St. David's Day 1889. It was only a small Eisteddfod, as very few preparations were made for it. But despite this, it was the planting of an excellent Welsh tradition in the confidence it would grow in time to be a tall, strong, fruitful tree.

Judging by the hundreds who have turned up today, with many travelling considerable distances, packing the substantial hall or gymnasium, the tree is now gloriously strong. There are competitions in singing, recitation, poetry and dance, going on well into the wee small hours, so that, by the end, I am quivering with tiredness. The people of Argentina are night owls, sure as eggs is eggs.

The first eisteddfod chair in Chubut was won in 1880 by T. G. Pritchard, and the adjudicator was minister Casnodyn Rhys from Treorcky. A decade later, Cymdeithas Cymry Fydd was established with the express intention of promoting Welsh literature, and to discuss topics of interest within the colony: they managed to use the popularity of the eisteddfod to subsidize an agricultural exhibition on the same day. The first crown graced the head of William H. Hughes, Glan Caeron, in 1909, for penning *vers libre*, which must have seemed like radical or even dangerous verse at the time, stripped of the strict and regimented rules of *cynghanedd*, the complicated pattern of rhyme and chime which lies at the heart of Welsh-language poetry.

The growth and consolidation of the eisteddfod in Patagonia contributed hugely to the development of choirs, with all the communitarianism (and occasional community rivalries) that that entails. There were three principal choirs: Moriah and Trelew, led by Llewelyn Williams; Canol y Dyffryn, or Middle of the Valley, under the baton of John Carrog Jones, and Dyffryn Uchaf, the Higher Valley, under the aegis of Dalar Evans. This was a serious competition: in 1914 it set choirs numbering no fewer than 40 members against each other for a prize of $100 with, additionally, a chair being awarded to the choir master. There was also an internationalist feel to things. In the same eisteddfod, there was a competition for translating from Esperanto into Welsh. But, by 1927, subtle changes were creeping in, such as adverts in Spanish in the day's programme. In 1929, the eisteddfod moved to Dolavon, with even bigger financial prizes, and as there was a medal for every member of every choir, this meant capping the numbers in each choir to sixty. In the 1930s, the eisteddfod was pretty peripatetic, moving from Teatro Verdi in Trelew in 1932 to visit the Gaiman in 1936, 1939 and 1942 before diverting to Dolavon in 1942. Also in the 1930s, a children's eisteddfod was established, and was followed by a youth version.

One of the most important eisteddfodau was that in the centenary year of 1965, when Dic Jones, the distinguished poet and west Wales farmer, won the chair, which was accepted on his behalf by Kenneth Evans of Drofa Dulog, with young girl dancers from Trelew performing the traditional floral dance which greets the newly honoured bard. It rekindled a tradition, not having had an eisteddfod at all for the previous fifteen years. The following year, a new pattern was established, with a chair being awarded to the best *awdl*, or long poem, and the crown being given for the best poetry in Spanish. Meanwhile, in the Andes, they started their own mini-eisteddfod, Y Cwrdd Cystadleuol, in 1977, which grew to be an eisteddfod in its own right in the mid-1980s.

As the eisteddfod audience grew bigger and bigger, new venues had to be sought, settling on the *gymnasio* of the racing club in Trelew. In 2001, the Gorsedd was re-established, bringing some further touches of pomp and pageant to the ceremonies, and to the event in general. But such changes were not instantly welcomed, as Walter Brooks and Geraldine Lublin explained in a learned journal, *Beyond Philology*:

> It is not surprising that some of the locals should mistrust the whole fancy ceremony, as well as the pompous robes and furnishings. Moreover, for those who perceived the legacy of the pioneers as deeply rooted in Christian values, the quasi-pagan ritual of the Gorsedd should remain a senseless mystery. As a result, some changes were introduced in order to adapt the ceremony to the Patagonian context and render the ceremony less alien. To begin with, the procession of the local bards towards Meini'r Orsedd is led by a horse-riding *gaucho*. Furthermore, as explained by the Archdruid of the Patagonian Gorsedd, Clydwyn Jones, whereas the members of the Welsh Gorsedd don blue, white and green costumes according to their status, there are no

hierarchies in the Patagonian Gorsedd, whose members wear a blue poncho, without any further ado. Nevertheless, despite the initial lack of understanding, the reestablishment of the Gorsedd was to prove a success in the long run.'

Looking at the eisteddfodic diehards who are still in the hall at three in the morning, it is difficult to argue with that contention. It must be a success for so many people to be awake, let alone clapping, at this very late hour.

Chapter 8

Making Tracks

> I remember standing with my father and mother, Edith and Auntie Neved by the front window of the house, watching the long train make its way past the hills, and the lights of the train pulsating merrily as they went past fences and poles before disappearing into the dusk. For a small boy, it was a magical vision, coupled to some great mystery.
>
> (Elvey MacDonald in *Llwch*)

The second half of the nineteenth century was a boom time, a veritable golden age for the railway, with enormous engineering projects bringing the modern world and its advantages within reach of millions of people. Empires extended their reach with the help of herds of iron horses: new frontiers were there to be sought, created or claimed.

In 1853, there wasn't a single kilometre of railway line in the whole of India, and yet by 1929, there were 66,000 kilometres, or 41,000 miles of track, a network of lines connecting Calcutta with Delhi, and Allahabad with Jabalpur. In March 1870, the line between Bombay and Calcutta was completed, inspiring Jules Verne to imagine a journey around the world in 80 days. The world was contracting, travel was connecting peoples everywhere, and the railways were the cause. Elsewhere in south Asia, the British Empire was getting its railways built, with Rangoon and Prome, in what was then called Burma, being linked by the Irrawaddy State Railway.

In North America in 1885, Lord Strathcona drove in the last spike of track for the Canadian Pacific Railway, linking two oceans and helping to turn a colony into a country, while between the 1830s and the 1860s, there were enormous railway building projects in the United States. The railway was changing the world. Everybody wanted one. Everybody *needed* one.

Argentina was no exception to the railway boom, and the wealth that derived from wheat and meat powered the expansion of the early rail system, which, by easing the movements of goods, generated even more wealth. The Retiro station in Buenos Aires became the grand, indeed ornate, hub of the new railways, with three trains leaving every week to cross the continent to Chile. An American talked about this network in arachnid terms, suggesting that if Buenos Aires was like Paris, it was the railways that made it thus: 'Like the colossal web of a spider, it sends out its strands of steel north to the border of Paraguay and Bolivia, east to the Atlantic, south into Patagonia and west across the Andes'.

Little wonder then, that the early settlers of y Wladfa craved a railway line. Their desire wasn't to join the modern age so much as find an effective way of speeding their goods to market. With the markets being so far away, this seemed a good priority for their labours. Captain Love Jones-Parry's report about the area had stated explicitly that, 'should it be decided that the river Chupat be the place of settlement, the port must be in New Bay, 30 miles to the North, and I suggest that a railway be built between the bay and the valley, as ships pulling more than 12 feet of water are unable to navigate the river'.

Serendipitously, a straight track linked the valley with New Bay, unlike those that meandered through the valley itself, which followed the watercourses and the shape of the river. Travel on horseback was gruelling for both beast and man, and negotiating the gravel tracts of the plateau were particularly testing, and it would be a special horse indeed that could walk 150 miles across this sort of terrain without ending up hopelessly lame. On horseback, the trip between Puerto Madryn and the lower end of the Chubut valley lasted hours. In heat and wind, it was a trial verging on torture. Human ingenuity helped, with the creation of small carts made out of willow and driftwood, with wheels two feet in diameter, which could be loaded up to half a ton. There was a fleet of nine such carts by 1870, but they took twelve to fourteen hours to make the journey from bay to valley, or vice versa.

In 1884, the Argentine Government granted Lewis Jones the concession to build and operate a railway linking the lower Chubut valley with Puerto Madryn, on the southern side of the Valdés peninsula, as well as granting a league of land on either side of the tracks. Jones set up a company in Liverpool to finance its construction, but despite his efforts in addressing Cymdeithas y Cymmrodorion in London and approaching a range of potential backers, all the necessary money was not immediately forthcoming. Indeed, of the £200,000 capital needed in the 1880s, only £85,000 had been raised by the early years of the next century, so the venture was undersubscribed. Yet, for all this shortfall, Lewis Jones was very fortunate to be able to draw on the services of a gifted engineer, Edward Jones Williams, who became the principal architect of the line, and had drawn up the original plans presented in Buenos Aires.

Ingeniero Jones Williams

Edward Jones Williams was born in Durham in 1857, in the year of the second Opium War and the Indian Mutiny, to Welsh parents who subsequently moved back to Wales. Edward's father was an adventurer who, in 1862, left his wife and four children in a cottage in the village of Hewl to look for gold in California. The gold fields had been well and truly pillaged by the time he arrived, so he sought his luck elsewhere, spending eleven years on Vancouver Island. Meanwhile, son Edward attended the National School in Mostyn. Like Robert Stephenson, the father of the Age of Steam, the young Edward worked on local farms as a young boy. At the age of eight, Edward left school and went to work in the lamp-room of a local colliery, and because he was too scared to walk there alone in the dark, his mother would have to accompany him all the way to the pit head, despite the hour. For his labours, Edward Jones Williams was paid six shillings a week, but before long, he had the temerity to ask for a shilling extra a week, which the manager granted him, even as he pointed out that the salary, if paid in pennies, would form a pile higher than the young lad himself.

Edward also frequented Sunday school, and in chapel, he had the opportunity to hear both Michael D. Jones and Edwin Cynrig Roberts speak. They would, no doubt, have seeded a desire in the young lad's mind to visit Patagonia.

Edward went back to school, attending the small grammar school in Holywell, where he received a high standard of education. On turning eighteen, he gained an apprenticeship to become a mining engineer, under the tutelage of Joseph J. Williams. His father contributed the substantial sum of £30 towards this practical education, which suggested that his labours abroad had not been in vain. In the third year of his apprenticeship, the young Edward won a medal and ten pounds in the National Eisteddfod at Birkenhead, for writing a handbook of Geology.

After completing his apprenticeship, Edward travelled back and forth to Liverpool in search of gainful employment. But despite Liverpool being Britain's second city at the time, with half a million inhabitants and a very busy and successful port, the young man searched in vain. His father suggested they should both leave for Argentina, responding to the calls for emigrants and to a visit they had paid to Bod Iwan, Michael D. Jones' home in Bala. Because of their undoubted skills, he was able to secure them a passage on a steamship bound for Buenos Aires. Edward bade farewell to his love, Mary Price, promising to return in order to marry her.

And so the Williams family eventually found themselves in Rawson, where they spent a month in quarantine because of an outbreak of smallpox. The Welsh colonists were by now pretty well established. Chubut was an enormous state, almost a quarter of a million square kilometres, or eight per cent of the entire land mass of Argentina, and the third in terms of size after Buenos Aires and Santa Cruz. There was plenty of room to expand.

The challenge of building a railway here was suitably enormous, crossing parched plains where there was little water. But Edward set about the planning process. Taking two or three companions with him to hold the posts which marked the route, Edward started to plot a railway in earnest, in spite of shifting sands, whipping winds and punishing heat. He would need help, lots of it, but then there was a supremely qualified workforce back home. All he had to do was entice a lot of them over to South America!

In 1845, there was an enormous workforce of no fewer than 200,000 navvies in Britain. It would take a small army of labourers just to keep up with Isambard Kingdom Brunel alone, the visionary and hyper-energetic engineer who drew up the map of British railways. Overhearing a conversation in Spanish between Lewis Jones and his daughter Eluned on a train as it approached Liverpool was an engineer called Azahel P. Bell, who joined in the conversation, and duly offered to help Lewis achieve his goal of creating a railway, both as an engineer and in furthering the aims of the company. Bell then visited Patagonia to assess the prospects, and was pleased with what he saw.

The resulting company, known as the Ferrocarril Central del Chubut, was established in 1886 and, despite a slow take-up of shares, managed to raise enough money to buy 6,000 tons of materials to help build the railway. The town of Trelew grew out of this railhead, and the railway later helped service an important aluminium plant at Puerto Madryn, with links to the oil refineries at Comodoro Rivadavia.

In July of the same year, a total of 375 men, equivalent to one in every six persons in the colony, were tempted to leave for Puerto Madryn to begin to work of driving a 50-mile long railway through the desert. A working capital of £105,000 was amassed from £100 shares, and later the bank of capital rose to £200,000.

The railway company started advertising for labourers in a range of publications including *Baner ac Amserau Cymru*, *Yr Herald Gymreig* and *Tarian y Gweithwyr*. 'Wanted', it proclaimed, in Welsh, of course, '300 workers to build a railway from Puerto Madryn (or New Bay) to y Wladfa – a distance of about 50 miles. The wage is five shillings a day, or its equivalent in national currency. Enquiries to the supervisor, J. H. Lamb, Water Street, Liverpool'. The inducements went far beyond the five shillings a day for their labour, and included an offer of parcels of land on which to settle once they had been in Argentina for a total of three years.

The Ferrocarril Central del Chubut had a tacit agreement with the supervisor, Lamb. He arranged to transport materials, along with 462 able-bodied passengers, on a ship called the *Vesta*, which set sail in May 1886, with the biggest contingent coming from Neath, a dozen from the slate village of Ffestiniog, and the rest drawn mainly from the valleys of south-east Wales. By sheer coincidence, the doughty workers arrived 21 years after the arrival of the *Mimosa*, passing Punta del Gano and Punto Ninfas, so named after the flying fish and porpoise spotted here by earlier travellers. They had paid for the long trip out of their own pockets, and theirs was hardly a luxury liner. But they could console themselves with the prospect of becoming landowners and farmers: seldom did a building job come with such substantial perks. They had been promised 240 acres of land after the construction work came to an end. But most of the irrigable land was already in use and under ownership, so half the workforce eventually left the area, to be replaced by new Italian labourers.

It took twelve days to unload the 500 tons of tracks and sleepers from the

Vesta before the work of creating a railway through the desert could begin. The navvies didn't need to be agriculturists to realize that the land next to the tracks, which they'd been promised, was hardly fit for cultivation. There was also the small matter of their belief in *bwganod*, or ghosts, horseback spirits which rode across these dead reaches at night.

Apart from the spectres, conditions for the workers was far from satisfactory, and the 150 men who laboured at the Puerto Madryn end of the line said they were forced to 'live in tents, like gypsies', with food being nothing more than 'biscuits, tough meat and tea'. Food was expensive, too, which ate into a family's meagre budget in double-quick time.

The workers lived in groups of four or five under the shelter of rudimentary huts, which they would move along as the railway extended. The hut wasn't just a place to sleep, but also a base for brief hunting trips, seeking animals and birds for the pot. Each hut, known as a *batch* – after bachelor – would own a dozen or so dogs which were at liberty to roam, catching hares and so on by day, and guarding the horses at night.

By dint of sheer hard, physical work, the line was built quickly and efficiently, but even so, the cost of laying each mile seemed to grow and grow. On 11 November 1888, a 70-kilometre line was opened between Trelew and the quay in Puerto Madryn. The railway was formally opened by Governor Fontana at the new station in Trelew on 25 May 1889. On 12 June, the governor enjoyed a trip to Puerto Madryn and back, the first non-stop trip by a passenger on the line.

But the line didn't chug easily into profitability, or as one observer put it, 'the hopes of the promoters were to evaporate like a chance shower on the parched land of Chubut'. After all, there were very few passengers in the whole of Patagonia, and those who would take the train would probably only be getting a one-way ticket. The most the investors in the line could expect it to carry would be 8,000 tons of wheat, seeing as only a fifth of the available land had been turned to farmland, but only then if there had been a good harvest. With an average load of 100 tons, it would take only eighty trips to transfer the whole lot from the grain piles to the port. But the cost of doing so was prohibitive, with a charge of £1 for the 45-mile trip to Puerto Madryn. There was talk of taking grain by small boats, anything to avoid such punishing charges. But the colonists dug in, and refused to pay such fees, and by 1891, the train company was down to running one train a week.

This was enough to dampen A. P. Bell's enthusiasm for a grander plan, namely running the railway all the way across Chubut and on to the Pacific, proposing:

> a totally new system, unheard of in other countries that do not possess vast, deserted, and unproductive areas as this one has. This system could be appropriately called the 'Colonising Railway'. It is based upon the concession of land to be cultivated and settled, located in the desert, by which the State will compensate the Company for the cost of the construction of the railway across regions that are totally unproductive today. In this way, the railway makes the desert pay for its own settlement, at no cost to the Nation.

Bell was trying to fix a deal in which he would be given five square leagues, or 12,500 hectares, for every kilometre of track. But this was a line that would only run through Bell's dreams. He had acquired Lewis Jones' railway company in 1888, and would then sell it on to the Ferrocarril Central del Chubut.

Neither did the line bring any good fortune to the navvies who built it. When the chaplain of HMS *Flora* visited the area in 1900, the only people he encountered who were truly destitute and living in hopeless conditions were those who had arrived on the *Vesta*, and he described their homes as being nothing more than hovels. But like most railway towns, Trelew grew like Topsy. There were 58 houses there in 1895, but by 1911, there were 315. By 1933, the population was almost 5,000 and houses were taking the town's edges in all directions.

From Trelew, the line was gradually extended by 50 kilometres to Gaiman by 31 December 1908, and from there to Dolavon by 12 October 1915. Dolavon had originally been nothing more than a tiny hamlet, comprising three farms and an inn to slake the thirst of cross-country waggoners. The railway allowed it to develop as the social and economic centre for the west of the valley, with a branch of the Co-operative Society helping to consolidate its growth. In 1920, the company was nationalized, and the line was later extended from Dolavon to Las Plumas. In an echo of the Beeching cuts in Britain – when Dr Richard Beeching proposed the closure of over 2,000 stations and 5,000 miles (8,000 kilometres) of railway line in the 1960s – this Patagonian line was finally closed in 1961.

Nowadays, little remains of the line, other than the occasional tunnel and the station at Trelew, which has been converted into a quaint and charming museum. Here, you can see an ornate wooden organ and silver cups that used to grace Moriah chapel, together with the chair won by one Morris ap Hughes in the Dolavon Eisteddfod, and one from the more prestigious Eisteddfod y Wladfa in 1945. In another of the atmospheric and orderly rooms, there's a pluviometer, or rain gauge, from Estación Bocatoma, together with a clock that used to belong to one James Peter Jones, the first man to be born in Trelew. There are portraits, too, of some of the early settlers, such as Lewis Humphreys, whose hipster beard would put most modern equivalents in London's Hoxton to shame, and John Murray Thomas with his wife Enriqueta Underwood, along with a clock bag belonging to the pioneer Abraham Matthews, along with a record of the funeral of John Howell Jones on Calle Belgrano in Trelew in 1937. In the various portraits of the early settlers, a steely determination seems to glint in their eyes, as if to say: we are here to stay, we are making this land ours.

There were other rail lines the other end of y Wladfa, too, one running through the Andes. Paul Theroux's almost-classic book, *The Old Patagonian Express*, starts with a rush-hour subway ride to South Station in Boston to catch the Lake Shore to Chicago before starting an epic journey from North America to South America, which ends when Theroux winds up on the poky, wandering *Old Patagonian Express* steam engine, which comes to a halt in a desolate land. Along the way the irascible, curmudgeonly, but nevertheless very entertaining author, meets an engaging parade of characters such as the monologuing Mr. Thornberry in Costa Rica, the bogus priest of Cali, and the blind Jorge Luis Borges, who delights in having Theroux read Robert Louis Stevenson to him. But the blind author also wants to dissuade Theroux from pressing on to Patagonia.

> As he fished out his door key, I asked him about Patagonia.
> 'I have been there,' he said. 'But I don't know it well. I'll tell you this, though. It's a dreary place. A very dreary place.'
> 'I was planning to take the train tomorrow.'
> 'Don't go tomorrow. Come and see me.'

> 'I suppose I can go to Patagonia next week.'
> 'It's dreary,' said Borges. He had got the door open, and now he shuffled to the elevator and pulled open its metal gates. 'The gate of the hundred sorrows,' he said, and entered, chuckling.

Theroux finds that Borges was right about Patagonia when he comes to the end of his journey, the town of Esquel, southern Argentina. He arrives there on the final 'teeny-weeny steam train', the *Old Patagonian Express*. He has arrived precisely at Nowhere, at 'enormous, empty spaces'. 'The nothingness itself,' he concludes, 'a beginning for some intrepid traveler, was an ending for me. I had arrived in Patagonia, and I laughed when I remembered I had come here from Boston, on the subway train that took people to work'.

When he boards the *Old Patagonian Express* for the very last leg of his journey, Theroux is disappointed to find that 'express' is a misnomer, as a journey he estimates would take only three hours on a straight track is a fourteen-hour ride. And the train itself doesn't exactly inspire confidence in this by-now weary and wearied traveller:

> The whole contraption creaked, and when it was travelling fast, which was seldom, it made such a racket of bumping couplings and rattling windows and groaning wood that I had the impression that it was on the verge of bursting apart – just blowing into splinters and dropping there in one of the dry ravines.
> The landscape had a prehistoric look, the sort that forms a painted backdrop for a dinosaur skeleton in a museum: simple terrible hills and gullies; thorn bushes and rocks; and everything smoothed by the wind and looking as if a great flood had denuded it, washed it clean of all its particular features. Still the wind worked on it, kept the trees from growing, blew the soil west, uncovered more rock, and even uprooted the ugly bushes.

Theroux's gift for miserabilist commentary comes to the fore as he tries to capture the monotony of a place that had no landmarks, 'or rather, it was all landmarks, one indistinguishable from the other – thousands of hills and dry riverbeds, and a billion bushes, all the same. I dozed and woke; hours passed; the scenery at the window did not alter. And the stations were interchangeable – a shed, a concrete platform, staring men, boys with baskets, the dogs, battered pick-up trucks'.

He does, however, meet one Welshman. 'His name was Renaldo. His surname was Davies – he was Welsh. This part of Patagonia was full of Joneses, Williamses, Powells and Pritchards, Welsh families who had migrated across the plateau from Rawson and Trelew and Puerto Madryn with the intention of founding a new Welsh colony. They are tough, independent, and undemonstrative people, not the singers and dreamers one associates with Wales, but a different breed altogether, churchgoers, sheep-farmers, tenaciously Protestant, with a great sentiment for a homeland they have never seen and for a language few speak'.

Nowadays, the train just runs for tourists.

Chapter 9

Ariel and Martha

I first met Ariel Hughes in Washington D.C. in 2009. He was preparing a traditional *asado*, busily barbecuing an entire lamb on the Mall, that proud statement of American-ness, a national monument that runs as a great green rectangle between the dome of Congress and the Lincoln Memorial. Ariel had travelled from his farm on the outskirts of Trelew to take part in the annual Smithsonian Folk Festival in the year when Wales was one of the three featured countries or cultures. His energy, his sheer dynamism, won over the crowds who watched this bright-eyed man explain the principles of *asado*, which involves making a fire on the ground or in a fire pit which is then surrounded by metal crosses – the *asadores* – that hold the entire carcass of an animal splayed open to receive the heat. His long hair pulled back into a sort of pigtail, his red beret at a jaunty angle, the deep fan of laughter lines radiating out from his eyes brought to mind the French singer Sacha Distel, this born communicator seemed to keep going, to lubricate his very sentences with copious swigs of *mate* from his silver flask.

Ariel is a *mate* connoisseur and enthusiast, and freely admits that he gives the leaves of green Paraguayan tea some extra pep by adding coca leaves, giving that slight stimulant fizz and energy boost that Bolivian tin workers get from chewing them. The preparation is a quotidian ritual. The tea is placed in a gourd and then the *mate* and hot water poured onto it. The hot mixture is given enough time to stew and is then passed around from drinker to drinker and the liquid is drawn into the mouth through a metal pipe or *bombilla*. You can offend your *mate*-drinking companion if you wipe the *bombilla* before sucking in some mate for yourself, even if he or she seems insalubrious.

I next caught up with him a long way away from Washington D.C. in

Trelew, in the company of his wife Martha. It is a delight to see them together, as they are clearly in love. He does those little things – playing with her hair, or picking a single strand from her shoulder – grooming, attentive, unfussy tokens of affection. Martha was born in Trelew in 1950 and came from a Welsh family. Her father was William Hughes and her mother was Maria Luisa Vidella from Portugal. Maria's father, in turn, came from Portugal and her mother was a Mapuche Indian from Chile. The two of them were brought up together in the same area, as Martha recounts:

> I used to recite, and he sang, and we started courting when we were both in the choir together. Ariel's grandfather taught me recitation, and I would meet him on the farm as well. Osian Hughes, Ariel's dad, also led the choir. Then we started going together, having known each other all our lives. Now we've been together for forty years, married for 35 years. Ariel is a very happy man.

She says this with great fondness, wrapping the affectionate words around him like a poncho. Martha lists her children. They adopted Margarita and Segundo and also had Cecil, Roy and Alan. Cecil was the first, then Roy, then Margarita, then Alan, then Segundo. Martha tells me about the circumstances of adopting the two children. As someone who was himself adopted, I'm always keen to hear such accounts:

> Margarita came to the house looking for work when she was very small, only 11 years old. She came from a very poor family and was simply looking for work. She didn't have a father, only a mother. She stayed with us, and stayed with us, and finally we arranged with her mother that we should adopt her. We were living in Esquel at the time, and the only way to arrange it was to adopt her. Her Mapuche mother had five other children, half-brothers to Margarita. One day, Cecil was speaking to a friend and he came to ask me, 'Mam, Margarita is my sister, but she didn't come from your belly?' 'Yes, that's right.'

Margarita heard this exchange and asked Martha,

Can I call you 'Mam'? She was choosing to call me that: I'd never asked her to do so. She was 14 years of age by then. She felt she was part of the family. She had learned Welsh, had learned to play guitar with Osian, and he treated her fondly. She also sang in the choir. But then, in 1993, she died. She was living in Cordoba, she had married and she was expecting a baby. Two or three men came to the house to steal things and they killed her. They shot her dead. She was 24 years old.

Segundo came to work in the garden. He had a complicated history. He was looking for somewhere to stay because the court had told him to leave the house, because his father used to beat him and made him work only to bring him money. He was 16 when he first came to our house. He knew our children, and would come to work in the garden and one day, when we were living in Esquel, he came and told us that he had left home. We asked him where he intended to go. He said some friend's house, and I said, you can't just go anywhere, and offered him a place with us, and he accepted. The other children asked him where he would sleep, and we said they had to choose, and Roy said he could sleep with him. Three or four days later we went to arrange the papers. It wasn't so easy because of his father. We were scared of him. He hung around with bad types, and he came to a violent end. Segundo's father was very nasty, and we used to try to hide Segundo and the other the children from him. Segundo and Cecil live in Esquel. We lived there for 27 years.

Now in Trelew, Ariel Hughes professionally advises farmers about seeds or which stock to choose, encouraging organic farming and exploring ways to diversify. 'We as farmers talk to each other. We talk to farmers on their farms, and I give them advice via my radio show, which I host once a week. And some come to us, where Alan works the farm, while Roy works in the hostel attached to my grandfather's farm, Pen-y-gelli.' The farm is near Highway 3, which runs from south to the north. The highway used to run behind the hills, but the new road was built in 1976. By now, the town encroaches on the farm as the town has grown so quickly, with as many as 120,000 people living there. Ariel thinks it's grown far too quickly.

There were floods in northern Argentina in the 1970s, and many people moved to Trelew as a consequence. Some of the industries didn't pay tax, and in the 1990s, many closed, but people stayed on in the area anyway. The highway passes through Trelew, and some people simply decided to stay here. People are also leaving the countryside and moving to Trelew, leaving the farms behind, and the Bolivians are taking their places.

Vegetable-growing is popular and important, and Ariel wants to effect some change, bring in more organic agriculture but it's an uphill struggle.

People from the towns want to know how their vegetables are grown. They want to buy organic and will pay more for them. So, sometimes people head down the organics route, but more often than not they grow veg using a lot of chemicals and pesticides. Then there are the gang-masters looking after many workers who live in very poor conditions. They eat only food from the farm. They don't have decent housing, and work like slaves from sunup to sundown.

Some of the other bad agricultural practices in the area also exercise Ariel.

In Chubut, we have clean animals. but we also import meat from the north, and it's harder to know where it came from and how it was prepared. Here, we eat more lamb than beef. We eat lots of fat and meat here. It would be good if we could change that, for our health. You see, some places just don't care about the animals, or the meat they produce. In Tir Halen, there's a place that breeds pigs where the animals seem to be eating meat. There's a lot of rubbish, attracting seagulls and vermin.

Pen-y-Gelli Farm is in two parts. It is 12 hectares (26 acres), and a ditch crosses the land. This is the main canal crossing the southern side of the valley, very near to the hills. Ariel explains:

So here, we can produce grass, while three and a half acres are given over to grow sorghum for foraging animals. There is also a water-wheel, such as they have at Dolavon, to help us move water around. We eat flowers from around the house. Not many people do that. Water transformed the valley. Thanks to the water, all sorts of crops grow. Before they created the Panama canal, ships had to go all around Patagonia and cross along the Pacific. Before then, there were all sorts of fruits landed in Patagonia. It's a good place to keep genetic stock for all over the world.

Plant life

Ariel is very interested in herbal lore and wisdom as well. 'Tehuelche women used plants to live, and medicinally, just like the Celts. The Tehuelche people mixed culture and information. To know what's safe to eat or use, you always need to look to see what the birds eat'. Some of this folk knowledge has been lost, but happily much has been written about it. Dilys Jones, Bernardo Jones' mother, wrote down the history of plants. '*Celyn bach*, or *cilunbay*, is very interesting as a medicine for cancer. Other plants from the *paith*, such as *chuqiraga*, are very good for treating sheep'.

He says that you can still find wormwood everywhere, from which you can make the bitter drink that would have been a medicinal staple for many of the early Welsh settlers. It's a real connection with Wales. Wormwood was found growing outside many Welsh cottages, with its use noted as far back as the ledgers of the Physicians of Myddfai, the medieval keepers of herbal wisdom. Osian, Ariel's father, 'taught me how to make wormwood tea, or eat a little bit of the leaf, which is bitter, but very good for the stomach. Wormwood was often hung near the door in dried bunches to keep out insects. We would also use it to treat roses. Tobacco, soap and wormwood would all be boiled together. It creates an organic pesticide which we can use every day'.

Ariel often opens his radio programme with talk about plants.

> We have to educate people. We have travelled a lot with the Mapuche and the Tehuelche, and have also learned from the Celts. We have learned to eat food that isn't cooked, but there's so much other information out there. Tamarisk, for instance, is used for many things. It grows in very salty soil. It gives very good firewood, is excellent for *asados*, and very good for fences. It

provides shelter for animals, as do the *alamos*, or poplars, which make excellent wind breaks and can be used to make boxes, roofs and fences. *Olmo,* too, that's very interesting, and also the oak, carried here by the Welsh. You can find almost all the plants that are connected with Celtic cultures here.

As he tells me this, I remember how I saw blackthorn in the graveyard yard hedges at Moriah chapel in Trelew. Another connection.

Ariel then starts to talk about the Celtic plant calendar, in which Ariel is an apple. Martha is grapes. 'Sorbus grow very well here. They kept spirits at bay in Wales. Elder, *ysgawen,* is also very useful for its herbal uses'. I tell Ariel about Twm o'r Nant, the itinerant and uneducated writer from Llannefydd in Denbighshire. When he was writing his short theatrical works, his *anterliwtiau,* or interludes, he was so poor he would write using a thin black ink made out of elderberry juice.

Just as his Welshness empowered Twm o'r Nant, helping this haulier, who had had little more than a few weeks' schooling in his life, to become the most important figure in Welsh theatre between the Middle Ages and the twentieth century, Ariel is a Patagonian through and through, and it's a force within him.

> Being free is the spirit of Patagonia. We feel we are a different country to Argentina. We have to live with the wind, the sun, the dryness. Here the *estancias* are always further away, everywhere's farther away, indeed everything is further away …
> But we know how to live. In 1958, during the floods, we had to move to the hills, where we lived with rats. We Patagonians like clouds and wind, because the wind sings, even when it's cold. And we like the night sky. The stars in Patagonia, they give energy to your soul, the whole great firmament of stars. Sometimes, our children stand on the edge of the canal in the middle of the night, until three in the morning, to see the sky, to enjoy the night sky. It's one huge, glorious energy source.

Chapter 10

El Hospital

While Ariel and Martha Hughes are great believers in old, indeed ancient lore, and the efficacies of herbal goodness, more conventional medicine featured in the lives of some of the women of y Wladfa. In a letter from Evan Thomas to R. Bryn Williams, the correspondent writes that 'the children of the Welsh migrate to seek obsequious wages in the cities, and the women go to wash pots in the British Hospital'. And go there they did, in considerable numbers.

At the beginning of the Second World War, a matron from the British Hospital in Buenos Aires visited y Wladfa by way of a one-woman recruitment drive. Many English nurses had returned home to Britain to attend to the needs of soldiers, and so there was a real skills and labour shortage, and young women from y Wladfa were enticed to take their places. They would be given comfortable lodgings as well as a small salary during their three years of study, after which they would be given a diploma. Lizzie Lloyd, from Esquel remembers the colour coding on the eating utensils – green cups and plates denoted syphilis, which was very prevalent among sailors. It was hard work, day in day out. Day shift: sutures, ward rounds, wound-cleaning, the delivery of enemas, the administration of pills. Night shift: disinfecting, reassuring patients' families, dealing with illness and its emotional fall-out. As it says in the so-called Florence Nightingale pledge, a version of the Hippocratic Oath, 'With loyalty will I endeavour to aid the physician in his work, and devote myself to the welfare of those committed to my care'. Yes, *caring*, most of all, caring.

Former nurse Norma Hughes comes from Trevelin. This opera-going, music-loving denizen of Buenos Aires displays her allegiance to Wales in the form of an exquisite red dragon on her necklace. She explained why it was called the British Hospital, and tells me of her experiences there.

> An Englishwoman started nursing here. It grew and grew and grew. Good nursing school there. For those who weren't used to duty, it was a tough regime. I came here when I was almost 18 years of age. My eldest sister was already here, living in the nurses' home at the hospital, and she was a great help when I was settling in. I used to cry every day because of *hiraeth* for home. I still take tea every afternoon like we did at home fifty years ago. The hours at the hospital were very long, and after a night shift, there'd be lessons. We had to be in by 10:30 every night, or we'd get a talking-to from the matron. We had to fill in our names in a ledger if we were going to be back late. I had to hide in a doctor's car to sneak back in once. I started in 1961, finished my studies in '63 and stayed there until 1969. After that, I went to work with a cancer surgeon and stayed with him for 14 years. Then I went to look after an old lady in her home.

Another of the nurses was Erie James, who contacted the Scottish matron asking for a place on the nursing course. She was told she would have to send a full-length photograph of herself, and a letter of recommendation from her chapel minister, as well as one from her doctor, attesting to her health. It was a 70-hour trip from the farm to the big city, and when she arrived at the station at nine in the morning, she was greeted by a deputation of half a dozen nurses who had been sent by the matron, even though they had all just worked a full nightshift. Erie knew them all personally, which helped her settle in quickly.

Erie was joining a cohort of 100 trainee nurses, all living under a strict regime. Her uniform, complete with white socks and white shoes, didn't fit her when she first tried it on, and a friend had to help her pin her cap in place – not a single hair was to touch her heavily starched collar. In the process of changing her clothes, she also changed her name. She was now simply 'nurse' to all and sundry.

Her first job was answering the summoning bells of the patients and answering the telephone, a task made even more difficult by her lack of

English. Luckily, that first day, most people's attention was elsewhere: a patient from Pakistan had bolted from the hospital and sought sanctuary by climbing up into a palm tree in the square, where his lack of English and Spanish helped keep him ignorant of what the various people below were shouting at him. Finally, the Pakistani ambassador was summoned to help.

Soon, Erie was on the night shift, working from midnight to eight, even though she hadn't yet been trained to use syringes, and those patients who were on penicillin had to be injected every three hours. She also had to deliver enemas to those who were due to have surgery the next day. This was no bother, other than when a handsome young man from y Wladfa, with a reputation as a bit of a Don Juan, had to be given one. The fact that he kept on breaking down into helpless mirth didn't help the intimate process at all.

After three years came graduation, a sensitive ceremony in which the matron lit the candles the graduands were carrying. They each vowed to be faithful to the teaching and example of Florence Nightingale. Schubert's 'Ave Maria' was sung by one of the nurses, there were hymns and speeches, and the wife of the British Ambassador handed out the diplomas. Erie was given hers, along with the matron's prize.

The British Hospital gave many young women from y Wladfa both gainful employment and experience of city life. Many chose not to return to Patagonia, the allure and excitements of life in Buenos Aires proving much too strong.

Chapter 11

The Artisan

> Artesano. Artista. Pintor.
> Que te inspira cuando creas
> Maravillas con tus manos?
>
> Artisan. Artist. Painter
> What has inspired you to create
> Marvels with your hands?
>
> From the poem 'Preguntas',
by Juan Morgan James

At the farmers' market at the Colegio Agrotécnico de Bryn Gwyn near Gaiman, I met Juan Morgan James, a native sculptor whose long facial features brought to mind pictures I had seen of the Tehuelche, though he is, in fact Mapuche. I bought one of his sculptures, which sits on the desk in front of me – a dignified, tall woman, summoned out of a piece of hard wood, she seems to be able to see far, to scan very distant horizons. There is a word inscribed at the base. It is 'Ka', or 'spirit', such as the Egyptian 'Ka' and 'Ba'. Juan sees his job as being 'to connect, as if in a dream, the earth and heavens'. For the Mapuche, he says, the spirit is what the white people, or Spanish, call the soul. When somebody dies, the spirit stays with their things. This is the reason why, in part, when a person passes, they are buried with all their belongings, whether it be a dog or a horse, anything they owned. All this is done in preparation for their next journey, when they go up to the sky and need all of these things.

Juan works as a porter in a junior school, Escuela 122, in Trelew, where he cleans, gives the kids their breakfasts, sees himself 'at the service of the children'. He likes children and their special energy and innocence. He has now been a sculptor for twenty years, and he shrugs off the label 'artist', choosing rather to plump for the word 'artisan'. 'An artisan,' he maintains, 'is a person who stands up for himself. If I lost my job tomorrow, I'd be able to carry on working in pretty much any space – I'd be able to survive. When the world finishes, comes to an end, the ones who will survive will be the artisans – and the cockroaches'.

Later, he gave me some details about his life. On a piece of paper, Juan drew a simple genealogy. His *ñuke*, or mother was Anita Ñanco from Paso de Indios and his father, was Adrian David James, from Dolavon. He knew his father, but kept away from him and grew up in the care of his grandmother. Despite his mixed pedigree, he sees himself as firmly Mapuche, as he sees himself connected to the earth – another name for the Mapuche is *Gente de la Tierra*, People of the Earth:

> The Mapuche have a very special relationship with the earth, because it is the *mother* earth who provides everything, so this is why they believe that if you treat the earth badly, it's because you don't love it. And you have to love the earth as you love your mother, look after it and protect it. If you have the earth, you have everything. Nowadays, the majority of Mapuche live on the edges of cities because they have had their lands taken away from them.

Juan, like many Mapuche, has been radicalized by what has happened to the Mapuche over the years. Historians believe that the Mapuche have made Patagonia their home for 13,000 years. But they were chased off the land and reduced to poverty by the Spaniards, and have been the victim of invasions, massacres and land grabs ever since. The most notorious was in 1879, when more than 1,300 Mapuche were killed and their lands confiscated for British settlers.

One of the most recent conflicts, in 2007, saw the Mapuche taking on Benetton, the Italian clothing company famous for its often inflammatory 'Colours of Benetton' advertising campaigns. It is one of the biggest landowners in Patagonia, having bought a staggering 2.2 million acres or 900,000 hectares.

Free market reforms, backed by President Carlos Menem in the 1990s, encouraged wealthy North Americans and Europeans to invest heavily in

Patagonia, tempted by its low prices and Argentina's newly open economy, with celebrities such as Sylvester Stallone, Ted Turner, Jerry Lewis and George Soros, as well as a clutch of faceless corporations, buying up land. When Benetton bought out the British-owned Argentine Southern Land Company at the beginning of the twenty-first century, it became the biggest landlord of them all.

Much of its land was used to graze 280,000 sheep, whose wool went into the firm's brightly-coloured sweaters. The company opened the Leleque Museum, in the village of that name, 'to narrate the culture and history of a mythical land', while Carlo Benetton was reported as saying that 'Patagonia gives me an amazing sense of freedom'. But the word 'freedom' had a seemingly hollow ring to it.

Atilio Curinanco was born in Leleque, less than a kilometre from where Benetton's new museum now stands. He moved to the nearby town of Esquel with his wife Rosa and their four children to look for work, but, battered like so many in the slump that followed Argentina's economic slump of 2001, they decided to go back to the land, to try to scratch a living again in the old way.

They set their sights on 740 acres of unoccupied land called Santa Rosa, land that had traditionally belonged to the Mapuche, located next to a Benetton holding. In December 2001, they went to the state-managed property agency to ask for permission to occupy the land. Eight months later, the agency gave Mr and Mrs Curinanco an apparent green light. They presented themselves at the local police station to say they planned to occupy the land, and the same day, they and a group of friends moved in and started work.

As Mr Curinanco later told the press, 'We went to the land without harming anyone. We didn't cut a fence. We didn't hide. We waited for someone to come and let us know if it bothered them'. But Benetton objected, and took them to court in a case that attracted widespread media attention. The couple eventually had to give up the land, browbeaten by Benetton. It's cases such as this one that have radicalized the Mapuche, including Juan Morgan James. They see land which was once theirs wrested from them by people whose only interest in it is pecuniary. For the people of the earth, this is pretty much akin to stealing their souls.

Chapter 12

Gaiman

The Chubut river gives its shape to Gaiman, a linear settlement and perhaps the most Welsh of the Patagonian towns. Here, Welshness is a commodity, in the shape of an array of tearooms offering scones and *bara brith*, homemade jams and the signature *teisen ddu*, a cake that can last a lifetime, a bit like that famous Big Mac that never decomposed. A bilingual police sign proclaims both 'Policia' and 'Heddlu'. Tŷ Te Caerdydd sports an enormous white teapot in the garden, under the shadow of a yucca tree. You can buy bread in the Siop Fara. Gaiman is clearly the go-to place if you want a great cup of char, or if you want to stir up your romantic life with some love spoons or, indeed, acquire the same sort of gifts that are piled higgledy-piggledy in tourist emporia all over Wales, like tea towels with the welcoming 'Croeso' writ large everywhere, amid a red fluttering of dragon wings.

It wasn't always this genteel. In a letter from Thomas Benbow Phillips, written in 1900 to a potential colonist, he advised that, 'if you are fond of shooting, a fowling-piece would be handy, and one always feels a greater sense of security when travelling by having a Smith & Wesson revolver with one. Mine is a 38 calibre'.

Now that it's less of a Wild West frontier-town, Gaiman is a fine place to gently wander, and you certainly don't need to pack a piece. There's the oldest house in the town, built for people who must have been short, and not at all claustrophobic. There are redbrick cottages and Bethel, a redbrick chapel just an Argentine frog's hop away from the river, here crossed by a modern, metal bridge. By day, it's often possible to just enjoy the slow running of water through the canal as it passes through the park in the middle of the town. Rush hour might bring a dozen cars to irritate the tranquillity, but then it can all settle back, as if the motors were just mirages, Gaiman once again dozing as the sun dapples in through the park. Here, the sound of the slow, steady flow of the bottle-green canal waters mixes with the bright chirrup of sparrows.

To the west lies New Gaiman, nowadays still attracting new immigrants, who live in grey, concrete-block houses. In his autobiography, *Llwch*, Elvey MacDonald recalls how the eastern edge of town, between the hospital and the town's second cemetery – standing on the site where Gaiman's first chapel was erected in 1877 – was nicknamed Jerusalem. This reflected the presence of many Arab settlers, originally from places such as Syria and Jerusalem. When Elvey was growing up, development on the southern side of the town was scant, with the exception of some farms lying between the town and the petite settlement at Bryn Crwn. To the north lay the railway line that led away towards Dolavon, Las Chapas and Dol y Plu.

During Elvey's childhood, Gaiman was a squat town of single-storey buildings, with the exception of three houses and then, latterly, the two-storey Water Company offices. In those days, there was no tarmac or concrete, the soil of the roads impacted by the passage of what little traffic there was. There were the Patagonian equivalents to boy racers, though, such as Elvey's cousin, Chapi Williams, and a hot-blooded engineer called Pronsato, who would scream through town in their powerful pick-ups and jeeps, throwing up a dangerous spray of chippings. In the rain, the roads would churn into mud baths. The town is much quieter today, the wide thoroughfare through the middle animated by only one car and a bus. The silence is broken only by a smiling gang of schoolchildren, lining up at a *parada*, waiting for the bus, chattering excitedly.

Calle Michael D. Jones used to have another name, Hafn y Gweddwon (Widows' Gap), because so many women who had survived their husbands lived there. Women didn't just outlast their men, but lasted a long while, too. The longevity of women in y Wladfa prompted some to see it as a phenomenon, such as Bronwen MacDonald writing to *Yr Enfys*, the journal of Cymry a'r Byd (the Welsh International Union), in 1969. She noted how Mrs Powell Jones of Trelew was 90, Mrs Robert Roberts, Bryn Gwyn, 91, Mrs John A. Jenkin was 92, with Mrs William Jones, Mrs Samuel Hughes, Gaiman and Mrs Richard Williams, Bethesda all being healthy nonagenarians.

Gaiman museum, run voluntarily for decades by the late Tegai Roberts and her nephew, Fabio González, is a treasure trove, with a great deal of the material as yet unclassified in any methodical manner, bringing to mind *The Old Curiosity Shop*, with its Dickensian abundance. Here's a photographic record of the day President Julio Roca visited the settlement in 1899, and of the first ever eisteddfod in Trelew, when the town looked like nothing more than a few Lego houses (Argentine edition) set in a dust bowl. There's the 'Act of Establishment' for the town of Rawson. One of the displays is an extract from a book by the colony's third schoolmaster, R. J. Berwyn, in which he posits that, 'in this century, emigration has become a necessity for survival to many of our race. Of those who left Wales, some felt like aliens in the country to which they went, others became integrated with their surroundings and lost their national identity'. This was the same identity maintained within the displayed and sepia-tinted pages of early newspapers and magazines such as *Y Drafod* and *Y Gwerinwr*. Elsewhere, stern faces, perched above Victorian Sunday best costumes stare out from faded photographs, hard work and stern endeavour etched into the rigid lines of their faces; the unwavering chins, the defiant stares into the camera's dead eye.

Chapel-going

Bethel chapel in Gaiman is full on a Sunday morning, the morning's hymns a selection of favourites – 'Hengoed', 'Penmachno', 'Arwelfa' and 'Sirioldeb' – which will be sung solo by Alejandro Hughes, then 'Coedmor' and 'Rhosymedre'. The visit of a minister from Wales, Tegid Roberts, has helped ensure a good congregation. As the voices raise in unison, the words heavy, sticky somehow, I am transported back to my childhood, to Libanus chapel in Pwll, where such sombre songs underlined a seeming seriousness of purpose. There, the deacons seldom smiled. Luckily, outside, in the pelting Patagonia sun, the crowd mingles like the old friends they are. Soft words of Welsh patter down on the yard outside like leaf dapple as they exchange the week's news. Of the chapels in the valley this is one of the best attended and many of the others have closed their doors, or only hold services sporadically. The persistence of chapel-going in Patagonia, and of singing hymns in Welsh, is a minor miracle. The sometimes drab but always serious songs in a minor key reverberate in the mind as I walk back into town.

Randal, day by day

After chapel, I return to Gaiman's past. In one of the boxes in the museum, I find the diaries of Randal B. Phillips, son of Brazilian pioneer Thomas Benbow Phillips, which give a vivid glimpse of Gaiman in the past. At the beginning of the diary, he's drawn a picture of a red dragon coiled around and protecting an egg, and there's a piece of doggerel verse to go with it – 'So up with the Ddraig Goch, Up with our flag / Down upon the ground we'll never let it drag / Patagonia i'r Cymry shall still our motto be, / Patagonia i'r Cymry, till our people are free'. The entries are full of quotidian rhythms and the sort of tiny threads of incident that make up life's tapestry. 'Visiting friends, drinking *mate*, playing cards and drinking more *mate*'. He goes looking for lost cattle, castrates bulls, salts meat, melts tallow for candles, and accidentally stabs himself in the thigh while trying to kill a bullock.

Inevitably, perhaps, given the tough lives they lived, Randal Phillips also registers the passing of many people. 'Old Williams Howells died this afternoon, poor old fellow was sick for a long time. He was laid up in bed only six days, but it would have been better if he had gone to his grave these last twenty years ago.' One of his neighbours, Gwilym Walters Hughes, drinks himself to death – 'the poor fellow has been drinking too much grog'. On 26 October 1898 he reports how 'those boys have been out on the camp hunting a lion last Sunday and they killed the lion, too, and they said it was a very large one. 'A few days later there's another burial – 'poor Peter Jones', and three days later, 'poor Mr Morris Humphreys'.

There are signs of the coming great flood on 1 February 1899, when it 'came to rain something like of bursting of hundreds of clouds in the sky'. The next day, he is busy 'throwing earth to the top of the roof ... The rain was coming through'. The following day he ventures as far as Drofa Dulog where he sees that Owen Roberts' wheat is 'all under water'. By July, the river is in full flood. On 22 July, Randal reports that:

> The river rose somewhat two feet from last night till this morning, and rising fast all the time. At 8 a.m., the water was coming down the ditch fast, the riverbank had burst, or gone over, in Tir Halen. At all appearance, we shall have a flood all over the valley. At 9 a.m., I called at Schultz's house. When I got there, he was busy moving his family and goods to the hills. The water was just at

his door and at the back of the house. From the top of the house, I could see a lot of people moving away as fast as they could, and the water was coming at the foot of the hills on the north side. In Tir Halen, almost everyone was moving away to the hills. They rescued Adna Davies and his family in Schultz's boat, finding them on top of the corral, but the two chapels have fallen down, and others are destined to do the same.

One of Gaiman's residents nowadays is Milton Rhys, the great-grandson of William Casnodyn Rhys, an ultra-nationalist Baptist preacher from Port Talbot. The grandfather was born here in the valley – David Rhys, a carpenter.

In a newspaper interview with the *Telegraph* on 28 March 2012, Rhys' half-Welsh, half-Argentine identity became apparent, although any talk of the Malvinas made it very clear which side he was on. In April 1982, as a young conscript of 19, he was told by his colonel that he was going to the recently invaded islands on account of his good English (Milton's father was an English teacher). Wearing civilian clothes, with one uniform in his bag, he stepped off the plane in Port Stanley and took up residence in an outbuilding at Government House, the home of expelled governor, Rex Hunt.

Here, Rhys was given the job of monitoring radio broadcasts and relaying orders, allowing him an insight into the campaign. For a week or so he wore his civilian clothes, walking around Stanley trying to reassure the population, though some of the locals took him to be a spy. The locals, known familiarly as Kelpers, were offered new colour televisions by way of a peace offering, but this made the troops angry, as the plane was meant to bring in supplies. (The British also poked fun at the islanders. After getting into the habit of referring to them as Bennies, after the dull-witted character in the television soap opera *Crossroads,* an edict went out from the General Staff ordering the men to stop referring to the islanders in this derogatory way. The men obeyed entirely, referring to them from that day on as 'Not Bennies'.)

General Mario Menéndez had the thankless task of governing the islands as defeat loomed. In his newspaper interview, Rhys recalled him with admiration.

Menéndez was excellent, very intelligent, spoke several languages, very calm, a very good listener. But he was not in charge. He was the political man, not the head of the military operation. He would say: 'Hey you, Welsh soldier, can you play?' And I would play the piano for him, or sing a song.

He was a wise man. When the British arrived, he said: 'This cannot be, it will be a civilian as well as a military massacre.' I was there when Galtieri telephoned and said: 'You are all cowards! Jump out of your foxholes and fight!' Menéndez said: 'My general, you do not know what we are fighting here ...'

Taking tea

Plas y Coed teahouse is right next to the main square in Gaiman. Here, in 1968, Kyffin Williams met Dilys Owen de Jones as she busied herself in her small parlour, feeding her cardinal finches. She told him how she first came to Patagonia, and what life was like for her thereafter:

> There we were, landing at Madryn and nothing, nothing, nothing but desert. Well, I sat down in the dust and tears rolled down my cheeks. Whatever were we doing in this dreadful place, where there was typhus and dead animals and dust and wind. The more I looked around, the more the tears came, and it was all because of my brother, who was sick, that my father brought us here. My brother had tried to lift a heavy weight, and bang went a blood vessel in his chest, so my father sold everything and out we came. After a year, my brother went back and got married. I suppose we just got used to the place. And, oh, it was much, much hotter then, and there weren't so many trees, and it's funny how the weather has changed. The floods were dreadful years ago, and the house was under ten foot of water and I was wet, wet, wet, and that is why I have rheumatism and have to walk with two sticks.

After Kyffin left Gaiman, he ventured as far as Tierra del Fuego, stopping off in Gaiman on his return. There, he found that someone had won a fancy dress competition by masquerading as an artist called Kyffin Williams, presumably sporting a moustache and maybe brandishing an artist's palette!

The tradition of tea-making at Plas-y-Coed started properly in the 1940s and 1950s, when Dilys Owen's friends would call in on her when visiting Gaiman from their farms. She and her second husband, Evan Jones, would make them a substantial tea and they would give her dairy produce and eggs in return. This slowly seeded the idea of establishing a teahouse, of having one's cake and eating it, as it were.

Plas-y-Coed was then taken over by Dilys's daughter-in-law, Marta Roberts de Rees, and nowadays it is run by her daughter, Ana Rees. Ana's great-grandmother came to Patagonia with her family from Bangor when she was about ten, in 1900. Her brother had asthma and couldn't live in Bangor, so most of the family decamped to Patagonia for the sake of his health. Her mother came from a Welsh family, her father from an Italian family who came to Comodoro Rivadavia, where he worked in oil. Her grandmother lost the Welsh language because her mother died when she was young, and she went to live with some South Africans. She learned Afrikaans very well, and spoke it perfectly. (The Afrikaaner colony in Patagonia is a whole other story.) Ana remembers three things about her grandfather – his working in the garden, the way he tended the roses and his yellow cat. She also recalls how he would try to teach her and her sister to play a Welsh hymn on the piano, and remembers trips in the old orange car to the chapel in Treorcki. Sitting on the hard wooden pews, she strained to understand as much as a single word of the service. That discontent must have seeded her later desire to master the language, to finally be able to understand those old, old hymns.

Ana studied for a degree in Welsh in Lampeter, so I had to ask her why she wanted to learn the language, and to degree standard at that. 'As a child, I loved listening to adults talking in Welsh, and I wanted to understand. I felt there was something missing in me, I needed to learn it. I feel complete now. I can read and write it now. *Mágico* is the word. That's what I feel.' She has clearly delighted in journeying through the world of Welsh literature, and her favourite books include Islwyn Ffowc Elis' *Wythnos yng Nghymru Fydd* and Mihangel Morgan's *Dirgel Ddyn*, while her absolute love is *Y Stafell Ddirgel* by Marian Eames.

The *magia* was there in the mantric words 'Croeso i Gymru' as she first crossed the border into Wales. 'I felt that my great-grandmother was with me then, travelling home. She was a big character, but I think there's something in my heart which is like hers'. Ana takes me back to the start of the tea-making tradition in this house, back in 1941.

> There was a farm here, with cherry trees. Something happened to all the trees, they all died at the same time, and they had nothing left to live on. Farming was in the blood. My great-grandfather farmed Pencarlan, near Aberdulais, in the Neath valley, right on top of the mountain. My great-grandmother would go visiting on horseback on Saturday afternoons, and she would make all sorts of cakes, including wedding cakes. Friends told her she should do this for other people, and she could charge for it. This would give her an income. People came, then she built the place where the tearooms stand now. The first part of the house was built in 1887. It was the first tearoom in the area.

Ana explains that teas are different from the ones in Wales, as there are lots of cream cakes, specifically to use up the abundance of milk produced by local herds. She also extols the virtues of *teisen ddu*:

> Every farm had a different recipe for this; each one is similar, but no two are completely alike. Some put more raisins, or more sugar. It's a sort of hybrid between *bara brith* and Christmas pudding. You cook it and leave it for a bit. When I married, I kept a small one for years. One of these can easily last a quarter of a century or more. In fact, eight years ago, a girl came to see my grandmother and they found a piece of cake my great-grandmother had made 36 years previously, and they ate it and it was perfect.

Ana studied Spanish at university, but one summer she came to Gaiman, met her husband Phillipe and never went back. Does she see a future for the language in y Wladfa? With the school, now, there are a 100 people coming to classes at all levels of WLPAN in Trelew and Gaiman. 'I've been teaching WLPAN for three years … three or four courses each year. In Ysgol yr Hendre they're trying to get more parents to come to lessons, so they can shadow their children as they learn the language.'

Ana benefits from having the family treasure trove of books around the place, just as Irma Hughes, editor of *Y Drafod,* benfited from her hermit father Arthur's library in Treorcki. This contained volumes representing some of the world's great literature, with Shakespeare, the poems of Dafydd ap Gwilym and tomes of philosophy and history standing proud next to books in Greek, Latin, Arabic, Hebrew and many other European languages. He spent so much time poring over his books that he had no time to cut his hair, which grew long and would drape and brush across the pages.

The hermit Arthur Hughes was born in Bryn Melyn, near Harlech, on 2 January 1878, and for a period in his youth, worked in a mill belonging to his uncle before going to Llanbedr College. After graduation, he intended to join the ministry, but doubted his own convictions, changed course and became a teacher in Bangor. During this time, he published two volumes about poetry, *Gemau'r Gogynfeirdd* and *Cywyddau Cymru*. Unfortunately, he started to suffer periods of ill health, and after the death of his novelist mother, Gwyneth Vaughan, decided to move to y Wladfa. He is credited with raising the standards of literature in the colony, even though, as a critic, he was berated by some for being too strict.

Arthur Hughes wasn't the only poet in this part of Patagonia. There were a number of others, often autodidacts, or taught by other self-educated bards and versifiers. There was James Pitar Jones, for instance, a tough-boned pioneer who worked the hard land at Tir Halen. He was someone who could freely recite the poetry of Goronwy Owen from memory, and work in three languages. Jones had only ever had three months of formal education in his entire life, but benefited from poetic guidance at the hands of Glan Aeron, another of y Wladfa's bards.

Darkness settles. Unfamiliar arrangements of stars pinprick the sky's velvet. Gaiman is quiet. Arel Hughes de Sarda once recalled a walk, on a quiet night, over the land between Trelew and Gaiman, where the path runs over the hills before descending down towards her farm in Treorcki. She delighted in listening to the sounds of silence, a cricket offering up its small music to the night's silence, while above, the stars inked in what her grandmother used to call 'Jesus' great roof'. When she arrived in the farmyard, the peace would simply envelop her.

Night must fall. Long shadows lengthen further. There are very few ghost stories told in y Wladfa, in keeping with the chapel-going, superstitionless nature of its people. There are country beliefs, of course, and weather sayings, as you'll find in all communities which depend on agriculture for their livelihoods. But there is one cracking ghost story from Gaiman, gathered in one of Mari Emlyn's collections of letters from y Wladfa.

A teacher called Owen Williams had come to live in Trevelin, leaving the love of his life back in Gaiman, fully intending to return there to marry her one day. But she met a man called Elias Owen, and in due course, married him instead. About a year after the wedding, Owen was riding his horse from Trevelin in the direction of Cwm Oer (Cold Valley), where some friends of his lived. The path wove through deep woods and suddenly, on reaching a bend in the path, the horse pulled up, lifting its head and pricking up its ears in alarm. Owen saw, quite clearly, and to his great horror and awe, a coffin, lying on one side of the path, and in it the body of his love, who had married another. No-one is sure whether he lingered or tarried there, or whether the apparition itself simply disappeared, but when Owen reached the sanctuary of his friends' house and said what had transpired, the woman of the house duly noted both the hour and date of the coffin's appearance. A few weeks later, someone came from Gaiman bearing a letter, and from it, Owen Williams came to hear how his former love had died giving birth to her first child, on the exact day and at the precise time he had witnessed the spectral coffin in the forest.

The cemetery

There was considerable anger in Gaiman in 1951 when the government disrespectfully announced they were going to build a new primary school on the site of the town cemetery. The protesting voices were loud and determined, but they had to accede to the government's wishes, having to move the gravestones and the bodies to a new site to allow the school to open. The new cemetery is on a hill overlooking the town, and as I walk there, schoolchildren in identical white coats are marching to class.

Much history is captured in the cemetery headstones, with memorials of young deaths such as six-year-old Nest, the daughter of poet Gutyn Ebrill and his wife Elen, and centenarians such as Elisa Evans de Williams, 1831–1931, and there are a great many inscriptions and poems in Welsh. One headstone connects us with the mid-1870s, when prospective settlers from the United States bought a ship called the *Electric Spark* to travel down to South America. It was a small vessel, weighing 66 tons, which set sail with just 33 passengers, who were sufficiently well off to be able to share ownership of the vessel between them, and be able to carry a good cargo of agricultural supplies and equipment, along with ample items of furniture. The passengers were complemented by six crew, and the man in charge was a redoubtable sea dog called Captain W. E. Rogers, who was born in Pembrey in Carmarthenshire, south Wales on 28 April 1827, and was buried here, in Gaiman. Rogers had fought as a sailor in the battles of Alma, Sebastopol and Inkerman in the Crimean War, winning a shining variety of medals for acts of bravery in the heat of battle.

Standing there, looking at the headstone for this Pembrey sailor, my mind drifts, indeed *has* to drift, to the most remarkable man I have met in my life. My paternal grandfather, Thomas John Gower, came from the same village as Rogers, and became a sailor when he ran away to sea when he was just fourteen years of age. He, too, went to Russia, but much further than Captain Rogers, as *Tad-cu* went all the way to Kamchatka in Siberia as part of the British military involvement of 1918–1920. It was just after the Russian Revolution, and the Bolsheviks were in charge. They had come to an agreement with Germany that it could have control of large areas of Siberia. This made countries such as Britain and France more than nervous, and they would have sent strong forces to impose themselves. But they were countries that had been, and still were, fighting on many fronts, so the British only had 1,500 men to send there. My grandfather stowed away on a boat as a young lad and went to one of the northernmost rims of the world to take these men supplies. He was a great hero of mine in many other ways, an uneducated man who could hold me spellbound with his stories, a coal miner who owned a one-man mine he chiselled out under the waters of the Burry Inlet.

I think he and Captain Rogers would have got on roaringly well – two old sea dogs who would have been most companionable swapping yarns over pint pots in a Pembrey hostelry. I imagine their animated ghosts ordering another jar just before stop tap, or before yet another story starts, another voyage into language, these two men enjoyably well into their anecdotage.

Like Thomas John Gower, Captain Rogers was a hero. The South American voyage hit the rocks, quite literally, at midnight on 26 March 1874, when the *Electric Spark* was wrecked on a sandbar in Tutoya, Brazil.

Miraculously, no lives were lost, and they even managed to carry forty boxes of goods and cargo to shore.

The cemetery is full of Welsh inscriptions and hints at all manner of histories. But I have come here principally to seek out the place where y Wladfa's finest writer is buried. I find it. The name on the grave is, simply, 'Eluned'.

Chapter 13

Eluned

> The Patagonian Welsh are not ones to wring their hands in despair, and proclaim that the world is at an end, bur rather a people who have braved many storms and learned to make the best of things.
>
> (Eluned Morgan, *Dringo'r Andes*)

Eluned Morgan is the Welsh-language travel writer who most resembles Bruce Chatwin, writing tight episodic accounts of her trips to the Andes and her voyages across the South Atlantic. She, like Chatwin, is not averse to being fanciful, or adding little flourishes of detail where they serve her art. When her biographer, R. Bryn Williams, sailed into Buenos Aires, he was expecting to see a light-filled city on a hill, but was surprised to see such a flat assemblage of buildings, albeit with some low hills rising as a backdrop. Then he remembered that he was actually recalling Eluned Morgan's description of the place as a city built on a hill with a lighthouse right on top. He thought this further proof of literary critic and playwright Saunders Lewis' assessment of her as a 'romantic'. In *Crwydro Patagonia*, Williams recounts how Eluned would answer the question why she wrote so many lies quite simply by saying, 'I was making a book'. Williams goes on to suggest that she could be amply forgiven, because the lies she told were so beautiful.

In 1870, Eluned was born at sea, as her surname suggests. 'Môr-ganedig', shortened to 'môr-gan', meaning 'born from the sea'. Her mother, Ellen Griffiths gave birth to her on the roiling seas of the Bay of Biscay, waters famous, or infamous, for the crashing power of their waves. Later in life, Eluned recalled how its was the Atlantic that rocked her cradle, and the sea is a constant undertow in much of her work, not least in the titles of books such as *Gwymon y Môr* (*Seaweed*), and *Ar Dir a Môr* (*On Land and Sea*), with its graphic depictions of wild storms on the Sea of Galilee, or Lake Tiberias, in Israel. As the daughter of one of the principal architects of y Wladfa, the trilingual Lewis Jones, she had much to live up to – not an easy task. It was to be a mantle of responsibility that weighed rather heavily on her shoulders over the years. From him, though, and from his reputation, grew much of her early confidence, but his status within the society of y Wladfa also isolated her. She was brave, tough and resourceful, and there is one image above all others that sums up her courageous spirit. In *Gwymon y Môr*, she recounts how she once travelled through a violent storm, and completely ignored the Irish captain's orders that everyone should avoid the deck and batten down the hatches. Not only did she thwart his commands, but she demanded that she be able to better see the storm and feel it on her skin, so, with his grudging blessing, she was strapped to one of the masts as the wind battered the sails and thrummed through the rigging. She must have been a most perplexing figurehead, this living masthead, lit up by the galvanizing strokes of lightning and the sub-sonic booms of thunder, which seemed to rise up from the ocean deep.

Eluned Morgan's earliest education was received in the small township of Rawson, in a schoolroom built from the cabin of a shipwrecked vessel. This was equipped with little more than a few rudimentary benches. Here, if a child received an extra big piece of slate on which to write, he or she would feel mightily privileged. Her favourite reading was the *Mabinogion*, and later in life, she would be amazed to find that children in Wales hardly knew the tales in which she had encountered Olwen, Gwydion, Blodeuwedd, Pwyll and Pryderi and all the rest of the magical cast she had 'encountered at the base of the Andes'.

At the age of fifteen, Eluned went to Wales, to a school run by a Dr Williams in Dolgellau, and she stayed there, somewhat reluctantly, between 1903 and 1908. Dr Williams organized the establishment on the model of the English public school, and this was a niggling source of irritation to Eluned, not least because she struggled with her broken and elementary English, and was mocked accordingly. The scorn of the English contingent in the school – not to mention the patronizing attitude of the teachers – led to a simmering resentment within her. In time, this had to boil over, and so, one day a veritable procession marched on the head's study and demanded that the head respect their country and their culture. The protests led to Michael D. Jones coming over from Bala to calm things down. Leading the charge was a young lady called Winnie Jones, and it was she who articulated the pupils' complaints to the head. Later, Winnie and Eluned Morgan would become close friends, a friendship which would allow Eluned to get to know Winnie's brother, T. E. Ellis, a distinguished politician. Eluned would also spend a fair amount of time with Michael D. Jones and his family in Llanuwchllyn, and it is surmised that it is through that connection that she came to know Elin Davies, who would eventually become O. M. Edwards' wife. These friends of hers gave her access to some very influential men of the age, who would become personal heroes of hers.

Eluned returned to y Wladfa as a young woman, taking a sea journey that took her to Bordeaux, Lisbon, Rio de Janeiro and Montevideo in Uruguay, a voyage that gave her ample and vivid source material to shape into *Gwymon y Môr*. The years after her return to Patagonia were fruitful ones in literary terms. In 1891, she won a prize in an eisteddfod there, and the following year, a little book was published, featuring an essay by her and two other women. This was despite the fact that there was no literary society, or literary busyness in the Wladfa at the time. Life was too hard and too testing for frivolities, versifying included. One of the three contributors to the book of essays was a teacher from Wales called Esther Emmet. It was through her that Eluned was able to reacquaint herself with the Owen brothers, a pair of publisher/printers whom she had first met in Dolgellau. They had moved to Abergavenny, with Esther Emmet lodging in the house next door. The Owens would publish Eluned Morgan's three principal works, and do so with great care and flair for detail and design, as the three volumes are beautiful and finely wrought.

In 1893, Eluned Morgan was acquiring a new set of skills as a printer. As we know, her father, Lewis Jones, was a printer by trade, and had become a very small-scale newspaper magnate by publishing *Y Drafod*, y Wladfa's daily newspaper. His compositor and setter had been lured away by the prospect of gold in them there Andean hills, so Lewis conscripted Eluned and her cousin Mair to do the work. Meanwhile, Eluned complained that finding Welsh reading material in Patagonia was as difficult as finding nuggets of gold, although she must have read her way through her father's bookshelves, heavy as they were with the works of Homer, Strabo and Pliny.

When she wrote to friends in Wales, her letters would often include a plea to send her some books, any books.

Meanwhile, *Y Drafod* was a spur to both publishing and writing action on her part, and she began to write regularly, sending articles to O. M. Edwards to be published in the magazine *Cymru*. The first of these appeared in 1896, coinciding with Eluned's return to Britain, where she worked copying Welsh manuscripts in the British Library, and spent some of her spare time fraternizing with other young Welsh people who were living in London at the time. But the experience of city life, its pace and crowds, its hemmed-in buildings and urban swagger, were alien and inimical to her, or, as one letter put it, taking her to Chancery Lane was akin to trying to grow moorland heather in a hothouse. She really didn't, and couldn't, appreciate such populous places, the speed, the rain, the smoke and the smog. She didn't set much store in material possessions, in all the trappings of capitalism. Give her the riverbanks of the Camwy any day, where someone could 'get his breath back, and feel, sitting in the shadow of a humble willow and in the sound of the Camwy murmuring as she slowly meanders towards the sea, that *there is a higher* purpose to life than gathering riches'. Little wonder she kept on returning to y Wladfa.

One of those higher purposes she dreamed of was campaigning for a Welsh medium secondary school in y Wladfa, so that local young people wouldn't have to travel overseas to receive a decent education, as was the case with her. After the death of Abraham Matthews, she had to take the reins as editor of *Y Drafod,* at a time when she was already being burdened with a great deal of extra work on the farm as her parents grew older. Then the great flood of 1899 hit the valley, and lives were overturned and literally inundated. She described how the water levels rose like angry waves in the Bay of Biscay in a storm, banging against the walls of the old house until the white spume washed over the roof. It was a period, as she describes it, when nobody saw the sun or the stars for many a long month, such was the persistence of the rain at a time when the contents of entire houses were washed away downstream.

Courtesy of a stint working for the Welsh department at Cardiff Free Library under Ifano Jones, and her experiences, positive and negative, within her own schooling, on her return to y Wladfa, Eluned was an enthusiastic educator. She was also much in demand as a lecturer, and enjoyed peregrinating around Wales, staying with Welsh families and seeing the green land. During her travels, she also got to spend time with O. M. Edwards, who gave her help and advice on editing, which would have been warmly welcomed by Eluned, who thought her own written Welsh, her Wladfa Welsh, was shot through with mistakes.

Taking stock of a reputation

Eluned Morgan's best-known works remain *Dringo'r Andes*, *Plant yr Haul* (*Children of the Sun*), about the Peruvian Incas, and *Gwymon y Môr* which, as we know, details an ocean voyage such as the one she would have undertaken from London to Patagonia. *Dringo'r Andes*, first published on St David's Day 1904, was well and warmly received by critics, swiftly selling at a shilling each, from a total print run of 2,000 copies. Eluned herself had to sell them, so she drummed up the support of 100 subscribers in advance of publication, including David Lloyd George, and an array of poets such as Gwili, Elfed and Alafon.

Dringo'r Andes is composed of 14 tight little chapters, the writing itself conversational and somewhat epistolary. This was quite natural, according to E. Wyn James' insightful account of her life in the magazine *Taliesin*, since the letter form was held in high regard as a genre in y Wladfa, and Eluned set great store by missives, forever admonishing her friends for not sending her more. The letter was, after all, the main form of communication between the colonists and the old country. Indeed, children were given tuition in letter-writing in school.

Parts of *Dringo'r Andes* were published in *Cymru*, a magazine established expressly to encourage ordinary people to read and gain skills in writing. Eluned was a case in point: her writing is crystal clear and reflects the relative simplicity of her own education. Sales of her Andean travelogue were looking good when bad news arrived from Patagonia: her father was very ill. She left Wales just as it was being announced that *Dringo'r Andes* was to become a set text in schools. Eluned arrived home in time to attend to her dying father, who passed away on 24 November 1904. The following year she was back in Wales – a pattern of coming and going that led up to her last visit to Wales in 1912. This one lasted until 1918, and was possibly extended because of the exigencies of war, or the difficulties of travelling at the time. War claimed an unexpected casualty when O. M. Edwards' arguments that young Welshmen should enlist was seen as a betrayal of basic Christian values by his erstwhile friend Eluned. It led to a deep fracture in their friendship, and Christianity became the core of her life for the last twenty years, fuelled by the effects of the 1904 Revival, which saw faith run through Wales like wildfire.

Her handful of books collectively established quite a reputation for Eluned, with Saunders Lewis saying that 'our prose never had a personality as exceptional and rich as Eluned Morgan'. He was referring not only to her unusual upbringing, but also to what the most recent editors of her work, Ceridwen Lloyd-Morgan and Kathryn Hughes, describe as the 'strong and complex personality which is reflected in her work'. She was a Romantic in keeping with many Welsh-language poets such as R. Williams Parry, T. Gwynn Jones and W. J. Gruffydd, who subscribed to this school. In writing in the tight essay form, she was also reflecting works by her friend and mentor O. M. Edwards, who penned books such as *O'r Bala i Geneva* (*From Bala to Geneva*) and *Cartrefi Cymru* (*Welsh Homes*). She is also an ebullient nature writer, with epiphanic descriptions of nightlife in the woods, the perfumed scents of flowers or the convivialities of bees. She tells us about 'majestic mountains and their ever-green, forested mountainsides', flamingos 'dressed in their beautiful colours, basking in the sun' and rivers 'carrying crystal clear water from the eternal ice'. One might even go as far as to say she is a Pantheist, positively Wordsworthian in her relationship to nature and its majesties, the way the lightning wraps its burning arms around an old tree and caresses it to death. She was a keen reader of Thoreau, and there are many places in her writing where you sense the way she craves for her own Walden Pond, its still and healing solitude. She also read Thomas Pennant, the Welsh naturalist, and the Norse sagas, in fact, anything she could lay her hands on: she was nothing if not a voracious reader.

'Or are the ribbons flowing through dawn's skies just lies?' Here she is, Eluned at her most rhapsodic, as she describes the bright procession of daybreak. 'There, the lord of day sends out his missionaries – whoever dressed them so? Some have silver mantles, others have purple and scarlet with edgework of pearl; the occasional maiden in snowy white …'

Some might find the purple splashes in the prose a bit too royal and overwhelming, but her James Joycean raptures and epiphanies show a woman who can find signs of the Creator just as easily in the natural world as in the confines of a chapel or church.

Her last book is seemingly out of the kilter with the others. *Plant yr Haul*, which first appeared in 1915, is not a tight, terse travelogue but rather a history book, chronicling the rise, development and subsequent fall of the mighty Inca civilization of the Peruvian highlands. It has been variously pilloried and dismissed, and the critical jury collectively finds it guilty of authorial misjudgement and of talent misapplied. But she remains the best writer to come out of y Wladfa, a fine chronicler of nature, who would willingly strap herself to the mast in a storm to fully experience the depth and danger, the vim and vigour of life lived to the full.

Chapter 14

Little Nell

> 'I'd better begin at the beginning. My father was a bookseller in the Rhondda in the middle of the last century … There was, in those days, a tremendous demand for Welsh-language books in the valleys, because thousands of Welsh speakers had flocked to the coal mines. Bibles, testaments and songbooks were sold in the main.'
>
> (Ellen Davies, via Marged Lloyd Jones in *Nel Fach y Bwcs*)

My Patagonian sojourn begins to feel like a bit of a literary pilgrimage as, the day after visiting Eluned Morgan's grave, I find myself at Llain Las, a farmstead I'd read about in sufficient detail to have a very pronounced feeling of *déjà vu* when I walk onto the yard. I've not only read about the farm, but also seen it on TV in a documentary about Ellen Davies, a.k.a Nel Fach y Bwcs. Ellen was a friend of Eluned's, so it feels as if I'm following the trail of literary women of y Wladfa.

The current owner of Llain Las, a clean-lined and simple adobe farmhouse, about ten miles from Gaiman, is Edi Griffiths, who works the place with his son Mauricio. Edi is a busy, bright-eyed man with bushy hair, dressed in the sort of blue overalls that are a fashion statement about working hard, their material caked hard. Edi lives in Gaiman town, but farms here, where he grows crops of alfalfa and buys calves from the highlands of the Andes to fatten them up before selling them on. He also keeps Merino sheep, that stalwart breed of the Australian outback. Edi, without stopping working on a range of little jobs, tells me farming is what he knows. I ask him about the farm's previous occupants.

> Yes, this is where John Davies Books and Nel Fach used to live, then it was bought by my grandad, then my father and then by

me. In my *Taid* and *Nain*'s day, they lived here with all of their nine children. There were only three bedrooms, so it must have been a bit of a squeeze. Sometimes someone would sleep outside so there would be more room. Many people would show up and simply sleep in ponchos, sitting down.

The house is in some disrepair by now, not least because salt is eating away at the foundations of the brickwork. Outside, there is an old oven for baking, where, after taking coals out, the bread would be put in. It's the one Ellen used, and I touch it as if connecting with the past.

The bricks of Llain Las were manufactured in self-built ovens. The first houses in the area, Edi explains, were built with bricks made of clay, but nowadays cement is used. He mournfully points out that there are now many empty houses falling into disrepair locally, and there is much to do to restore Llain Las. The roof is made of soil placed over a bed of rushes, some having been replaced with wood or zinc. But the place is immortal as long as books themselves last – the two books which feature, and thus immortalize, this homestead.

Ellen Davies gained the nickname Nel Fach y Bwcs because her father, John, ran a bookshop in Wales before emigrating to Patagonia in 1875 with his family, and his cargo of books. She would eventually return to live in Wales, where her daughter-in-law, Marged Lloyd Jones, fortuitously decided to note down her recollections and write her story in two volumes, the eponymous *Nel Fach y Bwcs* followed by *Ffarwél Archentina*. They are chronicles of a childhood chock-full of incident and *brio*. We hear about her brother Dyfrig's extraordinary present on the occasion of his fourth birthday. It was a pony. Nothing particularly extraordinary about that, I hear you cry, but this pony was called Kingel, after one of the indigenous Indians, and was exchanged by them for two loaves of *bara brith*. Kingel himself was the son of one of the native chiefs, and he taught Nel and her brother to use the *bolas*: she also recalled him singing Welsh in chapel, albeit a tad out of tune, sometimes screeching fit to drown out everyone else. Kingel couldn't read, so he had memorized each hymn.

One of the most tender stories in the book concerns Nel's other brother William, who, one night, heard the sound of a child crying, far out in the wilderness, many miles from anywhere. It was an Indian child, about four years of age, who was wet, cold and coughing incessantly. William tenderly lifted him up and carried him back to Llain Las, where it transpired the child was too weak to stand up. Milk and warmth helped him sleep, although the cough nagged him for a very long time. It turned out that his name was Tugel, and everyone on the farm grew to be very fond of him. Tugel and Dyfrig became firm friends, delighting in riding Kingel around the place. Then, one day the sound of galloping hooves was heard as the two boys raced away, only to be chased by William. On catching them Tugel told William, known familiarly as Dic, 'Tugel cariad Dic', his ungrammatical, but no less sincere way of telling him he loved him. This made the eventual appearance of some Tehuelche people, including his mother, to reclaim young Tugel, all the more painful for all the members of the family. But there was an awful lot more pain on the way. One night, Ellen's mother, in great pain, asked her young daughter to rush to fetch a neighbour, Mrs Jones, but the young girl got lost, snagging on thorns, afraid of night creatures. When she finally returned, she found out that her mother had died giving birth. Later, some Tehuelche calling at the house to ask for bread joined her in mourning the passing of her mother. The leader, Gallech, gave her his poncho as a sign of eternal friendship. Life went on, albeit cruelly. 'After Mam died, I had to learn how to milk all of the cows, seven of them, and that would take hours of my time. The men of y Wladfa milked only infrequently, and neither did they feed the pigs and calves, nor tend any single animal. That was women's work …' The poncho, meanwhile, is now a family heirloom, transported to Wales and kept with pride.

Another testing episode came with flooding of the valley in 1899, which terrified her friend Eluned Morgan as well, and almost inundated them both. Ellen recalled 'running for the hills, hearing children crying, animals braying plaintively and people singing the hymn "O Fryniau Caersalem", the water boiling around us. As I looked back, I could see pitiable creatures swimming against the flow and being carried toward the sea. I heard one home after the other being pulverized by the force of the waters'. The following morning, the whole valley was one big lake, and Bryn Crwn chapel was found to be completely destroyed, as if taken apart brick by brick.

Ellen moved back to Wales in 1900 and found it hard to adapt, even though she lived a long life, dying at the age of 95. However her aching nostalgia, her *hiraeth* for Llain Las and Patagonia, never left her. She is buried in Drefach Felindre, although her heart probably lies elsewhere.

Chapter 15

To the Yellow House

In his book *The Conquest of Nature: Water, Landscape and the Making of Modern Germany*, the Harvard historian David Blackbourn explores the ways in which controlling water, from straightening the courses of rivers to canalizing rivers, including the wildest reaches of the mighty Rhine are, collectively, an expression of the German national character. In a similar way, the building of a system of canals in ditches in Chubut demonstrates a certain gutsiness, a stubborn resourcefulness of character on the part of the Welsh who settled here. The network of man-made watercourses and drainages certainly helped make the colony sustainable and, at times – when they found a world market for their wheat – managed to make it properly profitable.

It was all made possible by accident. In 1866, one of the *Mimosa* pioneers, Aaron Jenkins, had half-heartedly sown some seeds on a piece of land near the place where Moriah chapel stands today, not all that convinced he'd have anything like a viable harvest to show for it. Seedlings speared up from the ground, but then the tiny shoots withered, just as great thunderclouds gathered and a storm emptied huge balloons of water over everything.

The level of the river water rose and rose, threatening to over-run the banks, which made Aaron's wife, Rachel, think that it might be an idea to open up a channel from the river into their fields, to let the floodwaters in. After doing so, they plugged the gap and, even though the river didn't rise again that season, Aaron garnered a fine harvest of wheat. This suggested that the soil wasn't as poor as they had thought, but rather, that more water was needed to produce a bountiful harvest. Other settlers benefited from this knowledge, although the following year, river levels didn't rise sufficiently to allow irrigation.

By the time new immigrants arrived in the period between 1874 and 1875, the community decided to implement the vision of an irrigated valley to the best of their abilities. Over fifty people put in Stakhanovite amounts of labour for five gruelling months, and managed to open up a canal three metres in depth, four metres across and 11 kilometres in length. This was a monumental achievement, especially when one considers that they were creating the canal system without ditching tools more sophisticated than spades and rakes. Not only did they have to dig the channel, but they also had to build up the high sides of the canals. Entire families mucked in, quite literally, opening up further stretches of canal by scooping up the mud, while also planting seeds in the soon-to-be-wetted areas.

In 1878, the flow of the river Chubut wasn't strong or high enough to fill the canals and channels properly, which made them realize they needed to build dams higher up, and corral the waters. They would also needed to create a canal whose bottom was as deep as the river itself. The work of designing it fell to a young engineer, E. J. Williams from Mostyn, Flintshire, and the resulting canal ran straight for 21 miles. As cheese and butter were in short supply at the time, the workers had to subsist on bread alone, which led to this canal being known as Ffos Bara Sych, the Dry Bread Ditch. As other canals were opened, they were each given their nicknames – Three Attempts Ditch, the Petticoat Ditch, Blue Ditch and the Flat Ditch, which started some three miles from Gaiman and was designed to supply water to the Lower Valley. Meanwhile, dam building proceeded apace, the men working like, well, beavers.

One erstwhile dam spanned the river in 1876, utilizing a thousand pounds' worth of wood and iron, not counting the cost of the labour, but this wasn't strong enough to cope with the pressure of the water, and was swept away like a matchstick model by the current. A more redoubtable stone dam was erected near Gaiman in the same year, but this was breached in the middle by the weight of the water.

But for every setback, there was an advance. A new trenching tool, imported from America, eased the work. It was a bit like an enormous spoon pulled by two or three horses, and soon the Patagonians had made their own version. Soon, they were scooping out the earth at a fair rate of knots, and extending the canal system throughout the valley, where, by this time, no fewer than three irrigation companies were working to keep the waters moving. By 1886, the Argentine Government estimated that the three principal canals extended over 187 miles, with thousands of acres benefitting from the replenishing and sustaining wash of irrigation water.

Chacra 233

I am standing canal-ditch side with Ieuan Williams, in the lee of his neat farm, Chacra 233, known familiarly as Casita Amarilla Williams; a neat, yellow house with a bright red roof, a Patagonian farmhouse as if constructed from Lego. With broad sweeps of his arms, almost as if he is conducting the landscape, Ieuan points out the man-made water features that helped tame and fertilize much of the lower Chubut valley, making farmable land out of salty, grey, arid scrub. The water in the main ditch is a deep bottle-green, and moves slowly: this is turgid, treacly, heavy water. The water quality depends on the season, on the rains and on the sun's moistness-evaporating powers.

Ieuan's Welsh moves more briskly the more he talks. It is exquisite Welsh – Spanish inflected, of course, with quiet overtones of William Morgan's Bible. The words are steadily spaced, as if he is moving stones, or writing the words as much as speaking them, veritably building his sentences. Years on, as I transcribed our conversation, the euphony of his diction mixes with the sadness of his passing, a fact recorded in my copy of *Y Drafod*, which came through the post on the very day I listened back to the recording. It makes me glad I met him, the ghost in the voice on tape a genial one, a man willing to take his time with his answers to my many questions.

He points out one of the two principal canal ditches, each one running on one side of the river, then dividing into smaller branches, on both the northern and the southern sides.

> My grandfather used to set out on a Monday, taking enough provisions for the week, and he would spend the whole week opening ditches, joining other men who had often left their wives behind to look after the children. Initially, there had been natural channels they could follow, but increasingly, they had to create ditches on higher ground. They had enough horses by this stage to import machines from North America to clean the channels,

clear them of weeds and so on. Eventually, a company was set up to regularize this and share out the work, and the profit when it came.

A breeze flutters the shimmering leaf pennants of the willows and poplars which grow on the banks of the canal-sides as Ieuan expands on the history of the Camwy Irrigation Company.

> People could buy shares in the company, with voting rights. Bridges were constructed to cross over all the necessary paths, and each farm on this side of the river was divided into 1,000 square metre blocks. The first constructions were pitch pine bridges, which were built to take a fair weight, but then the lorries came, and they had to be strengthened with concrete. The company used to charge six pesos for every hectare they irrigated. A man would come by every summer to measure how much land was watered, and then they would work out how much you owed. The water-men would earn three pesos a day if they worked using shovel and hand, and ten or fifteen if they used horses.

Cleaning by hand, he tells me, was taxing and disgusting work, as one had to stand in the ditch itself and lift the detritus out before compacting it on the ditch-sides, thereby helping to strengthen them. Often, a few farmers would gather together to do the work, bringing a horse and plough, or shovels, or, later, that specialist trenching tool from America – followed by pirated copies – which made the work much easier.

The irrigation system itself involved ensuring that one side of a field was higher than another and levels, or squares, were created, with an earthen hedge around it. Water would be moved from one level to a lower level by opening up the hedge, which would then be closed after the water had flowed in. Square by square, much of the valley would be irrigated in this way, the skill being to ensure that there was enough water to cover the whole area, but not too much either, as it was a precious commodity which had to be used wisely.

Ieuan knows the whole story, and has time to tell it. The shadows lengthen from the poplars as he sketches out the rest of the watery history. The money stayed in the company as shareholders were given credit. That system worked until 1945, when the government intervened, and introduced the *Ley de Agua*, the Water Act or Law. They summarily took over the ditches and canals without notice, and the company lost control of them.

Many farmers felt that the new nationalized company cut back on basic maintenance, so that the river bed was no longer diligently cleared, and neither were the ditches which gradually filled up with dead vegetation from the plants and trees that grew on its sides. Because of this lack of attention, the level of the river rose gradually, and there was less room for water-flow between the canal banks, increasing the risk of flooding. A legal dispute between the company and the government went on for years, and the company was eventually compensated. Unfortunately, inflation had eaten into the value of the money by this stage. The federal government filled the company offices with workers, and employed people to look after the ditches, and the owners, sadly, had no voice in the matter.

Water affected the Welsh in other, more damaging and less benign ways, too. Ieuan tells me about the historical floods that wrought havoc, such as the one at the very end of the nineteenth century that reduced the regional government to functioning from a tent and, according to Governor O'Donnell, 'In a few hours, there has been destroyed in the Chubut valley the work of 34 years of perseverance and strenuous labours on the part of the Welsh who were its founders'.

Sadly, the great flood of 1899 wasn't the only inundation. Another, in 1932, flooded the entire valley, and many families were dispossessed of their homes. As a consequence, many young people left, some heading for the oil fields of Comodoro Rivadavia, some decamping to Buenos Aires – especially young women, who found as work as nurses – whilst others moved much further afield, with some emigrating to the USA.

Nearby is Bod Iwan, the farm where Ieuan grew up. His father, Ifan Owen Williams, came from the slate-quarrying region of north-west Wales, where the Snowdonian foothills are pockmarked by mining. Ifan benefited from a reasonably good schooling, and managed to stay on until he was 16 years of age before moving first to the slate quarries, and then spending two years underground in the coal mines of south Wales. Ieuan tells me, 'There used to be a farm hereabouts called Tyddyn Du. People thought it was because of some blackthorns which grew there, but then we found that out that there's a village called Tyddyn Du in Ffestiniog, so we think my father brought that name with him'.

Ieuan's father sought employment in various places in Patagonia, and moved to Bod Iwan farm sometime before 1918. He married a woman called Gwen Morgan, who was from y Wladfa, of Welsh descent, and they settled in the house that had been built for Llwyd ap Iwan's family. 'That's where we were all raised – two girls and three boys. Owena was the eldest, then Ethel, Gerallt, me and Edmwnd'.

Ifan had come out to y Wladfa when he was 25 years old, following in the footsteps of his brother Richard, who had adventured out to Patagonia two years previously, and had settled in Trelew, where he too was raising a family. Richard was the father of R. Bryn Williams, who penned a small shelf-full of books, including *Y Wladfa* and *Crwydro'r Wladfa*. Ieuan and his siblings worked on the farm from a young age, he tells me:

> We started work when we were thirteen or fourteen, in the summer, of course, then we went to school in the winter until we were sixteen, then back to the farm, if we chose to work there. The girls got married, but we lads stayed on the farm. Over the years, trade changed and other things were sown – *garbanzos* (chickpeas), and some peas too, and they sold well for years until a blight affected the plants. Then we carried on with alfalfa, which grew in value as lorries came to collect it from here to take to the cattle on the flat lands around Comodoro Rivadavia.

Chacra 233 was Ieuan's grandfather's 100 hectare farm to begin with, and it was called Tŷ Newydd. Edward Morgan, originally from Llantrisant, followed his brother Thomas out to Patagonia in the 1870s. He was already married, and he and his wife lived with Thomas for three or four years until they moved to Tŷ Newydd. It was desolate, hard land to farm. As place names such as Tir Halen suggests, the earth is very salty, which severely limits the crops that can be grown. Nevertheless, Ieuan's *Nain* and *Taid* raised twelve children there, and were together for sixty years.

As we stand there, the wind picks up and starts whistling through the *alamos*, the tall poplars that stand sentinel in serried ranks throughout the valley. The Welsh settlers planted these trees as windbreaks and as shelter from the summer sun. It can be a searing 30 to 35 degrees during December, January and February – months of unbroken, unmitigated heat. Ieuan tells me the only brief respite would come at about four o'clock in the afternoon, when a fresh breeze licked in from the sea 40 kilometres away, which in turn freshened the air until sunset at eight or nine o'clock. It was impossible to work in the middle of the afternoon, so workers would have a *siesta*, then start work again when things cooled.

The wind is a constant in Chubut, able to flail the skin off your face when it really whips up, and requiring a stiff backbone in a people to stand up straight in it. Little wonder, then, that we start to talk about the various kinds of winds what bluster, barge and billow through. Ieuan tells me:

> The seasons have changed over the years, but a wind that came from the north was normally a hot wind. The wind comes from the south in the winter, and that's a cold wind, that brings snow. From the west, they're strong winds and can be cold. They come from the Andes, bringing rain, and even snow at times, and then from the east, you get a wind that only blows in the summer. It's a pleasant, freshening wind which sets the zinc sheds clicking at night.

Before we head indoors, Ieuan names some of the local farms – Bod Iwan, Graig Wen, Ffarm Mostyn, after the owner William Mostyn, Llain Las, where Nel Fach y Bwcs lived, Rhymney, Ffarm Isa, Tan y Bryn, Tŷ Croes, Treborth, Cludfan and Tyddyn Du. This last, of course has a direct family connection to Ieuan.

After a few cups of heart-stirringly strong coffee, Ieuan takes me to the nearby chapel of Bryn Crwn, which takes its name from the surrounding area, typified by round hills, *bryniau crwn*. In its heyday, the Sunday school here attracted 100 people, adults and children. Ieuan remembers that there would about sixty people in attendance in the 1930s and 1940s.

> The chapel was full. There were three services – Sunday school at ten in the morning, hymn meeting at two and then people went home for dinner, as most of them lived within three or four miles. Some came back in the evening, especially the older people – the

ones between, say 30 years of age and 50. Then, in the night, a minister would preach and the place would be full to capacity, with over 100 people listening. Some walked here, some came by carriage and some on horseback, especially the young men. That was until the first cars appeared, sometime after 1923, when the Model T Ford came out here. In the 1940s, there were still only ten cars in the area in total.

Now, the carriages are long gone. Cars and trucks have replaced them completely, and buses run throughout the valley. Bryn Crwn chapel now holds services just once a month. Ieuan walks out to the car, letting me savour the silence, and the faint tang of bat droppings in the porch enters my nostrils, ammoniacally. I pick up a hymnal, thumb through its list of nonconformist hits. Outside, the warm zephyr of a breeze gently animates the tamarisk bushes: the sound is like the jazz musician Buddy Rich drumming very, very softly with his brushes. Accompanying, spectral voices drift out into the noon-day heat.

Chapter 16

Waldo Williams and Bod Iwan

Bod Iwan is the adobe farmstead home of the poetically-named farmer Waldo Williams and his family – poetic, because Waldo Williams was also the name of one of the most significant Welsh poets of the twentieth century. But that wasn't the only poetic connection.

Here, I felt I was treading a very well-beaten path to the door. A duo of Welsh troubadour poets, Twm Morys and the late Iwan Llwyd, had been here in 1998 on their South American adventure. In their book, *Eldorado: Llwybrau Dau i Le Diarth,* they wrote about the *asado* they had enjoyed here in the company of the three Williams brothers, Edmwnd, Gerallt and Iwan, the smoke drifting through the leaves while wives Mair and Martha brought in more and more wine. The two poets thanked their hosts by penning a poem in praise of the place, 'Cywydd Mawl Brodyr Bod Iwan', which ends with a line suggesting, or proclaiming, that the whole earth is to be found here.

Bruce Chatwin also visited this farm in Bryn Crwn, not far, as the *chimango* flies, from the town of Gaiman. And he subsequently wrote about it in the classic *In Patagonia,* so Chatwin fans have, in turn, followed him here over the years in droves, dutifully clutching their dog-eared copies of the Picador edition.

I should, perhaps, have clapped my hands outside the door, announcing my arrival, as is, or perhaps *was* the custom in these parts, but the welcome from Waldo is both genuine and warm without any clapping.

Waldo is a very handsome farmer, with a very beautiful wife, and their home, with its high-ceilinged, cool interiors does have something of the Welsh farmhouse about it, as described by Chatwin. It doesn't, of course, have the 'old wooden dressers covered in blue and white ornaments and china dogs, and women who asked if it was true that "the morals had gone down" in the land they still called home'. Anyway, Chatwin's account was as much projection as description. Little wonder it left the Argentine Welsh of the Camwy valley, somewhat aggrieved.

Before we can sit down, Waldo has farm work to do, and I watch him, busy on the land, the sun a fiery pearl overhead. Flocks of *chimangos* follow his every tractor move, acting like black-headed gulls do in Wales. These small vultures fly in flocks and are incredibly social birds. They have no claws on their feet, and walk in a slightly ungainly fashion, like chickens. Or, indeed, lame chickens. But in the air, the elegant vultures turn and veer, swoop and twist like European hobbies, thoroughly deserving the term 'aerobatic'.

Waldo stops to take a draught of water. There are more than the occasional echoes of R. S. Thomas' poem 'Cynddylan on a Tractor' as Waldo climbs back on, seemingly a 'part of the machine' as he rakes his three-disc harrow across the land, his 'nerves of metal and his blood, oil'.

Meanwhile Waldo's three dogs – Goronwy, Caswallon and Parri – lie supine in the shadow of the original wooden wagon that his grandfather had used to cross the Andes. Their master, his eyes fixed straight ahead, steadfastly turns the light brown dirt into die-straight corrugations. The earth is his.

Earlier, when I was writing down the dogs' Welsh names, Waldo had stopped me in my romanticizing tracks by explaining that the name Parri had nothing to do with Wales, but was, rather, an abbreviation of *parrilla*, or barbeque grill. The dog was called Parri because it stank to high heaven from eating sheep intestines.

Waldo has been to Wales, and even played rugby there, turning out for both Dolgellau and Porthmadog fifteens. While in the country, he had had the presumably not-so-rare distinction of being knocked unconscious by the Llanelli and Wales hooker, and subsequent Eisteddfod Herald, Robin McBryde. When Wales next visited Argentina to play the Pumas, word was sent to Robin that Waldo was looking for him! I don't imagine he quaked much in his rugby boots.

Nowadays, Waldo's land is mainly given over to the growing of alfalfa. Sadly, for him, the Welsh colonizers didn't just bring language, chapels and culture with them. One of them inadvertently introduced an agricultural pest species which grows right in the middle of Waldo's alfalfa crops. He shows me the alien invader, unbidden among the cash crops.

It's not a hostile-looking species at first sight. Hoary Cress, known in y Wladfa as *wansi*, was originally sown in the Chubut valley by a farmer called Owen Cadwaladr Jones, who lived on a farm called Pant y Barcud in Dolavon. Jones regularly escaped the bleak winters by travelling to Canada, Australia and sometimes back to his native Wales. On one of these vacations, he'd been struck by the idea of sowing this cress, which produced plentiful seed, for the benefit of the wild birds on his farm. It soon spread everywhere, becoming an invasive agricultural pest, the starch-white flower-heads soon appearing everywhere, and resisting all efforts to get rid of it.

The house, Bod Iwan, dates back to 1910, but the farm itself is much older, showing up on a map from 1886. Waldo tells me about the place's connection with Llwyd ap Iwan.

> In 1886, he worked on the railway line between Madryn and Trelew. After he married, he lived here in Bod Iwan, which had the same name as his father's home in Wales. He lived here for a few years, then they moved to the Andes because he had land in Cwm Hyfryd. They moved then to Nant y Pysgod, where he was murdered. This present house, Bod Iwan was built for the family a year after his death in 1909, and they lived here for two years. His wife got married again, to a Mr. Lewis, who lived three kilometres from here, then they moved to live at Craig Wen. One son, Mihangel, stayed here, then my grandfather rented the farm for nearly forty years.
>
> My wife and I moved here in 1998, because we wanted our two sons to have the same experience growing up as we did. I moved to Trelew to study, and then came here. It connects me with the place and with the family. I'm giving them an education, and then they'll have the choice to farm or not.
>
> Here, it's traditional production – alfalfa, sheep, cows. The Hereford is the commonest animal on farms around here, although there are also some Angus. In terms of sheep we have Hampshire Down although the merino is also common.

Waldo says they're certainly beneficiaries of the success of the early settlers with regard to irrigation.

> The water for the house comes from town, but the irrigation water comes from the *ffos*, the ditch, or from underground. The farm takes water from the northern main ditch, from a secondary channel. We go to a dam a kilometre from here, open the dam and take what we need. We pay the water company around thirty pesos per hectare per year, so not really a significant amount.

Waldo remembers Bruce Chatwin coming here, not least for what he was wearing at the time.

> Bruce Chatwin came here, and met my brother's friend. My family brought him here. Yesterday, a man from Uruguay came here just because of Chatwin. He met my grandmother, Gwen Morgan Williams, and Edmwnd. I was eleven when Chatwin came here. He was wearing shorts. In 1974, that was very strange, to see a man in shorts, and I was very surprised. He came to Bod Iwan, but no-one knew he was planning to write a book. He also stayed here, then went to chapel, and went to Llain Las with Edi. He was here a few days.

What he subsequently wrote spawned quite a reaction, according to Waldo. 'Some readers were angry and some not. He doesn't tell the truth, for some people at least. He didn't speak Spanish, so he must have been a very, perceptive man, because he knew things anyway ...'

It was Christmas Day when Bruce's guide Enrique, subsequently renamed Anselmo in Chatwin's work, took the young author to visit Waldo's uncle Edmwnd, or Edmundo Williams' home here at Bod Iwan, where he also met his brother Gerallt. They showed him around their adobe house, allowing him to see and photograph a collection of Welsh relics, which he appraised with those Sotheby's-trained eyes of his. 'The two Sheffield-plate trays – they were wedding presents – were on the mantelpiece, and the two pottery pug-dogs. On either side of the dresser were tinted photographs of her [Gwen Morgan Williams'] husband's parents, who came out from Ffestiniog. They had always hung there and they'd hang there when she'd done'.

After allowing Chatwin to create his mental inventory of the house and contents, Gerallt took him to the nearby church of Bryncrwn in his 1958 Dodge, even though Chatwin disliked cars because 'the spirit of generosity already threatened by the horse, evaporated entirely with the motor car'. That said, plenty of people offered him the generosity of a lift on his peregrinations, even though he might prefer to walk.

In Chatwin's biography, Nicholas Shakespeare explains that 'Edmundo took intense exception to the few lines Bruce wrote about him. It is not too much to say that they changed his life. His resentment illustrated a sentiment widely held: whereas V. S. Naipaul insulted the important, powerful people when he wrote about Argentina (in *The Return of Eva Perón*), Bruce upset the little people, those who could not answer back'.

So what were Chatwin's transgressions? Well, to begin with he changed people's names, calling Gerallt Ivor. He also gave Edmundo a new name, re-baptizing him as Euan and going a little further than describing him just as a bachelor, hinting, with the most delicate innuendo and suggestion, that he might be gay too. This made Edmundo nothing short of apoplectic, according to Shakespeare. 'He had received this stranger politely. He knew nothing about appearing in a book and suddenly, two years later, other strangers start coming to his door, asking personal questions he does not want to answer. Through his fleeting appearance in *In Patagonia,* people have assumed an intimate knowledge of him he was rarely prepared to give anyone'.

Bruce, in fact, cast Edmundo as himself, so that his own actions and attitudes toward the gay Enrique were ascribed to the Welsh farmer. With these things in mind, a seemingly straightforward description of Edmundo / Euan by Bruce starts to generate new nuance:

> 'No,' Mrs Davies said. 'Euan hasn't married yet, but he sings instead. He's a wonderful tenor. He made them all cry at the Eisteddfod when he carried off the prize. Anselmo was the accompanist, and they made a fine pair. Oh, how that boy plays the piano. I'm so pleased Euan gave him the nice plate for Christmas. The poor thing looks so lost and lonely, and it's no fun living in Chubut if your family doesn't help.

So what does Waldo make of Bruce's descriptions of Bod Iwan and of his relatives? Cautiously diplomatic, he sees both the positive and the negative in Chatwin. It's also the first time in our conversation that he switches from speaking English to Spanish, a telling switch of the tongue.

> He's very perceptive in some things – he recovers certain details. Probably they weren't said exactly how he wrote them, and in this case there are certain things that he perceives which aren't as they should be. He sometimes makes mistakes. His sensuality, in the way he interpreted certain things, perhaps makes them bigger than they are and, in some cases, I think he treats people badly. He changes some people's names, but not others … But people know who they are. We don't know his whole journey, but he dedicates a lot of his book to Gaiman and its Welsh colony – partly because it's more interesting, but also because he found a way of communicating. Quite a few people here spoke three languages, so that allowed him to communicate with them.

Nicholas Shakespeare, too, quite naturally, puts a positive gloss on things, suggesting that the book has had a liberating effect, which in turn attracts tourists, an effect which can be measured by comparing the two tearooms set 'within a dusty red grid' in Gaiman in 1991 with the seven tearooms in 1995, when Princess Diana stopped by for cakes in the ranch-style Caerdydd. Whatever people may think of Chatwin, he did help put the place on the map. And pinpointed the Welsh on it.

Chapter 17

The Welsh in Chatwinland

Bruce Chatwin was a deeply gifted, if problematic author. His reputation built very quickly in his lifetime, and when one great writer sings the praises of another, it's often time to pay full attention. Many writers praised Chatwin, from Graham Greene to Paul Theroux. In W. G. Sebald's collection, *Campo Santo*, there's an insightful gem of an essay called 'The Mystery of the Red-Brown Skin: An Approach to Bruce Chatwin'. Here, the great Sebald lists, pretty comprehensively, the ingredients of Chatwin's books. 'Their structure and intentions,' he avers, 'place them in no known genre', containing, as they do, 'anthropological and mythological studies in the tradition of Lévi Strauss' *Tristes Tropiques*, adventure stories looking back to our early childhood reading, collection of facts, dream books, regional novels, examples of lush exoticism, puritanical penance, sweeping baroque vision, self-denial and personal confession – they are all these things together'.

Sebald's essay title refers to a small scrap of fur, possibly from a giant sloth or a mylodon, which was kept in a pillbox, a Chatwin family heirloom. This sloth-scrap, something exotic found in a locked cupboard, is, for Chatwin, a real fetish, being an 'object without any real value, but desirable in great measure, which can thus inflame and satisfy a lover's illicit fantasy'. Sebald suggests that there is something of a fetishistic greed about Chatwin's mania for collecting stories and then 'turning the fragments he found into significant mementoes endowed with a wealth of meaning, reminding us of what we, as living beings, cannot reach'. Sebald goes on to suggest that the fact that Chatwin tended so much that way, creating or curating in his writing a sort of museum of extraordinariness, goes some way to explaining why his work was read far beyond the frontiers of Britain. 'The universality of his vision,' Sebald posits, 'lies in the way his descriptions evoke the recurrent themes of our imagination – an account, for instance, of an extra-territorial region where a community of Welsh settlers who emigrated over a hundred years ago still sing their Calvinist hymns, and where, under an ice-grey sky, the wind constantly blowing through the thin grass stunts the trees and bends them to the east'.

The Welsh settlers were just some of the rich parade of people that Chatwin, an *intense* traveller, observes and, at times, mythologizes in this wind-parched land. Some are historical but, as in the case of Butch Cassidy and the Sundance Kid, already near-mythological. This notorious duo, and some of their accomplices, came to hold up banks in South America when US bank jobs became simply too dangerous. In *In Patagonia*, we also encounter the Sect of the Brujeria, which made waistcoats from dead Christians, Thomas Bridges, who made it his life's work to construct a dictionary of the Yaghan Indian language, and the unsuccessful anarchist Simon Radowitzky, among many colourful others. The book, originally entitled *At The End: A Journey to Patagonia* gathers all manner of such stories in such a way that Chatwin managed to change the very idea of what travel writing could be, seemingly unshackling it from the forms, foibles and traditions of the past. It is a travel book where the traveller isn't centre-stage: it's not a first-person narrative. Neither is it complete, so whereas some travelogues offer lists and landscapes, detailed portraits of people met and the histories of the places passed through, Chatwin leaves gaps, hints at what's been left out, gives a partial, impressionistic account in sentences that seem cut and trimmed with a scalpel. So while some travel writers are baggy, their prose dragging along behind them with their luggage of facts, Chatwin travels light, a rucksack on his back, with just some clothes and a half-bottle of champagne – for emergencies only – passing through, moving on. In his prose, as in his peregrinating life, the nomadic restlessness that engaged him, or obsessed him intellectually, propelled his feet forward too, through dust and rain, sun and storm.

Chatwin was an inveterate walker. As he himself said, 'My god is the god of walkers. If you walk hard enough, you probably don't need any other god'. Walk on.

Lifelong fascination

Chatwin knew of Patagonia even as a small boy. One day in school, poring over a map, trying to decide on the safest place to hide in the event of a cobalt bomb, he plumped for Patagonia, especially when he coupled its remoteness with the information in the wind chart, showing how prevailing winds would dissipate radiation fallout. Plus, his distant relative, Charles Millward, had settled in that part of South America, which meant that he, too, was safe from the bomb. Later, when Chatwin was studying archaeology in Edinburgh, his lecturer, a Dark Ages specialist called Charles Thomas, first kindled Chatwin's interest in the Welsh settlement in Patagonia, whilst also setting him essays on the pre-history of buttons, scissors and trousers, so that Chatwin could see how wrong we can sometimes be by making the wrong inferences from material objects.

One could get it pretty wrong by believing in a paper object Chatwin claimed to have sent to Magnus Linklater, the editor of *The Times*, namely a telegram saying crisply 'GONE TO PATAGONIA FOR FOUR MONTHS'. As Nicholas Shakespeare points out in his biography of Chatwin, the message was probably relayed in a letter he sent to Francis Wyndham, who recruited him to *The Sunday Times* in 1972. The letter, posted from Peru, gave the explanation: 'I have done what I threatened / I suddenly got fed up with NY and ran away to South America / I have been staying with a cousin in Lima for the past week and am going tonight to Buenos Aires. I intend to spend Christmas in the middle of Patagonia / I am doing a story there for myself, something I have always wanted to write up ... it could be marvellous, but I'll have to do it in my own way'. Chatwin wanted, more than anything, to follow the story of his cousin Charlie's piece of petrified skin. This had been criminally thrown out in a house move in 1961.

The allure of Patagonia had been deepening for Chatwin over many years, not just its cobalt bombproof qualities, but also the qualities of its people, described in his sprawling university manuscript, *The Nomadic Alternative*. Charles Thomas' lecture about the Welsh in Patagonia still resonated, as did Darwin's reaction to the Yanghan Indians of Tierra del Fuego. Added to that was a chance viewing of two gouache maps of Patagonia painted by the Irish architect Eileen Gray, which prompted him to tell her that Patagonia was one of the places he'd most wanted to go to.

The place, or the *idea* of this remote place, most certainly had him in its thrall. In New York, he couldn't stop talking about Patagonia, and about his cousin's scrap of prehistoric skin, to the extent that his agent, Gillon Aitken, said he should simply go for it. And so he did, arriving in Buenos Aires at a nervous, uncertain time in the history of a country that had already had enough dark and jittery decades.

President Juan Perón had just died, leaving his widow, Isabel, at the helm as Argentina began its dark descent into torture, terror, military rule and widespread labour unrest. Chatwin would spend three and half months out there, down there, charting a huge southern sweep of country and, in the process, mapping his own inner terrain as a person, as an astute, imaginative observer, and as a travel writer. In the latter case, he would end up staking a claim to the whole bally territory, making it very nearly his own.

So, for Bruce Chatwin, Patagonia isn't so much a place as a tapestry of uncommon inhabitants and daring mythmakers who have lived in this southernmost region of South America. In Chatwin's hands, Patagonia is rendered as a pointillist panorama of people dotted here and there among great empty wastes, consisting largely of madmen, dreamers, everyday eccentrics, isolates and hermits who are marooned on huge *estancias* or in their own shells. Some drink, some think deeply, meditatively and usually longingly, of home. As he himself says in a letter to his wife Elizabeth,

> You would think from the fact that the landscape is so uniform and the occupation (sheep-farming) also, that the people would be correspondingly dull. But I have sung 'Hark the Herald Angels Sing' in Welsh in a remote chapel on Christmas Day, have eaten lemon curd tartlets with an old Scot who has never been to Scotland, but who makes his own bagpipes and wears the kilt to dinner. I have stayed with a Swiss ex-diva who married a Swedish trucker, who lives in the remotest of all Patagonian valleys, decorating her house with murals of the lake of Geneva. I have dined with a man who knew Butch Cassidy and other members of the Black Jack Gang. I have drunk to the memory of Ludwig of Bavaria with a German whose house and style of life belongs rather to the world of the Brothers Grimm. I have discussed the

poetics of Mandelstam with a Ukrainian doctor missing both legs. I have seen Charlie Millward's *estancia* and lodged with the peons drinking *mate* (with which I have a love-hate relationship) till 3 a.m. I have visited a poet-hermit who lived according to Thoreau and the Georgics. I have listened to the wild outpourings of the Patagonian archaeologist who claims the existence of a) a Patagonian unicorn and b) a protohominid in Tierra del Fuego (*Fuego pithicus patensis*) 80 cm high.

In a relatively short span of time, Chatwin garnered a fantastic amount of stuff for a book, 'from the Anarchist (yes, Bakunin-inspired) Rebellion of 1920, to the hunting of the Black Jack Gang, Cassidy, etc., the temporary kingdom of Patagonia, the lost city of the Caesars, the travels of the Musters, the hunting of Indians, etc. Everything I need …'

Everything he needed. Although, given his amplitude of material and vast array of stories and characters, *In Patagonia* should be a doorstep of a book, it is, in fact, a rather slender tome. It is written in 97 short chapters (some barely a page long), that Chatwin himself likened to photographs that capture a decisive moment.

Cutting back

Susannah Clapp, Chatwin's editor at Jonathan Cape, his very enthusiastic publishers, had the job of reducing the text with its 'characteristic style, a hovering between fact and fiction; a combination of a very spare syntax and short simple sentences, with a rich, flamboyant vocabulary, lots of arcane words, lots of peculiarities and a non-chronological, rather elliptical structure'. Clapp had to do her best to maintain the structure Chatwin called 'Cubist – lots of small pictures tilting away and toward each other to create this strange, angular portrait whilst introducing a sense of progression and drive'. Between them, they managed to hone down the prose and burnish it too, and the critical response was positive beyond, with the likes of Paul Theroux and Jack Lambert choosing it as their Book of the Year, while a stellar cast of authors, including Grahame Greene and Patrick Leigh Fermor, wrote to congratulate him. But there was still the little problem of veracity. The writer and war correspondent Martha Gellhorn, who was once married to Ernest Hemingway – and, incidentally, lived in a cottage in

Wales for some fifteen years – saw many similarities between Hemingway and Chatwin. Both had a wonderful memory, wrote in crisp and carefully structured sentences, used repetition and more repetition, and they were both also mythomanes. 'They are not conscious liars. They invent to increase everything about themselves and their lives and believe it. They believe everything they say'. But that still didn't mean they didn't lie.

Those 'lies' hurt people in the Welsh community, hurt some of them to the very quick. People who had never been properly considered found themselves not only written about, but scrutinized, fundamentally assessed. Chatwin's reductivist technique of summing up a whole life in a few brief lines had a scalpel sheen to it, and left blood. In Gerallt Williams' case, reading about himself in Chatwin's book was like hearing his voice played back for the first time on a tape recorder: he didn't recognize it as his own, he didn't believe it was him. And to compound his crime, Chatwin hadn't asked permission, hadn't even revealed he was writing a book when he visited Gerallt's home, so it was a sort of transgressive eavesdropping of the most intimate kind, with each fact garnered from the unwitting subject and then placed in the book a small betrayal. Luned Roberts de González' son, Fabio, suggested that someone should write something about the English who visit the place, brandishing their dog-eared copies of *In Patagonia* like bibles. Gaiman museum director Tegai Roberts told Marcus Tanner, author of *The Last of the Celts*, that 'we are all very surprised by the book … so superior, looking down on us … a very *English* way of looking at things'. Her sister Luned's vexation was with one of the photographs Chatwin took of a Welsh family, looking poor, dowdy and dishevelled, placed alongside a photograph of an Argentine family. 'This family was not photographed in their house. It was obviously taken in a *barn*!'

Once told, stories often recur in Chatwin. Butch Cassidy and the Sundance Kid, for instance, are revisited a number of times as Chatwin revives differing accounts – first, they die in a shootout in Bolivia, then they live quietly in the US after propagandizing that they were killed, then they're a couple of outlaws in the Chilean Andes. The stories often mix and meld together, sometimes contradicting each other, creating a meshwork, a tapestry, a tightly-patterned quilt.

These stories give *In Patagonia* a surprising range, allowing Chatwin to quickly change keys and register from the mythic to the realistic, from the allegorical through the comic to the tragic. While discussing the Sect of the Brujeria, for instance, Chatwin's prose takes a Borgesian turn:

> No-one can recall the memory of a time when the central Committee did not exist. Some have suggested that the Sect was in embryo even before the emergence of Man. It is equally plausible that Man himself became Man through fierce opposition to the Sect. We know for a fact that the *Challanco* is the Evil Eye. Perhaps the term 'Central Committee' is a synonym for Beast.

At other points, as when Chatwin is recounting the story of a failed anarchist or other type of political idealist, the stories feel something like the flyover biographies found in John Dos Passos' *U.S.A. Trilogy*. They crisply summarize a life in the span of a few pages, and short as these vignettes are, one can't help but feel melancholy over the inevitably sad fate doled out to these activists, these lemming-like anarchists, who seemingly had to follow their beliefs over a precipice into oblivion.

As with the people, so too Chatwin's penetrating descriptions of the land, which come in the form of sharp phrases, or via short paragraphs or a few explosive sentences. They are snapshots, not panoramas for, as the author once explained to his fellow travel writer Colin Thubron, 'I was determined to see myself as a sort of literary Cartier-Bresson going SNAP, just like that'. So Chatwin finds Patagonia a place of 'vicious' sunsets in 'red and purple', in which 'damp whiskey had bitten rings into the French polish'. Snap. It has towns of 'shabby concrete buildings, tin bungalows, tin warehouses and a wind-flattened garden' and train stations with a 'photo of a soft, middle-class boy with slicked-down hair, wanted for murdering the Fiat executive'. Snap. The beach is 'grey and littered with dead penguins'. A Welsh woman's dialogue encapsulates her character: 'I can't move, my dear,' she called through. 'You'll have to come and talk to me in the kitchen … I can't move an inch, my darling. I'm crippled. I've had arthritis since the flood and have to be carried everywhere.' Her taciturn son is snapped up in a couple of descriptive sentences: 'He ate too much cake for his own good. He called his grandmother "Granny", but otherwise he did not speak English or Welsh'. Chatwin compacts, summarizes, selects most judiciously, then sets off the flashbulbs. Still, Chatwin never comes off as heavy-handed, always retaining the plausible excuse that he is simply describing what he found.

Unlike most travel writing, Chatwin is hardly ever present in the book other than in a couple of samples from his journal, or when he'll offer an opinion such as 'albatrosses and penguins are the last birds I'd want to murder'. This oddball opinion is one of the very rare occasions when Chatwin allows himself to intrude directly into his restrained, pared-back, almost clinical prose.

> Walked all day and the next day. The road straight, grey, dusty, and traffic-less. The wind restless, heading you off. Sometimes you heard a truck, you knew for certain it was a truck, but it was the wind. Or the noise of gears changing down, but that also was the wind. Sometimes the wind sounded like an unloaded truck banging over a bridge. Even if a truck had come up behind you wouldn't have heard it.

Here Chatwin, always the nomad, wanders in his writing, and wonders at wandering and its pleasures, whilst also pondering the point or pointlessness of getting lost, or moving without direction. Yet these are all part of the allure of coming here. 'Patagonia is the farthest place to which man walked from his place of origins. It is therefore a symbol of his restlessness'. He argues that the redaction, and later selection of the various stories concertinaed into his book all tie in with this: 'All the stories were chosen with the purpose of illustrating some particular aspect of wandering and/or of exile: i.e., what happens when you get stuck'. This is an outgrowth of Chatwin's personal philosophy on humanity, as recounted by Sybille Bedford in *The New York Review of Books*, who said, 'he has a horror of houses, possessions, fixed abodes, counting himself naturaliser one of the nomads. He appears to believe that settlement is unnatural and degenerative for humankind'.

In Patagonia is the kind of book one would expect to get from someone so committed (at least nominally) to nomadism. In its essential plotlessness, its tumbling jumble of stories, travels, and people and places, it embodies the feelings of restlessness and wandering. Necessarily lacking much of a central narrative, the book nonetheless propels a reader forward with its episodic, short chapters and Chatwin's sharp prose, that rarely lingers on any detail for more than a few sentences. It is rightly viewed as a groundbreaking work in literature – travel or otherwise – a book described by the *New York Times* as 'a little masterpiece of travel, history and adventure'.

Chatwin arrived in Gaiman on Christmas Eve 1974. The local schoolteacher, Albina Zampini, whose father had arrived on one of the waves of emigrants who drifted in in the 1870s, realized that Chatwin was a man alone in a convivial season, and invited him to her sister Vally Pugh's house, where there was a party in full swing. 'Poor chap, he didn't have any presents, so I gave him a linen handkerchief. He was eating *turrón,* a candy, which he said reminded him of the mylodon. The main subject on his mind was that giant sloth'.

Chatwin wasn't just given presents. He was also introduced to a young musician whose real name was Enrique Fernández, although Chatwin transmuted this into 'Anselmo', who had a near-genius ability to play Chopin like, well, Chopin.

When Chatwin strayed away from truth in his travelogues, real people, with real feelings, got hurt. As we know, he had upset people in the lower valley, and he didn't leave the Andean Welsh unscathed either. Clery Evans, granddaughter of the legendary John Daniel Evans, still bristles at the description of her father, Milton, as a drunken, clownish sot who would yell out, demanding, 'Gimme another horse piss' every time he wanted another beer, before 'draining the bottle'. Chatwin also redacts a story Milton told him about sheep scab, with an off-colour punchline, but goes one stage further when he suggests that Milton tells the story over and over again. Little wonder his daughter Clery is aggrieved, still hurting after all these years. She thinks Chatwin's lack of Spanish led to a lack of sophistication. Her view of him is splenetic, the views of a cultivated, bookish woman who still feels the slight to her loved one, and dismisses Chatwin like sweeping a fly off her best china. 'Insignificant, a small insignificant man, dull and charmless. He was interested in people only if they could help him, or supply picturesque material. Or if they had good bodies like the Bolivians'.

Chapter 18

Naming the Land

Just as the aboriginal peoples of Australia sang the land into being, so too did the Welsh name their new homeland, with the map being full of euphony, story and information. And when they moved to Patagonia, the Welsh took some of their names for land features and farms with them. Luckily, Isabel Laporte collected names of farms for an MA thesis in the 1990s at Bangor University, with about three quarters of those collected being in the lower Chubut valley.

Most of them are no longer used, for two principal reasons. According to Argentine law, when one parent dies, the property is divided equally between the remaining spouse and the children. Thus, farms become subdivided, and often the name is lost into the bargain. Also, the slow decline in Welsh supremacy saw Welsh names being displaced or replaced by Spanish ones. Even the early Welsh settlers would eventually use Spanish names, or Hispanicized versions of Welsh originals such as *La Galesita*, or little Welsh one. Similarly, a sheep farm on the Valdés peninsula called Quilimbay is an adaptation of the Welsh *celyn bach*, their name for a native plant that grows there. Similarly Llyn y Gŵr Drwg – Devil's Lake – has today transmuted into Laguna del Diablo. Some names pass straight from the Welsh to the Spanish, such as Rhyd yr Indiaid becoming Paso de Indios.

Pant y Ffwdan became Partafuden, a valley where some of the settlers almost got lost when searching for gold. Sychlyn, the Welsh name for a dry lake, became Laguna Seco, a place between Telsen and Martires. Pico Thomas, meanwhile, is a mountain named after John Murray Thomas, and the name is still used for this lofty peak.

In the area west of Gaiman, settled by second or third wave immigrants – many from the USA – there were also English names, such as Hyde Park, that came there courtesy of Gwenllian Davies, who had in turn moved there from a place with the same name in the US.

The story of this farm is woven into the tapestry of texts that make up Brith Gof's haunting theatre piece, *Patagonia: Breuddwyd yn yr Anialwch*. In Scene 3, stalwart company member Lis Hughes Jones recounts how, when she was in Patagonia, she met the two sons of John Davies.

> If you travel on Ruta 25 which runs straight from Trelew to the Andes, 15 miles beyond Gaiman and just before you reach Dolavon, you will see a tyre half-buried in the roadside. On a smear of white paint and stencilled in red are the words Hyde Park. Turn off through the sand dunes and there is a single-story farm house of that name … It was in 1875 that John Davies arrived in Chubut from the coalfields of Hyde Park, Pennsylvania with all the ingenuity of the pioneer, and it was with the help of Thomas Puw (Gaiman), the architect of Tabernacl, Trelew, that the house was built: from mud, straw, rolls of sackcloth, home-made bricks, odd lengths of timber. It's still there. In fact, it's all still there. In the yard is every implement ever used – wagons, reapers, rakes, threshing drums. In the barn – scythes, horse tackle, *bolas*. In the parlour – Indian saddle blankets, Captain Rogers' sextant, an early Singer sewing machine, all in order, from first to last.

Of the Welsh names for farms, Isabel Laporte notes that roughly half of them are names from Wales, ones carried over just the same as goods, and the other half original names created in y Wladfa. Some came from further afield such as Castell Oneida (Oneida Castle, after Oneida, New York State). Names such as Antur, Gobeithfa, Rhyddid and Rhagluniaeth (Adventure, Place of Hope, Freedom and Providence) collectively tell us something about the spirit of the early colonists. Place names feature other essential qualities: *ymdrech*, *cethin*, *egni* and *ffyrnig* – struggle, unyielding, energy and fierce – reflecting, perhaps, the hardships they endured, and what it took to stay here.

Some names are in combinations not found in Wales, such as Bod Amlwg and Bryn Afallon – a reference to the Celtic paradise of Avalon, or more prosaically, to a hill of apples – Dolantur, Maes y Gamlas, Pant y Brwynog, Tŷ Zink or Tyddyn Morlaes. Other placenames were slowly subsumed, such as Aber Gyrants from the Welsh word for currants, *cwrens*, the name for what is now called Rio Corintos. The meaning and origins of some names are not so clear, such as Valle de los Altares – this may come from the Welsh word *allorau* (altars), describing the odd features of a range of hills, or may simply come from the Spanish. Meanwhile Doz Pozos (Two Wells) used to be known as Ffynnon yr Allwedd, the first well encountered on Hirlam Ffyrnig when travelling north toward Rio Negro.

There are many places that use the prefix 'Bod' – a permanent place to dwell – which is then qualified with the name of a person, so that we have Bod Iwan, Bodarthur, Bodgwilym, Bodowen, Bodruffudd, or otherwise qualified with an adjective suggesting other qualities of the place, so it could be beautiful or the view might be clear, or lonely – such as Bodamlwg, Bodeglur, Bodhyfryd, Bodlenog or Bodunig.

Some of the river names have flowed away, such as Afon Eira (Snow River), now known by its Indian name of Lepa, or Avon Ioan (John's River), now called the Tecka. But some persist, running over the map. Bagillt is the name of a stream south-west of Trevelin, initially discovered by one Edward Jones from the town of the same name in Flintshire.

Sometimes, a single incident gives rise to a name. Bocs Gin Mawr and Bocs Gin Bach are places near Paso de Indios, where an accident led to the loss of two boxes of gin. The gin in question was apparently sold to the indigenous people, who then partied hard, indeed spiritedly, and today the two places are known as Cajón de Ginebra Grande and Cajón de Ginebra Chico.

The name of Bryn Merched (Women's Hill), in the Bryn Gwyn area, is a bit of a joke. The man who lived here never married, and was known as Thomas Hen Lanc or Thomas Bachelor. There were other placenames or personal names that showed the Welsh had a sense of humour. There were nicknames, of course, some hard to understand, such as Dai Creadurbyw (Dai Livingcreature), while Ned y Ffos (Ned the Ditch), is a little easier to fathom. The same impishness is at work in the name Parc yr Esgob, (Bishop's Park), the name popularly used for the house where the Rev. Abraham Matthews lived, which was therefore more of a manse!

Drofa'r Llofrudd (Murderer's Bend)

The first martyrdom in the colony came at a time when prisoners were kept in Punta Arenas, 800 miles away, in the far south of y Wladfa. One day a riot broke out, and many prisoners escaped, killing several of their jailors. Later, one of the prisoners showed up in a place called Trebowen, and Aaron Jenkins, originally a Merthyr man, and a poet and huntsman, was asked to catch him and take him to the cells. On his way up the valley, Aaron met two Welshmen who had already managed to capture the man. Aaron insisted he could take him the rest of the way himself. The man had been disarmed but he wasn't chained, and when they were almost within sight of Rawson, the escaped prisoner plunged a knife into Aaron's back. While he lay supine on the ground, the prisoner stabbed him again before stealing his horse and equipment and making a run for it.

On discovering the murdered man, posses of young men were swiftly dispatched, with one group heading in the direction of Punto Ninfas, another to Madryn, the third heading for the coast and the other proceeding along the valley. This last party managed to get on the murderer's trail the following day, tracking him for miles in a northerly direction before heading west, hugging the hills.

They then visited the house of Siencyn Richards, who told them that the man had exchanged Aaron's horse for one of Siencyn's best beasts. On they went, doggedly tracing his progress back through the valley, and hearing how he had passed through Gaiman at dawn. Then his trail seemingly evaporated, so they placed men in strategic places to guard the various fords across the river. Near one called Rhyd Bowen (Bowen's Ford), a little house lay empty, and before daybreak, one of the posse members heard a door squeak on its hinges. He surmised that the fleeing man had hidden his horse in the house overnight. The pursuer ate a hasty breakfast and descended on the house, but it was found to be empty, though he picked up the trail again and followed it down to the river, where he started sweeping through the lush grasses and bankside vegetation. And then he spotted him. The man threw himself onto his horse, a knife between his teeth, but before he could make his getaway, he was shot through the throat.

On hearing this, the other men swiftly made their way to the place, where every single one them shot a single bullet into the dead man's body, so that each was guilty, and not one of them could be singled out for blame.

They then searched his pockets, finding religious imagery of the Virgin Mary, before heading for Rawson, where they lit beacons by way of sending news to the other search parties that had fanned out across the land. Aaron Jenkins was buried, as was his wish, on the land outside his smallholding, and he became known as the first martyr of y Wladfa, with poets such as Morris ap Hughes penning, or singing ballads to his memory:

> Fe'i claddwyd yn ein bröydd,
> Heb arch na'r un gobennydd,
> Mae enw man ei fedd mewn cof
> O hyd, sef Drofa'r Llofrudd.
>
> (He was buried in our lands,
> Without a coffin or a pillow,
> That place, his grave, remains
> In memory, as Murderer's Bend.)

The names of the farms in y Wladfa make a lovely litany. With the river flowing as such a prominent factor in life in the Chubut valley, little wonder there's a bank, or riverbank, of names such as Glan Dwrllwyd (Grey Water Bank), Drofa Dyllog (Broken Bend), Drofa Fresych and Drofa Gabets (both variants on Cabbage Bend), Drofa Hesgog (Rushy Bend) and Drofa Sandiog (Sandy Bend).

Some farm names are just transplants, such as Aberystwyth, Treorcki, and Dolddelan, derived from Dolwyddelan, but there are many others which locate the farm or seek to describe one of its principal characteristics. Here's just a selection: Plas Hedd (the Palace of Peace), once home to the seminal pioneer, Lewis Jones; Ffarm Wag (Empty Farm), Y Mason, Glan Alaw (Banks of the Alaw), Ffarm y Cwmni (the Company Farm) and Dyffryn Dreiniog (Thorny Vale).

Some names are quite naturally explicitly agricultural in origin, such as Y Fuches Wen (the White Milking-Fold) and Maes Comet (named after a famous mare which was imported from Cardiganshire), while others refer to birds, not all of them indigenous Patagonian species, so that we have Llys yr Eos (Nightingale Hall), Pant y Barcud (Kite's Hollow) and Nyth Dryw (Wren's Nest), being the first storehouse owned by the Co-op, which presumably was not very spacious.

Personal names can be quite telling, too. Richard (R. J.) Berwyn, the teacher, was originally Richard Jones, but there was another Richard Jones on board the *Mimosa*, so he changed his name. Others did the same, such as Hugh Hughes, who became Hugh Hughes Cadfan, and Rhydderch Jones, who became Rhydderch Iwan, with the names being handed on to their children.

One of the most hopeful names belonged to a little girl. Bryniau Meri, a small range of hills, was named after the first girl to be born in y Wladfa – a new name, a new beginning. Another baby, born on the long journey from the lower Chubut valley to the Andes, was called Mary Peithgan, born on the *paith*, in the same way as Patagonian writer Eluned Morgan was born at sea. The word *paith* itself, meaning prairie, is worth pausing over. John Davies of Mallwyd listed it in his *Dictionarum Duplex* of 1632, qualifying it with the words *desertus* and *vastatus*. Two hundred years later, another lexicographer, William Owen, was adding 'a prospect, a scene'. It was often a prospect the early settlers viewed with a sinking heart, another huge expanse to cross.

Dôl yr Ymlid (Field of the Pursuit)

Lewis Jones described the event in 1871 that led to the naming of this place. It could easily have been a scene from the Wild West. One Saturday night, a commotion was heard on the lower half of the river Chubut, and in the morning, it was found that many of the cattle and horses had disappeared overnight. Twelve armed men, with two horses each in attendance, went looking for the lost animals, tracking them to a place called Campamento, where they assembled a rude raft to cross the river, before crossing 60 miles of parched, gravelly terrain called Hirdaith Edwin to get to Dôl y Plu. The trackers found it hard to credit that the animals could have progressed across such waterless land without human intervention, when they spotted a heifer tied to a bush, a sure sign that the rustlers were nearby, although they had no idea how many of them there were. They went up a steep gorge, and soon spotted three or four horsemen urging their mounts on, going hell for leather, whilst aiming for some steep cliff ledges to the west. By now, all the riders were galloping out of the gorge, spurring on their horses, whipping them on, in one great, fanned-out line, until they lost sight of one another as they slalomed through outcrops and turns.

Soon, bullets were being fired by the lead pursuers, with the fugitives ducking and weaving, and all at great pace. One of the rustlers fell from his mount, so that all they could see of him was his hat. One of the colonists dismounted, and stealthily approached the fallen man, only to find that he'd been duped – the cunning man had used the various twists and turns to skedaddle, leaving his hat as a decoy.

The horses, which had been on the move for three days and three nights, were now bone tired, and their unshod hooves painful from traversing the rocky land. So they all slowed down, surmising that the rustlers were, by now, out of reach. They returned at nothing like a breakneck speed, and dallied in a meadow to watch the cattle. And that meadow was called, and is called Dôl yr Ymlid.

What's in a name?

The early settlers gave their children Biblical names – 38 from Old Testament books, 35 from the New Testament and 31 from the Book of Genesis alone, while there were 197 traditional Welsh names. Some have been not quite as traditional, and some interesting girls' names have been given over the years, such as Rawsona, the daughter of Abraham and Gwenllian Matthews, named after the first small settlement. Aviona Jones was born at exactly the time the first aeroplanes arrived in y Wladfa and was named after *avion,* the Spanish name for a plane. And then there's Aluminada, marking the arrival of electricity, not aluminium.

For some years in the twentieth century, Welsh names went strictly out of fashion. The status of the Welsh language and culture in Patagonia declined significantly, after the military dictatorship that held power in Argentina between 1976 and 1983 made it illegal to give children Welsh names, and it subsequently became undesirable to display any Welsh heritage or knowledge of the language. But luckily, the era of the dictators came to an end, and now babies are once again being given Welsh names in y Wladfa. Kiara. Winnie. Osian, Danna. Julia. Owen. Ionna.

Chapter 19

Frutas

> The woodlands of Wales are a carpet of moss, but here is a country carpeted with bountiful, sweet strawberries. I travelled twenty miles in all directions while staying here, and never lost sight of my pure companions: it is a place flowing with milk and strawberries ...
>
> (Eluned Morgan, *Dringo'r Andes*)

When the *Rifleros*, with their mix of Argentine troops, Welsh settlers and two Tehuelche guides, climbed the *cordilleras* of the Andes after their ultra-gruelling trek and beheld a beautiful valley, they called it Cwm Hyfryd. It was a vista green and lush, especially after the parched vastness of the endless dry scrublands they had crossed on horseback. Charmed, if not enchanted, by the view, they probably had no real idea of just how fertile this outstretched land could be. But there was a sense of natural abundance, judging from one of John Murray Thomas' description of Cwm Hyfryd. It is, he opined,

> ... one of the most beautiful scenes I have seen since leaving Wales. Picture a large pan, the bottom of which is rich pasture land, and the sides are forested hills, at the same time covered in good pasture. You can imagine what kind of land it is when strawberries and currants of many different types grow there, there are plants and flowers of the types to be seen in the Old Country ... Everyone rejoiced greatly that we had reached the good land of which there had been so much discussion. We camped that night on the banks of a small stream that sprang from the mountain behind us, and on its banks grow blackcurrants,

redcurrants, rhubarb, raspberries, watercress, birch and other trees … There are here trees of all kinds, red and white pine trees, ash, cedar, and birch.

Similarly, Llwyd ap Iwan, in his diary, offers, 'An illustration of the fertility of the place – a rhubarb leaf over seven feet in circumference brought to the encampment. Underneath this leaf, a man might shelter from wind or rain. The vegetable grew in abundance. Other visitors, too, underlined the fertility of the valley, such as the explorer and anthropologist Perito Moreno, who described how 'We went on the following day along the very beautiful valley of an exuberant fertility, where the settlers of the colony of 16 October live … Really, that land is a wonder of fertility, and the choice of the place to establish a colony could not have been better'. The town of Trevelin, with its 6,500 or so inhabitants, officially sits in the hyper-fertile Valle 16 de Octubre, or the Valley of 16 October.

If you needed any further proof of that fertility, you need only visit a hyper-abundant berry farm in the middle of the forest four miles north of Trevelin. The roadside sign at the entrance is a bit perplexing if you don't read either Indonesian or Welsh. It reads Pulau Pelangi, accommodatingly translated underneath as Ynys yr Enfys. They both mean Rainbow Island, and the island in question is run by a resourceful and amiable former oil-man, Arturo Lowndes, and his Welsh-speaking wife Rosa, whose maiden name was Jones. Rosa grew up on a fruit farm in Sarmiento, and gave her husband much of the knowledge he employs here, which he then supplemented with a bit of book learning.

Rosa came from a huge family: 'We were twelve – four girls, eight boys – and I was number eleven'. Her mother, Sephora Roberts, came originally from Dolgellau, and her father, Samuel Jones, from Bangor. They were brought up in Gaiman before moving to Sarmiento.

As befits its rainbow name, the farm certainly grows a kaleidoscopic range of fruit. Arturo and Rosa grow and harvest a luscious litany of *frutas* (fruits) – cherries, rhubarb (which they sell to all the local ski houses), apples and red and yellow raspberries. Arturo also harvests a cornucopia of currants, and has plenty of knowledge to share. He gives me a sort of open-air master class in matters of soft fruit. Their neat, trimmed bushes bear blackcurrants, used for making cassis, redcurrants and white currants, which are, botanically speaking, sports of the redcurrant, a sport being the part of a plant that shows morphological differences from the rest of it.

Wandering around the terraces and groves of fruit, past the greenhouse where they just grow flowers, or the stands of horseradish, it all seems a long way from the petrodollars and power play of the oil industry. Which is probably why Arturo likes it here so much. He's a bit of a wag. There's one odd tree, which a neighbour didn't like, who asked Arturo, 'Why have you got this horrible tree?' He answered, 'Because it gives flowers', which wasn't strictly true. 'So I bought a big sack of roses,' he tells me, 'and cut all the buds off and then glued them on top of the tree. The neighbour was amazed when he saw the blooms, and admitted he'd never seen anything like it in his life. He came back a couple of weeks later and said they still looked lovely. Then it snowed, and he finally twigged, when he saw the tree still flowering – with all those *plastic* flowers!'

The list of fruit they grow goes on and on – gooseberries and their cultivated avatars called Worcester berries, which are smaller, purplish, very thorny and considerably more disease-resistant than their wild antecedents. Then there are lingonberries – also known as cowberries, tayberries – similar to the loganberry (a cross between the blackberry and the red raspberry and baptised with the name of Scotland's longest river), not to mention lush vine-growths of plump cherry tomatoes and, unexpectedly, some black tomatoes, some grown from seed bought in garden centres in Wales.

All these are grown on a farm of some 15 hectares, or 37 acres. All the fruit is grown outdoors other than the cherry tomatoes, which are grown under glass. They're planted late, Arturo tells me, before moving on to show me onions and chard, planted for the family's use, and grapevines on the sides of the greenhouses. He also brought wattle tree seeds over, because they have nice flowers.

Some of their harvests finds its way to the shelves of supermarkets in Europe. Cherries are the main fresh export, and they come in a range of shapes, sizes and succulence, while other fruits are frozen before sale.

Arturo explains the slick operation involved in getting what is, after all, very perishable fruit, all the way from Argentina to places such as Aldershot and Aberystwyth.

> It takes six days maximum to get our fruit from the branches of the trees here onto the shelves of shops in the UK. We pick them, classify them, put them in boxes, then on pallets, then we promptly put them on trucks, which reach Buenos Aires in two days. The fruit is flown to London, which takes eleven or twelve hours. That's three days. They come off the plane, then the distributor takes a look at them. Appropriately enough, the company's called Utopia, and they're the ones who finally put them into packets for the retailer.

In the old days, the process was slower and more cumbersome, because they had to hand sort them, but now they have machines to speed things up. Luckily, they don't have many problems with pests.

> We're free of fruit fly. In the raspberries, we sometimes get a very small insect, like a tiny flea. We spray them with a sulphur product ten days before we pick them, then wash off the sulphur. That does the trick and helps us avoid using insecticides. There's also a small slug that gets onto the cherry trees after we pick the fruit, so we spray those, too. We used to plant pyrethrum between the cherries to keep away the bugs, but we don't get many bugs. We have a special room for my fertilizer, and there's a shower there to use after fumigation. Any water is used again to fumigate, so that none can leach out onto the fields.

Cherry picking

As you might expect, Arturo doesn't grow just one kind of cherry. With a sweep of the hand, he explains:

> The first 500 cherry trees were planted about twenty years ago, and we have Bings, the best-known ones, which started out in Oregon in the United States. Then we have the quintessentially bright red Vans, the British Columbian Celeste, the unsurprisingly heart-shaped Sweethearts, the New Star, developed as recently as 1998, again in British Columbia, and the Rainier, which is the preferred cherry – it's orange and yellow on the outside and it has yellow

> meat on the inside, but it's very, very sweet. It's the cherry of choice in the UK: here in Argentina they prefer the Bing and the Van, which are very dark.

There are 3,500-4,000 cherry trees here in total, and there are different ways of planting these trees. They plant the trees closer together, so they get fewer cherries, but it helps production. Each cherry picker is given two boxes, which are weighed, and a personal card is marked. The card can go through the washing-machine, because the ink is indelible. The quality of the cherries picked is assessed, as well as the quantity, and at the end of week, Arturo sees who's picked the most fruit and also the best fruit, and that picker gets paid an extra day's wages.

One young chap used to score more points than everyone else, week after week. His eyes were quick, too, so he was getting the prize every week, which was a bit of a disincentive to the others. Arturo and his wife had to establish a second prize too that year. They're served brunch at midday. Many of them move from place to place, finishing the strawberries, say, and moving on to sheep-shearing, which gives them work for most of the year. Training them is relatively straightforward …

Normally, the climate hereabouts is perfectly conducive to fruit growing, Arturo tells me.

> Further up the in the mountains, there's less freezing air, so the air moves like a river and goes downhill. Places lower down the hill are often actually colder. One of the things we do when it's freezing is wet the fruit. The ice freezes, protecting the fruit, as the ice rim on the outside may be five degrees, but the fruit remains at freezing point. Luckily, we're also blessed with plenty of water up here. You need freezing temperatures in winter to get sweet fruit in summer, otherwise you don't have sufficient sugar in your fruit. We measure the amount of sugar inside the fruit before we export it.

Arturo has an alarm system set up inside the groves, which transmits a radio signal to his bedroom to wake him up when it's freezing, or whenever the temperature falls dramatically.

You have to make decisions according to how cold it actually is, because the fruit has different phenomenological phases. The fruit can sometimes cope with cold, so I set the alarm according to the status of the fruit. If needs be, I'll wake up and get all my workers to help me. It's a bleary workforce then, I can tell you.

In the trees around the property, strange birds macaw their cries. The sky overhead is a cerulean curve, seemingly bending the mountains underneath. The animated bird-chatter on the farm margins makes me suddenly aware that there are no nets draped over the fruit trees and bushes, and no obvious signs of bird-scarers. There are no Chubut-ean scarecrows wearing *gaucho* hats at jaunty angles, neither are there camouflaged men with shotguns hiding in the hedges, guarding the perimeters. So, how, I have to ask, does he keep the birds from the berries? His answer seems, at first, to be nothing more than a tease: 'To deal with the birds, I put meat on the top of poles in the orchard'. He can see that I doubt if the fruit-eating birds are all that interested in leftover steak and mince. But then he explains that the meat attracts hawks and other birds of prey, and they are the ones who keep the birds away. It's an interesting Andean variant on using falcons to keep larger birds away from airport runways, thus warding off the danger of bird strikes. In Arturo's case, it's bird strikes against the loganberries.

As we amble gently around the farm, Arturo doles out some biography. He was born in Buenos Aires in 1937, his parents Edmund Lowndes and Doris Hullet. His father's uncommon name derives from Normandy, he avers, as a De Launde crossed over to England with William the Conqueror in 1066. In deference, perhaps, to the Celt he's taking around the farm, he tells me that his great-grandfather was a Scot, who built the railway from Cordoba. His father was born in Rosario in central Argentina, the country's second largest city, some 400 kilometres north of Buenos Aires. He explains that the city straddles the river Paraná, and has a big grain-exporting centre. There, Lowndes Senior worked for Royal Mail Lines Limited before progressing to become the manager of the company, which resulted in Arturo travelling around the world as a youngster.

His mother died when he was 17, then 'Dad got married to an Irish lady. She passed away, and then he married his third wife, Iris, from England'.

Arturo studied at the Belgrano Day School, St George's College and the University of Patagonia, and being a keen sportsman, he not only played rugby for Belgrano Athletic and the Old Georgians, but also hockey for Esso and Suri Oil, and sculled as part of a rowing team at the Tigre Boat Club. Even now, he still plays a mean game of tennis. Although 72 years of age, he entered a tournament this year and ended up playing a 24-year-old in the last match. He threw two or three dirty shots at him, and Arturo knew that would be enough to send the guy crazy, so that's precisely what he did.

We stroll through an arboretum, where he shows me some of the sheer variety of trees he's planted, such as the lime trees, the redwoods from the United States, the maples, hollies and the laryx, which are feathery trees, along with a deciduous palm tree from Finland, which loses all its needles. It's a nice tree to touch, really, he tells me, though I didn't have him down as a tree hugger.

He also tells me about the sort of problems English cherry growers wouldn't have to face: 'We've had wildcats from the back here, like the bobcat in America, which ate a lot of the lambs. We also have problem with red deer eating the cherry trees'.

We retire indoors, where Arturo and Rosa invite me to partake of some home-made raspberry liqueur, served in thimble measures in exquisite, demure crystal glasses. Half-past ten in the morning is way before my normal cocktail hour, but it would seem churlish to decline and, besides, the first sip is the gateway to many. Arturo assesses the drink as 'perfectly divine, the very nectar of the gods. We make some out of cherries and some out of sour cherries and redcurrants, but this is the best one. We mash the fruit with sugar, put it in a glass vase, and place it in the sun for ten to twelve days. It comes out a bit cloudy, then it's filtered and bottled. Then we drink it, with extreme pleasure!' It does seem like the very quintessence of raspberry-ness, each tiny taste warmly encapsulating a whole growing season, weeks of plumping moisture and intensifying sweetness. The sugar is sticky on the lips, which I imagine, by now, look slightly lipsticked. They have, yet again, harvested a vintage liqueur. Arturo says they probably have about twenty bottles in store at the moment. His three daughters like it, which always makes stocks dwindle. Liqueur isn't the only fruit by-product at Pulau Pelangi. Rosa makes a huge amount of jam.

She made 825 kilos this year and she sells it all, no problem. 'I sell it at an old folks' home, which is a British and American Benevolent Society in Buenos Aires, and when I go to the hospital, I take a little present from Patagonia'.

The room where we're sipping liqueur is full of fine pieces of carved, wooden, Asian furniture, all acquired on their travels. A beautiful bar is decorated with delicately fierce dragons. Lacquer tables are patterned in such a way that their provenance has to be Indonesia. Another piece, from Singapore, is decorated with no fewer than 100 delicate carvings of birds, the primary feathers of their wings sharpened with a paring knife, coupled with a gimlet eye.

Arturo then takes me into his studio, full of dark colours, teak woods: here a beautifully wrought cork carving from Bali, a phantasmagoria of storks and cranes and pagodas; there a collection of little ducks which he 'picked up from all over the place. This I exchanged for a T-shirt in Papua New Guinea,' he says, pointing at a miniature skull of a deer from the island. There's also an intricate ship in a bottle from Java.

One of the other connections with Asia was their friend Hiromichi Kokubu, a dentist from Sarmiento who moved to Comodoro Rivadavia, where he learned Welsh and would enjoy playing 'Sosban Fach' on the guitar. Arturo would like nothing better than to send Hiromichi to meet newly-arrived visitors from Wales, just to see the look on their faces when this Japanese dentist started to address them in Welsh with a cheery *'Bore da, sut 'dach chi'*!

In one corner of the living room is one of Arturo's prize possessions, namely a Roland E-500 synthesizer. He has been involved with Welsh choirs all over the world – in Comodoro Rivadavia, Indonesia, Australia, Trevelin, Tehran and Japan. He is a much, much travelled man, having resided in Tasmania, the United States, Singapore, Indonesia, Trinidad and Tobago and other countries. His hobby is music, and he has directed various choir groups and a jazz band not, to mention a steel band in Trinidad.

Arturo is as keen on genealogy as he is on music and furniture, and as we finish the last of the morning's Lowndes liqueur, he tells me how his grandfather was born in Cordoba. 'Hewlett was his surname. He put me in boarding school, and they were the best years of my life. It was at St

George's that I put powder in the pipe organ'. He recalls some of his early rebelliousness with relish …

He was kicked out of his first school by the headmaster. 'They had decided to install speakers in each classroom. On Inauguration Day, just before the system kicked in, I asked to go to the toilet, but went instead to fetch firecrackers, so the whole school listened as the headmaster yelled out loudly as all the firecrackers went off – Pap! Pap! Pap! Pap!' Arturo's laugh, as he finishes his tale, is as ripe as exploding fruit.

> The headmaster's brother then came back from the UK. He practised boxing, and said that if any of us had a grievance with him, we could settle it in the ring. I said, 'I have a grievance, sir,' so a ring was set up in the recreation area, and we put on gloves. The bell rang, and I didn't wait, I just went for my opponent, giving him a great big kick in the nuts which bent him over, then I kneed him in the side. I had no idea of the rules of boxing. That was probably the main reason I had to leave the school.

It certainly sounds sufficient. You might be forgiven for thinking that a berry grower's life is a tranquil one, but you'd be very wrong. Arturo and Rosa have had their fair share of natural disasters to contend with. The local *bomberos* – the men from the fire department – only just managed to contain one of the largest forest fires in the area during the past 20 years, which burned rapaciously, egged on by the breeze, to within 300 yards of their home. When the wind subsequently blew, it rained black ashes. 'The next thing that happened was that a volcano, located across the border in Chile, about 60 miles west of us, which has been dormant for approximately 9,000 years, exploded and started to spew ashes into the air. The column of ashes reached 70,000 feet'. The prevailing winds brought the ashes in their direction, and the fallout lasted for 15 days, covering the ground in light grey silica.

Arturo recalls how 'we had an accumulation of three inches'. The ashes even reached the city of Buenos Aires, 1,400 miles north of Trevelin. On top of that, it snowed five inches. As the snow melted, and the wind blew, 'we had white ashes and sulphur-smelling talcum powder even in our pockets. The melt off the snow carried ashes into the river Percy, which runs below our farm, and filled the river bed, so that the river started to flood. All airline flights were cancelled, and we planned on leaving by car as soon as the roads were opened. Luckily, we were in good health, as we had dust masks in stock for fumigating the fruit, and our water source is an artesian well, and wasn't contaminated.'

They had to wait to see what happened to their berry crop the following November, since the sulphur content raises the acidity of the soil, which might have been good for the raspberries, currants and gooseberries, but not the cherries. Arturo pauses at one specimen.

> That tree is gone. That one, too. When they're brown like that, they won't grow into good cherries. The rain washed the pollen off the leaves, so they haven't been pollinated. That's why they're turning brown. We've brought in boxes and boxes of bees to help pollinate them. There's a chap who rents them out like a service, and then takes them back home.
>
> The volcano did affect the fruit crop: the ash that fell on the leaves killed all the fungus, but now the water has mixed with the sulphur, and there's a lot of acidity in the soil. That may be the reason we don't have cherries this year. That, or strong rains. It'll be one of the two.

We turn a corner to find a little replica Scottish glen, with crystal water running through, fed from three streams, turning a waterwheel before passing the Oregon pines. It's paradise here, that's for certain, and I've just spent a day with a man who lives under a rainbow, and whose plans, no matter how ambitious, always bear fruit.

Chapter 20

Elvin and Amanda

As we shake up breakfast and, in the worst parts, rearrange our bones and facial systems bumping over some very rough roads, we talk, naturally enough, about the beating vehicles get around here. We had left Elvin and Amanda Roberts' compact house in Esquel after morning tea. They clearly enjoy their association with Wales as their listening material suggests, with music by Côr Godre'r Aran, Cantorion Cynwrig, Bob Roberts, Tair Felin, the singing shepherd, Trefor Edwards and *y baswr o'r bryniau*, the bass from the hills, Richard Rees.

We pass various farms, spaced out at substantial intervals. El Mirador, where they speak Welsh. El Condor. El Parque, which used to be known as Parc Unig (Lonely Field). There's also one called El Faldeo, which must derive, I suspect, from the Welsh word *ffald*, meaning sheep-fold among other things.

We hit a stretch of road so bumpy that it's like a mad fairground ride. Little stones skitter, in dangerous sprays, from beneath the heavy tyre treads. We spot another pick-up in the far distance, coming along the same track. It must be rush hour. Elvin explains that's the reason so many people drive Ford or Chevrolet pick-ups. 'Cars have to work hard here. They often break because of holes in roads'. I know the feeling. My breakfast has been churned into a smoothie, despite the vehicle's solid suspension. And this is one of the main tracks. Goodness only knows what things will be like if we go properly off-road.

Flying ahead of us along a hedge bank, we see a little bird which I identify as a rufous backed *negrito*, a species the Welsh in Patagonia baptised as *siôl fach goch*, or little red shawl, which seems to wrap it up in a little skein of charm. Another little bird, with black plumage was named *gweddw fach*, the little widow. The Spanish have some lovely names, too, such as the one for the little woodpeckers that beat out their presence on Andean tree boles: they are called *carpenteros,* suitable enough for such busy woodworkers.

Amanda was born in Buenos Aires, but the rest of the family was born in Trevelin, in Bodeglur, so named because her religious grandfather used to say that, by dint of his faith, 'he could see things clearly'. It was a big household, teeming with children, so her parents had plenty to do.

> We were 11 in total, but my eldest sister died when I was young, so there were ten children. Dalia was the eldest, Madryn Gwyn, Menna, Iola, Meinir, Irfonwy, Vincent, Esther Valmai, Gwennie, Nantlais and me, Amanda. I remember reading the novels of Daniel Owen when a girl. We had many Welsh books, but not many light books. There were serious books, religious books and so on. Dada read passages every night, especially in the winter. We would look forward to that, and everyone would enjoy the experience.

Elvin is 76 years old, but he doesn't look it. He has a characterful, rubicund face, with strong features – a solid jaw, deep-set eyes, and cheeks that are weather-worn around the edges. His hands offer ample testimony of hard graft. Their Cumberland sausage fingers have a grip that makes my pathetic typist's hands wince when he shakes them.

Elvin was born in Esquel. His grandfather, Benjamin Pugh Roberts, came from Llanuwchllyn, and his father was William John Roberts. 'We were five children,' explains Elvin. 'We have three ourselves. The eldest, Victor Kevin, teaches in the agricultural college and helps out on the farm, which is great, especially as he's a vet. The second is an accountant, while our daughter, who used to be a primary school teacher, then studied to be a lawyer. We spoke Welsh to the children when they were young, but since they've grown, we speak Spanish with them'.

Nowadays, Amanda and Elvin speak Spanish to each other in the main. 'But we love being able to speak Welsh,' Elvin says. Amanda adds:

> We take an interest in Wales. We have been there and visited with great pleasure. My brother-in-law Vincent went this year. When

we went, we went to see Bernardo, who is buried in Llandybïe, then went to Cardiff and on to Brecon to see Gruff and Eifona Jones. We then went on to Llwyngwril to see a relative of Elvin's before heading for Llanuwchllyn for the National Eisteddfod in Bala, before finally going to Bodelwyddan, near Rhyl. It's so very different. Wales is full of little villages with people living everywhere, with roads to get to them – even on the hills. You call them mountains, we'd call them hills!

Elvin has always worked on the farm, keeping a few cattle, but mainly looking after sheep.

> I went to school in Gaiman. My mother wanted me to go to college in Trelew, but I didn't want to. I wanted to come back to the farm. It's hard work, but the body gets used to it. You see, Patagonia is another country, for here we live differently, the people are different, the weather is different. There's lots of room here, and very few people.

As if to underline this difference, he tells me a story about his uncle, Madryn Evans, who was killed by a puma when he was just a child of eleven years. 'They'd come here to live in the hills during the winter, in June. A lioness had got him and by the time his body was found she had covered him with dirt, so she could return later on to eat him'.

Elvin's is a substantial, if lofty and rocky parcel of land, measuring 2,500 hectares. It is located eight kilometres from Esquel on the slopes of Mynydd Llwyd (Grey Mountain), in a farm called, with precious little imagination, Mynydd Llwyd.

> We love to look out at the mountain. It changes throughout the day as the sun hits it from various angles. The elevation of farm rises from 800 metres to 2,140, almost twice the height of Snowdon. In the summer, we take the sheep to the top of the mountain, and bring them down again at the beginning of winter. We have servants who go out every day on horseback to shepherd the animals, as we can't fence up there. The shepherds

take more than one horse each, changing animals every other day, as they tire from climbing up to two thousand feet. The men wear windproof clothes made from the skins of cattle or goats, which keep your legs warm, and sometimes a poncho too. We have two workers at the moment, though usually we have only the one.

We mark the sheep, the cattle and the horses. We have to have permission from the government for those, and we have to keep books of animal marks, each farmer's being a unique combination. The work of shearing is done on the farm itself, by contractors, at the beginning of October, before the lambing. They come from the north of the country and may move on, after finishing here, to Trelew. We usually have four or five shearers, who are here for four or five days, working from six in the morning to the end of the day, without stopping. They'll work nine hours without stopping once.

Elvin tells me – as did all the other farmers I met – that the job has now become very hard because of what the government is doing to the farmer. They want everyone to have cheap food, so little wonder, he suggests, that the farmers went on strike. Elvin takes a dim view of politicians, all politicians. 'Politicians steal money. When politicians sleep, the country grows!'

Unlike some of his agricultural colleagues and neighbours, Elvin doesn't have the option of diversifying, because the farm is only good for rearing sheep – the weather up here in the tops doesn't allow much else. Plus, the weather has changed. 'Rain patterns have changed, and snow patterns, too. We used to have a lot more snow and rain, but this year it's been very dry. Now we are in the spring, and it's still cold like winter, and it's snowing still'. As it happens, news of the official start of spring has recently been on television, with pictures beamed into the studio of the first penguin coming onshore in the southern colonies. It's the Patagonian equivalent to spotting the first swallow back home, that fork-tailed herald of summer.

Elvin and Amanda met in the Cyrddau Pobl Ifanc (Young People's Meetings), at Bethel chapel in Trevelin, though 'very little happens in Bethel anymore. Should a minister come from Wales, we'll meet them, but there isn't much more than that'. Elvin used to travel from Mynydd Llwyd to her home, Bryn Eglur, to come a-courting, taking him four hours to arrive. He'd stay the night, and be given a room and clean bed. After they married, the couple moved out here to the slopes of Mynydd Llwyd, named after Llwyd ap Iwan, who surveyed so much of Welsh Patagonia, and whose maps delight the eye with their detail and elegance. Their nearest neighbour was five kilometres away, but nowadays there's only one servant there. 'We like loneliness in a way, we enjoyed living here'. They no longer live on the farm, and have a house in the town, much closer to amenities and creature comforts. As Amanda explains, 'When Victor Kevin started to go to school in Esquel, we had to think about buying a house there. Would we rather live here than in town? Well, I like gardening, and keep a flower garden. Elvin comes to the mountain pretty much every day. I like to go to English lessons and go to the swimming pool. Last time we went to Wales, I felt I missed out because we didn't speak English. It also keeps my mind alert'.

They've both seen Esquel grow a lot, as she explains. 'There are now 40,000 people in Esquel – it's filling up. Many farmers have come to live in town, and outsiders have forced a rise in land prices'. There are other concerns too. 'Meat prices are so low that people are pretty fearful'. A cattle show organized by the Sociedadad Rural de Esquel, known as the *rural*, is the place for selling livestock and socialising in the local farming community. Amanda tell me, 'The best bull sold at the last *rural* went for 29,000 pesos, for an animal from around Trevelin. It's an important *rural*, selling a lot of cattle, though the one for sheep is much bigger. For that one, buyers and sellers come from all over the state'. At this last *rural*, Elvin bought five Angus heifers to cross with his Herefords, as the calves are heavier and fatter. He explains that he may move them to Bodeglur or to Corcovado. It's anything but sedentary work.

Do they have problems, being so remote? 'In the last few years, not so much. We do have to deal with pumas, and foxes eating lambs are another problem'. Elvin, resignedly, blames Los Alerces National Park:

> The pumas aren't hunted there, so they multiply in the park and come out to hunt people's animals. Meanwhile, we try and control them with bullets and dogs. We also hunt hares in winter, to skin them and then sell the meat for pretty much the same

price as the fur. An abattoir in Esquel exports the meat, mainly from European hares. We only see the big Patagonian hares way out on the *paith*. There were many, many hares this year, because the abattoir didn't buy at all last winter, so they weren't hunted and they've been busy breeding. We also have condors up here. They're lovely to see. We've seen many on Mynydd Llwyd – when an animal dies, they drift down. Enormous, they are.

Over coffee, Elvin and Amanda talk about the first settlers with great admiration. 'Now we know the history, we know how hard it was to work the land, and what they put into it. Had the Welsh not come here, this area would belong to Chile. That's why we celebrate the Plesbiscite every year'. Elvin is referring to a signal moment in the history of the relationship between the Welsh and Argentina. The escalation in tension between Chile and Argentina over their respective claims over Patagonia towards the end of the nineteenth century seemed to be ratcheting up to the point of warfare. The two countries had successfully reached a measure of mutual agreement in a boundary treaty in 1881, but had sought further clarity about the boundaries in a pact of 1902, with Britain brought in as arbitrator. A group of commissioners – including the distinguished Chilean historian Diego Barros Arana, the Argentinian anthropologist and explorer Perito Moreno along with the geographer and President of the Royal Geographical Society in the UK, Sir Thomas Holdich – visited the Andean valleys. They toured the area and met with various local inhabitants, whilst also pondering the contents of the substantial paper submissions made by the two countries that were in dispute.

The area had, of course, been settled by Welsh immigrants since 1885, and this fertile east-west aligned valley had initially been awarded to Chile. Subsequently, the commissioners visited Trevelin, and received the views of the inhabitants of the Colonia del Valle 16 de Octubre on 30 April 1902, one by one over the course of three days, in School Number 18, which had been founded in 1895 next to the river Corintos by the Argentine National Government. The arbitration group finally adjudicated in favour of the Republic of Argentina, and Trevelin, Esquel and other adjacent settlements were subsequently incorporated into Chubut province. The Welsh had asserted their rights, and their allegiance to Argentina.

Elvin explained that 'the *rifleros* knew they were coming to a good place, because the natives had told them, so they expected a beautiful place and good water'. Elvin's family have deep roots here. The family home, Bryn Amlwg, was one of the first houses built in the area. Elvin's grandparents' wedding was the first in Esquel. William John Roberts, his father, went to the farm in Mynydd Llwyd when he was about fifteen years of age.

We explore the sheds. There are piles of cattle and sheepskins, and hooks to hang animals. 'We have to kill some of them ourselves if the abattoir doesn't want them. Sometimes we sell the meat, sometimes the animal'.

There is a year's livelihood in the sacks in front of us, the wool stored in plastic sacks, each weighing 250 kilos, with about 30 sacks gathered, that's about 6,000–7,000 kilos. That's 1,300 or 1,400 animals' worth, although he never knows the precise monetary value until they sell them, as the price fluctuates, and it 'depends on the Australian market. We get what animals are selling for there. It makes life very uncertain, and we never know whether it will go up or down in value. At the moment we get three dollars 70 cents a kilo, although we get paid in pesos. The price isn't bad, but the costs have gone up'.

As the sun slants in over the woolpacks, conversation turns to a difficult subject, the Falklands War. Elvin corrects me straight away, underlining the name Malvinas, even as he says it. How did you feel then, as Argentinians, I ask, during a war when Argentina fought against some of the children of Wales in the British Army?

> We weren't conflicted. There was a man with Welsh roots, called Austin, who was killed in the Malvinas. Martin Dafydd, our son, was in the army at that time as there was conscription. Boys went into the services when they were 18. Before he could go to university in Buenos Aires, Martin was called up, and he went down south. When they got there, the plane that was due to take him to the Malvinas had already left. If he had gone on that plane, he might have been killed, or injured in a way that would affect him for the rest of his life. Margaret Thatcher was avoiding domestic troubles with that war. The generals here wanted war, even though the population didn't. But the Argentine soldiers really have been treated very badly. They don't get their pensions,

as if *Los Chicos de las Malvinas*, as they're called, were, and are, an embarrassment to the country.

Outside, as we prepare to leave, Amanda shows me wormwood growing in the yard, and offers me a taste of *calafate*, of their tiny black fruits, which are used to make jam and ice-cream. Legend has it that once you've tried these, you have to return here. I bite one, slowly savouring its dark astringency, resigning myself to my fate.

Chapter 21

Esquel

Esquel is a neat, fresh-aired town in the north-west of Chubut. The town's name derives from one of two Tehuelche words, one meaning marsh and the other, 'land of burrs', which refers to the many thorny plants including the *pimpinella* and other herbaceous plants whose fruits, when ripe, turn into prickly burrs that adhere to animal skins or people's clothes as a way of propagation, very much as goose grass does at home in Wales.

The settlement of Esquel was created on 25 February 1906, as an extension of the Colonia 16 de Octubre, that also contains the town of Trevelin. You can see the Welsh influence here simply by flicking through the local phone book. Among the Abitus, the Jaramillos, the Otarolas, Troncosas, Pinedas and Itxassas there are 37 entries for people with the surname Roberts, 10 Lewises, six Evanses and Jenkinses, not to mention the occasional Davies, Price, Rowlands, Griffiths, Pritchard, Lloyd, Owen, Powell and Williams, while there's a scattering of perfectly Welsh forenames such as Gwili, Arenig and Sulwyn.

To get a grand view of the city, it's possible to climb up to the giant white cross that looks down on the place, through plantations of pine alive with the bright chink of finch calls. There are white starbursts of alpine plants in the mossy tussocks underfoot, small galaxies of vivid petals. These would have been of much interest to Mr Arthur K. Bully from Liverpool, who exchanged seeds for such plants with a Mr Thomas Austin. Bully wrote to the Deputation from the Welsh colony asking for 'someone else in the mountain colony who could exchange seeds … I should especially value a correspondent who added to a love of wild flowers a habit or a necessity of exploring among the mountains, so as to reach the secluded glens and ravines in which these beautiful wildings live'. Wildings. Such a lovely word.

Near the top, there's a fire-watching hut spray-canned with the reassuring graffito '*Jesus Vives*', and at the base of the big cross are many home-made wooden crosses. In the distance, the pyramidal Mynydd Llwyd, animated by racing cloud shadow, is a deep rust colour, with patches of mildewy black, although on the tops, the snows glow incandescent white, like huge splashes of bird shit, a *guano* of snowdrift. It's sheep country, yes, but quite the most dramatic sheep country.

Historically, livestock from y Wladfa could command staggeringly high prices, as a letter from William Christmas Jones from the Primavera Estancia in El Pajarito, Chubut to Richard Griffith, a.k.a the poet Carneddog, in August 1946 confirmed, with the champion bull selling for 70,000 dollars, equivalent to 5,000 pounds, while another animal went for twice that amount.

In today's *rural*, there are animals from many *estancias* – Leleque, Rio Frio, Cencerro, Santa Elena, El Chalet, El Murmullo and Media Luna. There are Hereford bulls, Angus bulls and shorthorns in pens, while farmers stand around, chatting with gusto, avoiding the white plastic chairs which are scattered all around, as they look too flimsy to take the weight of these muscular men. The mountains in the distance form a dramatic and uplifting backdrop – sable crags in morning sunshine, drapes of pine snaking like dark green boas over the far ridges. The town centre is shaped in part by Esquel stream, and the whole urban centre is surrounded by mountains such as La Zeta, La Cruz, Cerro 21 and La Hoya, a well-known ski resort.

Imagine the Royal Welsh Show set in the Alps rather than Builth Wells, and you'll begin to get the picture. Risking one of those flimsy chairs, Elvin Roberts tells me some stories about Twm Harri, or Harry Jones, a member of the border police, had awakened my interest in its history. Borders always pulse with possibilities and tensions, and the men who patrolled those between Argentina and Chile must have been a special breed, tough as old boots, born to the saddle.

Twm Harri was a bit of a Jack-the-lad. Elvin tells me about an occasion when Twm was told by a man call Migens that he should not come to the house after midnight, or the door would be closed. Jones arrived late and went to the hen coop for some sleep, but the poultry became so animated that Migens thought there was a fox, and went out to investigate. Meanwhile, Twm sneaked round into the house, locked the door and got a good night's sleep while the house-owner fulminated outside. Another story tells how Twm Harri exchanged a whole league of land for a measure of tobacco. He was clearly a real character, a policeman with a difference.

The colony's first police station was erected on the left bank of the Corintos river in 1897, at a place called Súnica, and built right next door to the home of the chief of police, Eduardo Humphreys, presumably to cut down on his commute. Six years later, it became a real, modern telecommunications hub when a telegraph line was connected to it!

Humphreys might not have been the sharpest tack in the box, as he included among his friends Butch Cassidy, the Sundance Kid and Etta Place, although, admittedly, they were on their best behaviour when he met them, and not robbing too many banks. They would come around to Humphreys' house to enjoy musical *soirées*, just as the state Governor Lezana called round to visit Butch at his place. But if Butch kept the law, some of his visitors did not, attracting the attention of diligent Pinkerton detectives who came to hunt them all down. The slow spiral in crime in the area, which flummoxed the local police at Súnica and Esquel, led the Argentine Government to establish a new hard core special corps, the Frontier Police, a bit like the Canadian Mounties.

The Fronteriza, like the Canadians, usually got their man, especially under the leadership of Major Mateo Gebhardt, but the ways in which they actually got him, and subsequently treated him, were often questionable in the extreme. Some prisoners never made it to trial, dying in custody, while others were tied to posts and whipped with lassos in order to extract confessions.

Twm Harri's grave is set in a remote spot between Esquel and Súnica. It's not an easy place to find, and there certainly isn't any public transport. So I realize I'll most certainly need someone's help to get there …

When I visited the late artist, Republican and activist, Rhobert ap Steffan, at his home in Llangadog – by way of the first piece of research I did for this book – the one person he told me I had to meet should I visit the Andes was Jeremy Wood. As it happened, the first man I spoke to at the bar at the Trelew Eisteddfod was Jeremy, one of those rare men with energy as if it's coming off the National Grid, brim full of passion for all matters Welsh.

Not that he is Welsh, mind. Jeremy is the son of two hemispheres colliding, as it were. He was born in the 1950s to a southern hemisphere, New Zealander father, and a northern hemisphere mother of mixed Irish and Yorkshire stock. Jeremy's father came from a farming / rugby family from Lyttelton, near Christchurch, and was, in turn, the son of an Australian horse trainer, descendant of immigrants from west Wales. Jeremy has now been living in Patagonia for more than a decade, and is married to Cristina Luque, from Esquel. They have a son, Tomos, aged four. Cristina's great-grandparents emigrated to Patagonia in the early 1870s from Boncath in Pembrokeshire.

Jeremy's has been a restless life, peregrinating from one place to the next, although the destinations had been set on 'shuffle'. He was raised in Germany, where his father was stationed with the Armed Forces, before moving to Britain. His later life found him living in a clutch of various countries and places including Italy, Iran, the USA, Japan, Patagonia and the Netherlands. He worked for various government institutions – Iranian, Dutch, British – and travelled to over 70 countries, mostly on business, but some just out of curiosity such as Zululand, Oman's Empty Quarter, Cuba, Easter Island, Bora Bora and Fiji.

Yet, for all that, I feel I should describe him as an elective Welshman, someone with sufficient connections to Wales to be able to describe himself as Welsh should he need to, much like the writer Jim Perrin, the art critic Peter Lord, and the cinema critic Dave Berry – people who know and love the place most intimately well, and somehow *become* Welsh. Jeremy elaborates:

> I had never visited Wales prior to meeting my first wife. She was from Pembrokeshire, and her parents and grandparents from north Pembrokeshire. I spent much time down there, never heard much English spoken, and fell in love with the people and the countryside. I subsequently spent many years living outside the UK, and always joined the local Welsh societies, since they always seemed to have so much more fun! I travelled all over Wales, followed the rugby team around the world and learned many of its songs. I probably know just as many songs in Welsh as I do in English! When I first visited Trelew, the Welshness of many locals was quite evident. Similarly in Trevelin. But when I

> eventually settled in Esquel, I was puzzled that the town didn't wear its Welshness on its sleeve as much as the other Welsh towns in Patagonia.
>
> I suppose that was the main reason why I organised the twinning of Esquel with Aberystwyth – to make the people of Esquel more aware and proud of their Welsh history, as well as making the Welsh in Wales more aware of their heritage in my home in the Andes. These towns are remarkably young – this part of Patagonia has only been settled for just over 100 years. And all of its history is Welsh. Or Tehuelche. Not much of its history is written down in one place. I was very hungry to learn about Patagonia, and about the Welsh in Patagonia. This inquisitiveness brought me into contact with many interesting people and took me to many places very few local people had ever visited. It wasn't long before I started to write about the place, and soon began to be asked to take tourists around.

He is an indefatigable researcher into the history of Patagonia and, in particular, the Welsh in Patagonia. To this end, he has amassed a splendid library of books, quite envy-inducing in range and rarity.

> It's not just books of Patagonia I have, I also have maps and films. The interior of Patagonia was *terra incognita* until recently. With not too much effort, I discovered maps of the interior which are almost unknown! I have an original from Musters' journey through Patagonia in 1870. I have recently completed a project on the first book published on Welsh Patagonia by Hugh Hughes, which was printed in 1862 by the Emigration Society as a work to convince potential migrants from Wales that Patagonia could be their Promised Land.

He cites 22 sea captains, explorers, atlases, weather reports and much more to justify his somewhat over-cosy description of Patagonia, 'and I had to find and research every one'. Another treasure is *Los Rifleros de Chubut,* the diary of John Murray Thomas, presented to Jeremy by Héctor Garzonio, the President of the *Rifleros*:

I suppose that the story of the *Rifleros* is one which rivals the story of the *Mimosa* for its magical quality. Both were forays into the unknown, were of a similar length and distance, and yielded results which affected the whole country. Cwm Hyfryd is freakish, in that it is nurtured by rivers which flow into the Pacific and, as such, should rightfully be in Chile. If you follow the Andes down on the Argentinian side, the land is characterised by an almost immediate transition from arid steppe to mountains. Valleys like Cwm Hyfryd and Cholila are a bit like tiny green bubbles floating in an enormous bowl of becroutoned Brown Windsor Soup. Had the *Rifleros* had accurate compasses, they would have missed Cwm Hyfryd altogether and returned to Rawson in February of 1886 with nothing to report! The *Rifleros* society keeps the history alive, and the annual ascent to Craig Goch on 24 November gives all the opportunity to remember and to celebrate. There are few other events in the Welsh history of Patagonia so well remembered.

We change the subject from riflemen to frontier policemen. To follow the history of the Frontizera, we set out from Esquel in Jeremy's all-terrain Toyota Hilux SW4 to visit Estancia Esmeralda near Súnica. Twm Harri's grave seems about as remote as you can get, rivalling that of Llwyd ap Iwan out at Nant y Pysgod.

It's a simple slate headstone, corralled by iron railings in the shade of a tree whose skin is peeling from being battered by the wind. The memorial stone, made by D. J. Evans, was placed here to commemorate the death of Twm Harri, or to use his proper name, Harry Jones, by his friends. He patrolled a huge patch of wild place, which in his day offered safe haven for many a lawless soul. The inscription notes that he drowned in the Rio Gualjaina in the line of duty on 12 July 1913. A motif on the headstone shows two Remington rifles, crossed over each other.

We then explore the area, including the staggering beauty of the waters contained behind the Futeleufú dam. A small plaque at the viewpoint names the place Amutui Quimei (Lost Beauty), bringing to mind the beautiful lands that were drowned to supply electricity to the aluminium smelters at Puerto Madryn. We prowl around the huge but now deserted Hotel Futaleufú, where the workers who built the dam were housed, the whole edifice now pretty much visigothed and vandalised by visitors who seem to like spray paint and their own names.

We then move on to Chile for a quick spin, crossing the border Twm Harri patrolled. We see tremendous meltwaters, perfectly turquoise in colour, and Jeremy introduces me to a new word, namely 'dephlogisticated', a neologism coined by the great scientist Joseph Priestley, who called oxygen 'dephlogisticated air'. As the glaciers melt the waters, they change to the colour of limeade as the sun illuminates them, starting their long, powerful meanderings to the sea.

In the small community of Corcovado, we meet a beamingly smiley young *bombero*, or voluntary fireman, called Damien Griffiths, standing proudly in front of his 1,000-litre fire engine. He tell us that his family connects back to the *Mimosa* settlers, but that his uncle, who understood the connection, has sadly died.

We then loop back toward Esquel. On the way, we see an entire horse hanging from a tree next to the road which runs from Trevelin to Corcovado, quite near to the Mapuche community in Lago Rosario. It's another indelible image to add to the bank of mental images of Patagonia.

The strangest has to be the shrine to *Gauchito* Gil, which I saw outside Playa Unión on the coast. Gil was a rebel, a semi-legendary figure. The popular accounts of his life vary enormously, but in broad terms, legend has it that Antonio Gil was a farmworker, and that a wealthy widow fell in love, or had an affair, with him. When her brothers and the head of the police (who was also in love with the widow) found out about their relationship, they accused him of robbery and tried to kill him, but he enlisted in the army to escape from them. He fought bravely against the Paraguayans and came back to his village to be fêted as a hero.

But when he arrived at his village, he was forced to return to the army to fight in the Argentine Civil War, which often pitted brother against brother, and by now *Gauchito* Gil was tired of fighting, and decided to desert. During this time, he became an outlaw and acquired a reputation as a Robin Hood-type figure because of his efforts to protect and help the needy.

In the end, the policemen caught him in the forest. They tortured him and hung him by his feet on an *algarobbo* tree. Just as a policeman was about to kill him, Gil said to him: 'Your son is very ill. If you pray and beg me to save your child, I promise you that he will live. If not, he will die'. Then the policeman killed *Gauchito* Gil by cutting his throat. That was on 8 January 1878. When the policemen came back to his village, Gil's executioner learned that his child was, in fact, very ill. Frightened, the policeman prayed to *Gauchito* Gil for his son. And afterwards, his son got better. Legend has it that Gil had healed his murderer's son. And legends tend to swell with time.

Grateful in great measure, the policeman gave Gil's body a proper burial, and built a tiny shrine to *Gauchito*. Moreover, he tried to let everybody know about the miracle. Nowadays, you see such shrines all over the place, with lots of red objects and red pennants announcing their presence. I asked Ariel Hughes about them when I saw him in Trelew, and he explained that Gil has become a sort of folk saint, 'very popular with Indians, especially from the area around Corrientes, in the north-east of the country. He was a rebel who was killed by mistake. He then became almost a saint. The *gauchos* believe in him, that he is a real man. The shrines are sprouting everywhere. Patagonia is one of the last places for them to arrive. For us Protestants, such images are strange'.

The shrine I visited was indeed very strange. The items left here included a bottle of Gatorade, a pair of brand new, red, high-heeled dancing shoes, some red silk roses, some candles and some cigarettes, not to mention a half-full bottle of Torrontes white wine. These in themselves weren't that remarkable, but the fact that the candles were lit and the wine was chilled was a trifle disquieting, especially as there wasn't anyone around, and had there been, they would have had to be lying prone on the ground, given the horizontality of the landscape thereabouts.

I did take a photograph of the items, but the digital camera fuzzed over when I tried to replay the image, and has never worked since. So you'll just have to take my word for it, and maybe join me in offering prayers to Gil, the Patagonian folk saint responsible for such weird mysteries.

Chapter 22

Land of the Condor

> Its plumage is as black as the shadow of a mountain at night, and a collar of fine feathers about it throat which are as white as mountain snow under full moonlight, its eyes glint like stars of morning dimming, while the red of daybreak lights each eye-rim, its bill four inches long, like a two-edged axe.
>
> (Eluned Morgan, *Dringo'r Andes*)

There are many Tehuelche myths concerning condors, those huge, soaring splay-winged scavengers that patrol the craggy dentitions of the Andes, their primary flight feathers like black, leathery fingers. Many of the stories centre on the exploits of the hero Elal, the offspring of a cloud-woman raped by Nóshtek, the son of Night. In various tales, we hear how Elal kills the condor, and in a good handful of stories, how he managed to pluck the feathers from its head, leaving the bird bald. Here's one.

Elal walked along, and the first thing he came across was a condor. The bird was hovering over a ravine and they say that Elal asked him, 'Can you give me one of those feathers?' But the condor did not want to part with one. 'Get out of here, you rotten miser!' shouted Elal. Annoyed by the boy's persistence, the condor hurled a piece of excrement at him, and he fell down. After a while, he got up, somewhat dizzy, and washed his face. Using his own urine, he washed his eyes thoroughly. Then, Elal is said to have aimed an arrow at the condor. The bird came down, circling around the ravine until it reached the ground. There, Elal pulled out its feathers until not a single one remained on its head. Don't you see how the condor's head looks? It is so because he was artful. Elal did not kill the condor, but he surely plucked its head bald.

With its bald head, its pickaxe bill and huge wings the condor was certainly a strange bird for some of the early foreign adventurers to behold, with some believing they were seeing Zeus' eagle, and others, Sinbad the Sailor's roc. Neither eagle nor roc, the condor is a member of the vulture family, a symbol of these high places, an enormous bird to match the mountains, king of the thin Andean air. Its wings alone are about the size of your front door, and when those splay out, they fill even more sky, the big primary feathers growing to a length of 70 centimetres, like big black scythes.

I saw one for the first time when I was on the local bus which ferries people back and forth between Esquel and Trevelin. A spiralling spot in the sky grew larger and larger, and soon, the big bird was drifting in on a downdraft, having presumably spotted some carrion or suchlike. It looked as if it could snatch a donkey from a field, so it's lucky this is a carrion-eater, or the actual donkey in the field near the bus stop would be, well, donkey-meat.

This *Vultur Gryphus*, to use its Latin name, hardly moves its wings – two enormous palm fronds fingering the sky – letting the air do all the work. If a species is this big, it needs a little help, a little uplift, to get airborne, and then a sustaining thermal to keep itself aloft. And as it has to quarter and survey enormous tracts of land, travelling considerable distances whilst scouting for carcasses, it needs to avoid flapping its wings. Flapping burns up energy, and simply isn't good ergonomics. So the condor needs to find places where the air is rising, using what scientists call slope-lifts and rising thermals.

This vulture's aerial requisites are well understood by Dr Emily Shepard of Swansea University, who had been studying the bird out in Patagonia, especially in the province of Rio Negro. She says that this sort of ergonomic flight 'isn't unlike a game of Snakes and Ladders played in three dimensions. The air rises in some places, as thermals, and so to conserve energy, the birds seek these out, to help bear them aloft. In other places, the air is falling, so it's like the snakes in the game, taking the birds down with them'.

Emily – an unabashed vulture enthusiast – explains what happens when the bird spots a corpse or some carrion on the ground: 'It will circle slowly to fully assess the situation. If the body is close to the road, and therefore close to man, the condor will be wary. It also needs to work out how easily it would be able to get airborne if it needed to. And, of course, it may also see other birds, busily feeding there already'.

If the bloody feast has started, the bird will drop like a stone, using its large feet as airbrakes to slow down before touchdown.

One way the birds find food is to keep a vulture eye, as opposed to an eagle eye, open to study the other birds in the sky. Punctuating the blue yonder like full stops, the birds will know if something's up simply because a bird, a full stop, is missing, and the other birds will start to move across the firmament to join it. It's a sort of signalling system, where the main import of the message is carried by absence – an empty sky where a bird was formerly on patrol is a sure sign of rich pickings down below.

The birds used to be hunted by man, often by simply staking out a carcass, letting the greedy bird gorge and eat its fill, and then, when it was too heavy to fly, moving in to capture it. One unfortunate bird, caught in this manner – by setting out a dead calf as bloody lure – was sent to Buenos Aires zoo, there to sit disconsolately in its cage, dreaming of boundless acres of sky.

The bird above the bus moves elegantly now, reminding me of a verse told to me by Glyn Alun Jones, my next-door neighbour when I was growing up in the village of Pwll, Llanelli. It describes the slow spiralling of the red kite, seeing it as both a giant and a graceful helicopter, its wings, or rotors, barely moving as it turns in the air before heading for home:

> Cylcha'r nen, fel hofrenydd – ei edyn
> llwydion bron yn llonydd.
> Wedi hela'n y dolydd
> Try'r cawr at ei gartre' cudd.

And this bird, now gone from view behind a fence, is indeed a giant, and, after all, this is the land of giants, the legendary hobbit-footed Tehuelche who hunted across the dry expanses.

So the size of the condor is in keeping with the dimensions of the land, a huge bird that builds a huge nest on rocky ramparts and unscaleable crags. The nest, being usually safe on such a peak or other lofty location, is easily spotted, covered as it is with vulture shit, or *guano*, and the remains of many a dinner. On the cliffs above Trevelin, the condor nest looks like a child's chalk mark on the high cliffs.

Although territorial, like so many birds in the nesting season, these huge scavengers are pretty collegiate and convivial (inasmuch as road-kill-and-carcass-devouring vultures can be described as such) during the rest of the year. They will happily roost together, with up to 100 individuals gathering at a spot deemed both safe and suitable for an emergency take-off should that prove necessary. Not that the condor has many enemies. Just one, really and that is man. But that situation is improving, as conservationists deliver grass roots education about the bird and its habits to both landowners and agricultural workers.

Meeting Erik

Erik Iolo Green's log cabin in Trevelin is the sort of place in which one imagines Daniel Boone or Jack London would have lived, and of course, he built it himself, Boone-style, as you need to be resourceful around here.

Driving to the cabin, we talked about a range of things, including the spread of non-native species of birds and animals, which affects this part of the earth just as it does so many others. I'd just asked him about the difference in size between the native Patagonian hare and the invasive European species, when he stopped the car. As if on cue, this genial man had spotted a hare. He rolled down the window and reached for the Express Super Magnum Rifle he kept out of sight under the seat. Taking casual but unerring aim, with the barrel resting on the window rim, he bagged the animal with a single shot. The dogs in the back of the truck leaped out to retrieve it, with all the precision of a floor show. They would get the innards. Four dogs. Working dogs, working sheep and cattle. Young dogs. Which are having hare for tea and are tail-waggingly excited at the prospect.

We lock the gate before heading up the rocky track which runs alongside a bright little freshet of water. 'We have to close the gates because there's a lot of theft. The last ten years, we've even started to lock the gates. We used to leave the houses open in the old days. You wouldn't dream of doing that nowadays, and you have to pretty much lock up the farm'.

Sanctioned by whistled command, the dogs drag the hare's body from the back of the truck, the animal shot cleanly, hardly marked. How different, and how succinct, is this kind of hunting, as opposed to the ways employed by the Tehuelche Indians in the past. Iolo's father, Fred, had been told by a man called Gweirydd Iâl Jones how he had seen the Teheulche hunting *guanacos* on foot. Jones described the hunters lining up in two rows, which separated into the shape of a V, then waited for the young men to chase the animals into its open mouth, where the *bolas* would be aimed at their legs, or sometimes the rope would target the neck, in the hope that the gyrating balls would fell the fleeing animals that way. A successful hunt meant a meat supper for all. The intestines were particularly prized in the feast that ensued, as they contained vitamins not found in most meat-centric diets.

Erik Iolo learned to shoot as a child, and employs his marksman's skills on deer as well as hares. 'If there are too many stags, we have to kill them'. Culling in this way is an effective way of controlling numbers. He also learned to shoot geese as a boy. 'Then the bison came, and the mink, and then the hunters who came to hunt them'.

High in the robin's egg sky, a tiny speck, on being scrutinized, reveals itself to be another condor. Erik's father, Fred, remembered how they would be hunted because they were unfairly accused of killing livestock. Unlike the hunters, Fred admired the birds, and worried about the way they were moving slowly towards the edge of extinction. In his writing, he noted their individual cleanliness, and also the long hours they would spend maintaining and preening their plumage. Fred enjoyed those moments when one of these massive birds would spot something on their farm, Pennant, and come circling in for a slow *danse macabre* around a dead animal.

Iolo hunts boar in the mountains behind the cabin.

> When hunting those, we take dogs. We used to breed a special kind of dog for hunting pigs. They were white fighting dogs from Cordoba. It's not easy chasing boar: there are so many wild roses that the dogs can't get through. We started shooting them by going lamping – using the light reflected off the quarry's eyes as a way of getting on target, or dazzling them into stillness. They can be mesmerized by the bright lights. Their numbers have increased hugely. They were originally pigs brought here from Europe, and they've spread. It's a similar story in the United States.

As we stand outside the cabin, the light deepening into violet, Erik points out Mynydd Edwin, and the place where a Canadian company wants to produce gold. 'They want to use 20,000 kilos of cyanide every day to work. It will poison the water that comes down to Esquel and Trevelin. That's Mynydd Llwyd, named after Llwyd ap Iwan, who measured everything around here, and marked the fields. There's Troed-yr-Orsedd, too, under a cloud. Conico is the highest peak around here, about 1300 metres'.

In one sense, I'd met Erik Iolo before, in the pages of Kyffin Williams' pellucid account of his painting trip to Patagonia, *A Wider Sky*, in which the artist describes a younger Iolo riding bareback on the way to Gorsedd y Cwmwl, the mountain named Throne of the Clouds. Iolo remembers Kyffin being here when he was a boy.

> I remember walking with him into the woods. A spirited gentleman. He came with large papers with him to draw the mountains and the animals and lived for months with my grandmother, Gwenonwy, the youngest daughter of R. J. Berwyn, the first teacher in the valley. Kyffin lived in Trevelin and came to the farm, painting the people and the animals. He became a friend of Dad's, and he sent us Christmas cards for many years.

The Patagonian landscape and its vivid palette of colours made a lasting and indelible impression on Kyffin, and in some ways, so did he on the people of the place. In a letter from Barbara Llwyd Evans to Eiddwen Humphreys, written on 25 March 1969, she says that it was his appearance that really drew her attention, with his black and green shirt, his blue jeans, his dark-green felt hat atop his head, looking as if it was too small for him. His hair swept across his brow, and he had a real bush of a moustache under his nose. This is how Kyffin remembered Iolo as a lad, with his dog at his side:

> I followed, clinging to the large Yankee saddle, Gigo chased hares while *chimangos* dived to chase Gigo. In the sky, the *teru* wailed, and bravely attacked the small eagles that had disturbed them. Iolo picked his way through the trees to emerge at the top of a cliff above a torrent. He nosed his horse down an almost vertical slope and I followed, holding tight to the my saddle and sketchbook. Iolo gave a freckled grin and I gathered that I had passed some sort of test. Then up the cliff again, past the stumps of trees that

had been snapped in the ferocious winds, and into a field of large red thistles. Iolo leaped from his horse and attacked them with fury. Back on his horse, he told me they were a plague which they thought had come from Russia. On we galloped through the foothills of the *cordilleras* to a corral where stallions fought over mares. Iolo told me to draw them but gave me no time, for he was away again, chasing Gigo over the wild land that was his home.

Guiding artists seems to run in the family. Fred Green showed Richard Llewellyn around when he came here in search of inspiration and a new backdrop for his popular fiction, chasing after the elusive touchstone that would allow him, once again, to transmute words into success. Together, they hitched the horses and rode together towards Corcovado, a trip that offered open-air lessons in a majestic landscape. The place certainly gave Llewellyn that. Towards the end of a long trek, which forms the backbone of *Up Into the Singing Mountain*, the not-so-gripping sequel to *How Green Was My Valley*, we behold the mountains, in all their transporting and uplifting glory. After slogging though the endless monotony of thorn and grey scrub, it's little wonder that Huw Morgan's response to the mountain vistas is little short of epiphanic.

Llewellyn wasn't all that he appeared to be, though. The writer of some of the quintessential Welsh fiction of the twentieth century wasn't averse to adding some to his autobiography. He claimed to have been born in St David's. According to a birth certificate found in an archive of Llewellyn's papers at the University of Texas, the author was really born in London.

Richard Llewellyn Lloyd, or Vivian Lloyd – his real name – was born in the north London suburb of Hendon, and was the son of a Welsh publican. Apart from claiming Pembrokeshire birthright, he also claimed, right up to his death in 1983, to be the son of a Welsh miner who worked down the pits in Gilfach Goch in the south Wales valleys. In fact, the writer's first job was washing dishes at Claridge's hotel in London, and his knowledge of mining came from stories he heard from a family who ran a bookshop in the city's Charing Cross Road.

Despite these autobiographical manipulations, Llewellyn's incredible success with his *How Green Was My Valley*, which came out to the sound of trumpets in 1939, led to a classic case of second-novel syndrome. It was well-nigh impossible for him to follow one hit with another, and so he penned no fewer than another two dozen novels, some of which sold in great numbers, but without ever matching the towering reputation of the first, which sat among his other books as a cathedral amongst booths. The two further books set in Patagonia, *Up Into the Singing Mountain* and *Green, Green My Valley Now*, didn't come close to matching the critical or popular acclaim of their predecessor.

Mountain Man

Erik Iolo Green, now in his fifties, farms some of the high, wild land that acts as a backdrop to Llewellyn's novels. 'Well, we had been warned of steepness, but there is steep and steep, and the way we went, you would think that steep is flat'. Adjoining Iolo's steep land is his sister's steep land. Farming sheep is a staple activity. 'At one time, we only kept merinos, but now that their wool isn't worth much, we've crossed them with Texels and Romneys, from the Romney Marshes in England to produce lambs for meat'. Some of his agricultural knowledge was derived from a period in Wales, when he worked on a farm and attended Llysfasi Agricultural College in Pentrecelyn, near Ruthin in north Wales.

Here, on the farm, Erik Iolo wasn't that far from Bethesda, the original home of his great-grandmother, Elizabeth Pritchard. She came to Patagonia for a reason quite unlike many of the other settlers. One night, back in Wales, she and a friend had had to hide from a man who seemed to be stalking them wherever they went. Elizabeth agreed with her friend, Grace Roberts, that one way of avoiding him was to go to Patagonia, which they did, part of the very first party of settlers and venturers aboard the *Mimosa*.

Elizabeth married Twmi Dimol, a steward on the *Mimosa*, a man who enjoyed versifying, and a friend of the popular poet Ceiriog. A long letter written to Ceiriog by Twmi in June 1866 offers a full picture of the difficulties and trials of life in the early settlement, detailing the hunger that beset them after only a month, and how they settled the gnawing pangs by eating foxes, owls and hawks. If even such unappetizing food items as these weren't available to the starving people, they drank salt water mixed with a few oats or breadcrumbs, or combined with tea-leaves. Even obtaining the salt water involved a 12-mile round trip to the coast, and little wonder that sometimes the hungry settlers made do by eating cacti and their roots, grubbed up from the broken earth.

Some relief came for Elizabeth and Twmi when the colony was able to start trading, especially after the purchase of the *Denby*, a small boat which cost $30,000, or £250 pounds. It brought in much-needed supplies, such as wheat and flour, dried beef and sugar, along with promises of financial support from merchants in Buenos Aires. But two harvests failed in succession in y Wladfa, and a dearth of rain and hunger once again beset the settlers. The *Denby* didn't seem to cope too well with such inclement weather and, on a sailing from the town of Patagones, bound for Rawson, laden with goods from the government, not to mention four oxen, it was wrecked, drowning six of the settlers on board, including Twmi Dimol. Some years later, the wreck itself was located not far from Punta Tomba, including a body wrapped in sail canvas, who was identified as Twmi because of the buttons on his clothes. Elizabeth later healed her heart by marrying the educator R. J. Berwyn. In the early days of the settlement, women outnumbered men, so a woman could have two or even three husbands in a lifetime.

Talking sheep

Erik Iolo has a farm of 230 hectares not to mention a much larger tract of land at Rhyd yr Indiaid (Indian Ford). Here his animals roam across 20,000 acres. He notes my raised eyebrow at the mention of such a huge landholding, and explains that much of it is tough and rocky, with only thin grasses on which the sheep can feed. The previous year, he took 500 sheep up there, but despite the best efforts of a full-time shepherd, they lost half of them. It's harsh terrain under hard weather: snow can fall for three solid months, dazzlingly beautiful, but mercilessly deadly.

Iolo's great-grandfather, R. J. Berwyn, would have been fascinated by the changing weather patterns, since he dutifully recorded cold and warmth every day as well as diligently recording rainfall. He also studied the night sky, following the courses of stars and planets, using the data to predict events and even producing an annual almanac.

But now the weather changes need something more scientific than an almanac to predict. And other challenges have come with climate change. Iolo refers to the drought which has beset the farmers of Australia, leaving them powerless to save their skeletal animals. He suggests these huge shifts in the weather apply equally in the Andes. 'First, we have periods of too much snow, followed by periods of drought. We went to shear the sheep before the lambs were born, and a hailstorm started, and this happened two years in succession. It was cold day after day after day. I lost almost every animal, dying under a rain of hail'.

Big cats

As if pelting and persistent hail weren't enough, there are other lethal perils to contend with. One of them is the puma, the stealthy big cat also known as the cougar, mountain lion or catamount, which has the largest range of any wild land mammal in the western hemisphere, so the cats that worry Iolo are essentially the same as those which prowl the Yukon in Canada. Secretive and solitary, crepuscular and nocturnal, these animals are strong, stalk-and-catch predators, and the puma is second only to the jaguar in size among the wild cats of South America. Yet, it's more closely related to the domestic cat than the lion: it's simply one of the biggest of the small cats, as it were. Here near Trevelin, Iolo maintains, they find sanctuary, a veritable breeding-ground, in the nearby Los Alerces National Park – a preserve created, in part, to protect the eponymous trees, some of them 3,000 years old – from where they venture out to kill sheep.

Fred Green, in his writings, compared the puma to the domestic cat, especially when he heard the pumas mewing to each other in the depths of the woods. If domesticated as a youngster, the puma would take quite readily to life around the farm, behaving like an outsized moggie, albeit with sharper claws, so that it could open a tin of cat food all by itself. I jest. Fred knew of many families that had adopted a puma in this way, even though they then faced an uphill struggle to keep it fed, as it had a voracious appetite for meat (and, of course, there were no tins of food!). One of Fred's neighbours, Elias Owen, cut his puma's claws so it couldn't attack anyone, and put a chain around its neck to proclaim ownership. Elias' puma wasn't all that fierce – possibly because of the clipped claws – and would run and hide should strangers make an appearance on Owen's farm. A shy and timid puma: who'd have thought it?

The wild puma is another matter, able to smite a sheep dead with a single fatal strike of its paw. Thus dispatched, the cat will suck the blood, for starters. If it isn't satiated by the blood, its normal butchery strategy will involve opening up the chest-cage so that it can devour the tasty soft parts and fatty insides, before casually slinging the carcass over its shoulder, dismissive of its heft and weight, and heading for a more solitary dining space. It may even bury the animal under a coverlet of leaves to finish it off later on. This puma habit gives people the opportunity to set down poison, to properly arrange the poor beast's last supper. Farmers have no qualms about doing this, since pumas can cause carnage among their livestock. Therefore, poisoning and hunting with dogs are commonplace practices, even though the dogs have to be very cautious of those deadly claws, so, working in concert, two dogs against one cat is usually the necessary ratio.

One apparent weak spot is the puma's throat, and this is capitalized upon by *gauchos*, who throw a rope around the neck, which seems to paralyze the animal, which is then dragged across the ground until it is dead.

The puma would only very seldom attack a human, and then only if the person was sitting down, or had inadvertently startled it. In his memoirs, John Daniel Evans recalls how John Murray Thomas, the experienced settler-explorer, was attacked by one. Thomas had headed off in the direction of Creigiau Gwynion (White Rocks), when a puma leapt onto his shoulders. As luck would have it, Thomas was wearing a thick poncho made of *guanaco* wool, and even luckier, he was carrying a loaded gun. Even though he'd been thrown to the ground by the cat, the puma rolled further than the man, with the poncho firmly seized in its claws. Thomas took control of the situation, got to his feet and shot the animal dead with his first bullet. When he finally returned to the camp, the marks of the puma's claws were visible on his skin – only the thickness of the poncho had saved him. Little wonder that Clint Eastwood wears them.

Llwyd ap Iwan recounts an encounter with a puma in his diary, in which he not only faces up to the cat, but talks to it into the bargain.

> Lions more numerous as we went south, some of which were more bold than the generality of pumas are supposed to be. One day, when in search of water and several miles ahead of the party, I discovered one proceeding leisurely by slow bounds across my line of march a few hundred yards in front. Having galloped up to it, I found it crouched near a bush awaiting my arrival. Addressing

the brute in words not too forcible under the circumstance, I tried to get the horse to descry the enemy, but not being able to do so, I retried to tether it at a safer distance. Returning on foot to about 30 paces of the lion, I saw that it was stretching itself out to spring at me. Its tail was up in the air with about six or eight inches of the end slowly waving as if beckoning me to approach nearer. Its chin was protruded well forward and resting on its paws; a gigantic cat about to leap at its prey. My heart was in my throat. I felt it making energetic efforts to get there, and after firing, I found that the bullet did not strike the exact spot I aimed at, proving I was a little flurried at the time. The agitation passed off immediately, and the second shot finished its work.

There are puma stories galore in the Andes, tales of stealth, danger and surprise. They are often, in truth about manliness and manhood, tales of derring-do involving cats.

There's a story about the old man Edward Jones (called Bagillt), who lived alone in the Andes, hearing his dog whining outside. When he went to investigate the source of the commotion, he saw a puma-as-vampire slurping down his animal's blood. 'It didn't have time to pull its tongue back into its mouth before I shot it dead', Bagillt averred, with some pride.

Iolo once saw a story about a puma written in the snow. There were concentric but tightening rings of puma prints chasing after a smaller animal, a *pudu*, the smallest deer in the world. Usually this little mammal, just 60 centimetres long, will run away from a predator in a speedy zig-zag, or even climb up trees to escape, but this one was clearly trapped within an orbit of sharp and pounding claws. The increasingly frantic hieroglyphs showed the rings tightening and tightening until the conclusion of the story was marked out with a circle of bright blood, the *pudu*'s story having come to a full stop, its last chapter written on a white page of snow.

Iolo tells me how he built the place, how they carried stones on a loader for two years to build the road to reach here. He brought the electricity line and the water in a pipe from the stream before building the house. He cut down all the trees and sawed them. His father had a saw here to work timber, and Iolo used that to prepare all the building material. Little wonder that pride smoulders in his eyes as he surveys the place. 'It's built of cypress, which is an easy wood to work, but there's a lot of disease in the trees hereabouts, which means they have rotted on the inside. Half the trees I cut down weren't good enough to be used for building, especially when I needed thick planks to hold up the roof.'

How did he learn to build the cabin? He points out that the early pioneers did it themselves, but in his case, he waited for the arrival of magazines containing details of how to build a cabin. 'I made the plan myself, then took a chainsaw, and trimmed three sides of each trunk, leaving just one rounded side. I put half a metre of stones underneath to begin with, then hammered long nails through'. He has now lived here for over a decade. As we chat, he stokes the fire with big logs, building it up, making the rooms toasty. 'There's no gas supply on the farms here. We have to get gas in tanks, and it's much more expensive than in town, where it comes in pipes'.

Iolo is a keen reader. He grew up in a house with many books. There was no television, so the nights were long, but that all changed when the TV arrived. He speaks Welsh with his brothers and sisters, but his two sisters have married non-Welsh speakers, so when their husbands are around, they use Spanish to converse. He also used to speak to all the uncles in Welsh, but they've all passed away, and there are very few old people left who speak the language.

There are many other changes, not least in terms of the people who live here. 'There are many Bolivians here now. They produce the best vegetables. These natives of Bolivia have worked the land for centuries, back to the Inca cultivations. The locals here don't like to bend over using hoe and rake'.

It was different in his father's day, when many of the migrant workers who came to work on the farms came from Chile, and they would be allowed to hold land for five years. They would normally be given wooded areas to cultivate, and they would apply the slash-and-burn principle, leaving just enough wood for fences and hedges, and using oxen to pull out the stubborn, burned roots. They would choose the land where *mai teng* trees, a kind of tropical hardwood, were growing, as these were seen as a sign of good, fertile land. Here, they could grow potatoes for three years, then cereals for a further two before they would have to yield the land. Any profit they made would be divided between themselves and the owner of the land. They would then leave Argentina by boat, crossing Afon Fawr, a boundary river, with their horses swimming alongside them.

And there was another difference in Fred's days, such as the absence of vehicles to take animals to market. In his memoir, *Pethau Patagonia*, he summons up Cinemascope visions of huge drives of livestock, just as bold, dusty and determined to move on as any that crossed the screen in a Hollywood Western. In the 1920s, Green recalled, there would be thousands of sheep under the control of four or five *gauchos*, flanking the animals on horseback. There was a time when cattle, too, were moved like this, across the mountains into Chile but this was before Fred's time.

Initially, the animals were destined for big cities such as Buenos Aires and Bahia Blanca, but as the oil industry burgeoned in Comodoro Rivadavia, so too did its workers' appetite for a regular supply of fresh meat, so Andean sheep and stock were redirected there. Like the drovers of Wales, the men in charge had to be tough of spirit and unyielding to the weather – after all, the drive from the high fields of the Andes to the oil fields near the coast was some 500 or 600 miles. You had to have been born in the saddle to deal with the hardships of that sort of journey.

In this era, there were wagon trains, too, carrying flour and foodstuffs and loads of disinfectants to use on the sheep. It would take a whole month to journey down from the Andes to the Lower Chubut valley, and another month to negotiate the return leg.

In the 1920s, mule-power replaced horsepower. It would take 150 mules to pull a dozen wagons, attended by 15 men – a mixture of native Indians, who knew the terrain, and *gauchos*, adept with lassoes.

Surveying the sheep in the fields outside his log cabin, I have the temerity to suggest to Iolo – at the risk of sounding impertinent – that their fleeces are very dirty. The animals seem to be covered in the sort of fine grey dust one finds when emptying an ashtray. He tells me that it's volcanic dust, following the eruption of the Chaiten volcano in nearby Chile, which had recently blown its top, throwing an enormous spume of gas and ash twenty miles into the sky. Much of the powdery residue settled on the Argentine side, and in the absence of rain to wash it away, the fleeces remained dirty, the ash clinging on stubbornly, like old snow, to field edge and tree branch.

As if the ash wasn't bad enough, it's very hard to make a living in the Beautiful Valley nowadays, Iolo alleges. 'The government seems to be against the farmers. Last year, there was a strike for three months, with roadblocks everywhere. The farmers won, eventually, as they were objecting to a new government rule called Rule 125. The government wanted 65 per cent of the soya grown for export, and they were against exporting meat. The strike was mainly in the north, in Buenos Aires, Cordoba and Santa Fe'.

Falling prices can be devastating in a different way, and Iolo, like many of his valley neighbours, has had to diversify. He turned his hand to cultivating tulips, selling the flowers to the Netherlands, a very real case of selling coals to Newcastle, even if the goods were much more colourful. Growing flowers in Cwm Hyfryd took advantage of the difference in seasons between Europe and the southern hemisphere, but that market disappeared eventually. Even before the orders stopped coming in, there were other issues, not least the problems of getting fresh flowers all the way to Europe. Iolo recalls one consignment of flowers that left Puerto Madryn bound for Rotterdam that got diverted to Buenos Aires, where all the blooms wilted and died.

Iolo also diversified into growing garlic, with some success to begin with, certainly enough to expand a three-acre crop to a six-acre crop. But transport problems were still a blight. He sent a very substantial consignment of garlic to Brazil, which was then held up at the border, and perished during the bureaucratic wait. But the changing strategies and constant diversification underlines the resilience of this tough and adaptable community of farmers, with some turning their hands to fox farming for the fur, others to growing and harvesting soft fruit.

It's a hard, testing life in the high *cordilleras*.

Erik sets about setting the table for supper. Outside, in the high air a monster of a condor circles seemingly listlessly, its huge wings dwindling with the growing distance. The last thermals of the day carry it slowly, so that it looks like a piece of ash rising up from a bonfire. Higher and higher it climbs until it is a fly-speck spattered on a celestial windscreen. Soon it is so tiny, so shrunken by the surrounding magnitudes it is next to nothing. The great vulture, this huge-winged scavenger has become nothing more substantial than a *punto*, a final full stop.

Acknowledgements

I'm hugely grateful to Elvey MacDonald for casting an eye over the book at the eleventh hour, even as he was travelling in y Wladfa on one of his regular trips. Needless to say any errors or misinterpretations are my own.

I have found the almost daily e-mails from Ceris Gruffudd in Penrhyncoch, bringing news from Patagonia and about things Patagonian, a nourishing fix, and the company of the members of the committee organizing the 150th anniversary celebrations always pleasurable. Thanks also to the staff at Bangor and Cardiff universities for making some enthralling material available to me.

I should also like to thank Morfudd Slaymaker from Lampeter, theatre director Mike Pearson for useful information and documents and Dafydd Wigley for sending me his recollections of visiting Patagonia during the 1965 centenary celebrations, the theatre producer Siân Thomas for helping with translations from the Spanish and also Dr Emily Shepard from Swansea University for her specialist information about condors. Emily is a perfect combination of expert, enthusiast and teacher, and can make the big birds soar up from a conversation. On the subject of conversations, thanks to Fernando Williams from Buenos Aires, and to Marc Rees from Cardiff, for some very stimulating ones along the way.

My wonderful editor, Luned Whelan, has chosen to work with me again, winnowing out all sorts of errors, so my thanks to her for attentiveness, her diligence and her forbearance. Diolch o galon, blodyn.

A timely and much appreciated Creative Wales award from the Arts Council of Wales allowed me to undertake the fieldwork for this book, which took me into many Patagonian homes and to visit many inspiring places, always meeting people who were so unstintingly kind with both time and information. 'Butterfly man' Eos Griffiths and his friend, Miguel 'Becho' Mulhall, took me to visit all the chapels in the lower valley of the Wladfa in a single day, in an outsize RV emblazoned with the words 'Mochyn Du' and

'Sosban Fach', the vehicle well-nigh dwarfing every little place of worship we parked outside. It was a memorable excursion, no doubt about that.

Parts of the book have previously appeared in *Taliesin, Planet* and *Wales Arts Review*, so thanks to the editors of all three.

And, of course, my sincere and abiding gratitude to everyone who made me feel incredibly welcome in South America, including Ieuan Williams, Waldo Williams and Edi Griffiths in Bryn Crwn, Lizzie Lloyd, Elvin and Amanda Roberts and Jeremy Wood in Esquel; John Humphreys, Ariel and Marta Hughes, Elmer MacDonald and Juan Morgan James in Trelew; Tegai Roberts, Luned González and Ana Rees in Gaiman; Erik Iolo Green and Arturo and Rosa Lowndes in Trevelin; Alwina Thomas and Norma Hughes in Buenos Aires and to Virginia Sosa from Montevideo, Uruguay who was, and is an inspiration. There were many, many others who helped along the way, felly diolch yn fawr a gracias i chi i gyd.

Sadly, some of my interviewees have passed away since my visit, and news of each and every death in the Wladfa reminds one of what can seem like the fragility of the colony. It's been through tough times, as this present book reminds us, but y Wladfa still persists, unbowed and unbroken, despite all the punishing weathers and history's pitfalls.

As I've already said, writing the book was, in essence, a negotiation around all the other books that exist on the subject. Some have been essential, such as R. Bryn Williams' *Y Wladfa,* Elvey Macdonald's diligently researched *Yr Hirdaith*, and Chris Moss' germinal and engaging cultural history, cited below. I have also been the net beneficiary of Wyn James' writings about Eluned Morgan, and Wyn and Bill Jones' work on Michael D. Jones, and I need to acknowledge a real and direct debt to the Princeton University Library's wide ranging survey, 'Strait Through: Magellan to Cook & the Pacific' which is an invaluable reference on the subject of Patagonian giants, especially the literary references to the Tehuelche, which provided much of the source material for the chapter on giants in this book.

Meanwhile, the books keep on coming …

René Griffiths has just brought out *Ramblings of a Patagonian*, an engagingly anecdotal account of the energetic life of this talented guitarist, surely the only *guanaco* breeder to play the Albert Hall. Clare Dudman's historical novel, *A Place of Meadows and Tall Trees,* details the early days of the settlement in Rawson in quiet, languorous, almost tranquil prose, while the handsome coffee table book *Patagonia: Crossing the Plain / Croesi'r Paith* charts actor Matthew Rhys's bum-numbing horseback ride. In Welsh, the ever-industrious Mari Emlyn has published not one, but three books in a year, garnering a long and industrious correspondence between the satellite and mother-ship Wales and vice versa, and some of these letters are referred to in *Gwalia Patagonia,* with thanks for the sheer industry which underpins her two epistolary collections.

Imogen Rhea Herrad's *Beyond the Pampas: In Search of Patagonia*, meanwhile, is a vivid and spirited travelogue which finds this German-born writer questioning the true relationship between the Mapuche / Tehuelche and the Welsh, and questioning whether the Welsh did enough to defend the indigenous tribes when they were being hunted down in the nineteenth century.

And then there's photographer Ed Gold's astonishingly rich book, *Patagonia: Another World*. The images here truly haunt me, an account of a fading way of life, as sickness claims the elderly and time erodes, or erases, the old ways of life. A pig killing at Bryn Gwyn is all steam and glimpsed knives – quite silent, even though the actual squealing must have cut to the quick. Not a single part of the animal is wasted, and we see Neilor Morgan Evans meditatively stirring a small aluminium pot of blood, turning it into black pudding. Abandoned farms are quickly pulverized by the beating weather. Ariel Elis stares at the camera in his home in Lle Cul, and continues staring long after one has turned to the next page. Reading, or viewing, Gold's book made me question the power of words to match the visual image. Whatever. It's a real work of art, from the life-wearied eyes of the men drinking at La Criolla Bar in Bryn Gwyn to the startling image of Paloma Pugh, a young girl in her sexy red dress, standing in the middle of a field, the wheat waving all around her.

These volumes, too, have all given me a glimpse of different facets of life in y Wladfa, and for this, I thank all concerned.

Jon Gower
March 2015

Bibliography

Books

Chatwin, Bruce *In Patagonia,* London, Penguin, 2003

Chatwin, Bruce, and Theroux, Paul, *Patagonia Revisited*, London, Michael Russell, 1985

Chatwin, Elizabeth, and Shakespeare, Nicholas, *Under the Sun: The Letters of Bruce Chatwin*, London, Jonathan Cape, 2010

Clapp, Susanna, *With Chatwin*, London, Jonathan Cape, 1997

Davies, Gareth Alban, *Tan Tro Nesaf: Darlun o Wladfa Gymreig Patagonia*, Llandysul, Gomer, 1976

Emlyn, Mari, *Llythyrau'r Wladfa, 1865-1945*, Llanrwst, Gwasg Carreg Gwalch, 2009

Emlyn, Mari, *Llythyrau'r Wladfa, 1945-2010*, Llanrwst, Gwasg Carreg Gwalch, 2010

Erfyl, Gwyn, ed., *Y Teithiwr Talog: Cymry ar Daith ym Mhedwar Ban Byd, 2*, Llanrwst, Gwasg Carreg Gwalch, 1999

Evans, Lewis, *Adlais y Gamwy*, Caernarfon, Y Goleuad (undated)

Gold, Ed, *Patagonia: Byd Arall,* Llandysul, Gomer, 2012

Green, Fred, *Pethau Patagonia*, Penygroes, Cyhoeddiadau Mei, 1984

Harrison, John, *Where the World Ends: a journey beyond Patagonia*, London, John Murray, 2000

Jacobs, Michael, *Andes,* London, Granta, 2010

James, E. Wyn and Jones, Bill, *Michael D. Jones a'i Wladfa Gymreig*, Llanrwst, Gwasg Carreg Gwalch, 2009

Jones, Emyr Wyn, *Bysedd Cochion a'r Wladfa Newydd*, Denbigh, Gwasg Gee, 1997

Jones, Marged Lloyd, *O Drelew i Drefach*, Llandysul, Gomer, 2007

Jones, Joseph Seth, ed., MacDonald, Elvey, *Dyddiadur Mimosa*, Llanrwst, Llyfrgell Genedlaethol Cymru/Gwasg Carreg Gwalch, 2005

Kurlansky, Mark, *Cod: A Biography of the Fish That Changed the World* London, Jonathan Cape, 1998

Laporte, Nadine Isabel, *Welsh Place Names in Patagonia*, M.A. degree thesis, Bangor University, 1992

Llewellyn, Richard, *Up Into The Singing Mountain*, Harmondsworth, Penguin, 1966

Llwyd, Iwan and Morys, Twm, *Eldorado: Llwybrau Dau i Le Diarth*, Llanrwst, Gwasg Carreg Gwalch, 1999

MacDonald, Elvey, *Yr Hirdaith,* Llandysul, Gomer, 1999

MacDonald, Elvey, *Llwch,* Talybont, Y Lolfa, 2009

Miglioli, Jorge and Sepiurka, Sergio, *Rocky Trip: The Route of the Welsh in Patagonia*, Esquel, Balero Producciones, 2004

Morgan, Eluned, *Dringo'r Andes* and *Gwymon y Môr*, Dinas Powys, Honno, 2001

Moss, Chris, *Patagonia: A Cultural History*, Oxford, Signal, 2008

Musters, George Chaworth, *At Home with the Patagonians*, Stroud, Nonsuch, 2005

Owen, Geraint Dyfnallt, *Crisis in Chubut: A chapter in the history of the Welsh Colony in Patagonia*, Swansea, Christopher Davies, 1977

Rhys, Matthew, *Patagonia: Crossing the Plain*, Llandysul, Gomer, 2010

Rhys, William Casnodyn, *A Welsh Song in Patagonia: Memories of the Welsh Colonization*, (privately printed)

Sebald, W.G., *Campo Santo,* London, Penguin, 2006

Shakespeare, Nicholas, *Bruce Chatwin,* London, Vintage, 2000

Skinner, Kenneth, *Railway in the Desert*, Beechen Green Books, 1984

Tanner, Marcus, *The Last of the Celts*, New Haven & London, Yale University Press, 2004

Theroux, Paul, *The Old Patagonian Express*, Boston, Houghton Mifflin, 1979

Wilbert, Johannes, ed., *Folk Literature of the Tehuelche Indians*, Los Angeles, UCLA Latin American Center Publications, 1984

Wilkinson, Susan, *Mimosa: the life and times of the ship that sailed to Patagonia*, Y Lolfa, Talybont, 2007

Williams, R. Bryn, *Crwydro Patagonia,* Llandybïe, Llyfrau'r Dryw, 1960

Williams, R. Bryn, *Eluned Morgan*, Llandysul, Y Clwb Llyfrau Cymreig, 1948

Williams, R. Bryn, *Gwladfa Patagonia,* Llanrwst, Gwasg Carreg Gwalch, 2000

Williams, R. Bryn, *Y Wladfa,* Cardiff, University of Wales Press, 1962

Williams, Catrin, ed., *Agor y Ffenestri*, Caernarfon, Gwasg y Bwthyn / Cymdeithas Cymru-Ariannin, 2001

Williams, Catrin, *Bywyd yn y Wladfa*, Caernarfon, Gwasg y Bwthyn / Cymdeithas Cymru-Ariannin, 2009

Williams, Fernando, *Entre el desierto y el jardin: viaje, literatura y paisaje en la colonia galesa de Patagonia*, Buenos Aires, Promoteo Libros, 2010

Williams, Glyn, *The Desert and the Dream: A Study of Welsh Colonization in Chubut 1865–1915*, Cardiff, University of Wales Press, 1975

Williams, Glyn, *The Welsh in Patagonia: The State and the Ethnic Community*, Cardiff, University of Wales Press, 1991

Williams, Kyffin, *A Wider Sky*, Llandysul, Gomer Press, 2006

Williams, Kyffin, *Gwladfa Kyffin*, Aberystwyth, National Library of Wales, 2004

Yzurieta, Dario and Narosky, Tito, *Birds of Argentina and Uruguay: A Field Guide*, Buenos Aires, Vasquez Mazzini Editores, 2003

Magazines and unpublished material

Agozzini, Maria Teresa, Transplanted Traditions: An Assessment of Welsh Lore and Language in Argentina, *Journal of Interdisciplinary Studies, Volume 1: Diaspora*

Brooks, Walter A. & Geraldine Lublin, (2007), The Eisteddfod of Chubut, or how the reinvention of a tradition has contributed to the preservation of a language and culture, *Beyond Philology*, 4, 245-59.

James, E. Wyn, Eluned Morgan, *Taliesin*, Volume 148

Brith Gof, *Patagonia: Breuddwyd yn yr Anialwch* (unpublished, courtesy of Mike Pearson)

Other books by Jon Gower

History and psycho-geography
A Long Mile
Real Llanelli
The Story of Wales

Travel
An Island Called Smith
Wales: At Water's Edge

Short stories
Big Fish
Breision
Too Cold for Snow

Novels
Dala'r Llanw
Norte (to be published in 2015)
Uncharted
Y Storïwr

As editor and contributor:
A Year in a Small Country
Clymau (to be published in 2015)
Encounters With Dylan
Encounters With Nigel
Homeland
I Know Another Way
Wales: In Our Own Image